History Wars

THE
PETER RYAN – MANNING CLARK
CONTROVERSY

History Wars

THE
PETER RYAN – MANNING CLARK
CONTROVERSY

DOUG MUNRO

PRESS

To my granddaughters
Rose Teloma Martens (b. 2011)
Adelaide Wanda Munro (b. 2021)

&

Belle (Maltese Terrier, b. 2008),
my constant companion during
the writing of this book

Published by ANU Press
The Australian National University
Acton ACT 2601, Australia
Email: anupress@anu.edu.au

Available to download for free at press.anu.edu.au

ISBN (print): 9781760464769
ISBN (online): 9781760464776

WorldCat (print): 1269298900
WorldCat (online): 1269193661

DOI: 10.22459/HW.2021

This title is published under a Creative Commons Attribution-NonCommercial-NoDerivatives 4.0 International (CC BY-NC-ND 4.0).

The full licence terms are available at
creativecommons.org/licenses/by-nc-nd/4.0/legalcode

Cover design and layout by ANU Press

This book is published under the aegis of the Social Sciences Editorial Committee of the ANU Press.

This edition © 2021 ANU Press

Contents

List of Illustrations ... ix
Acknowledgements ... xi
Referencing Conventions ... xv
Foreword ... xvii
Prologue ... xxvii

Part 1. Wider Setting

1. Manning Clark and Peter Ryan ... 3
2. The Australian History Wars ... 17

Part 2. Contention and Dissension

3. Criticisms, Reaction and Counter-Reaction ... 29
4. Errors, Great and Small ... 45
5. Justified or Not? ... 63
6. A Complicit Academy? ... 75

Part 3. Ruminations

7. Deliberation: Manning Clark and the History Wars ... 101
8. Reflection: Peter Ryan's Motives ... 119
9. Aftermath: The Dissembling Publisher, *Quadrant* and the History Wars ... 135

Appendices

Appendix 1: Pre-Ryan Material in *Quadrant* that Critiques Clark (1968–93) ... 163

Appendix 2: Selected Pre-Ryan Assessments of Clark's Life and Work (apart from reviews and contributions to *Quadrant*) ... 165

Appendix 3: Articles that Discuss Manning Clark in Peter Ryan's
Quadrant Column (1994–2014)   169

Appendix 4: Academic (and Quasi-Academic) Coverage
of Manning Clark's Life and Work (1993–2021)   171

Select Bibliography   189

List of Illustrations

Figure 1. Caricature of Manning Clark on the front cover
of *Quadrant*, September 1993.   xxiv

Figure 2. Peter Ryan—drawn from life—on the front cover
of *Quadrant*, October 1994.   xxv

Figure 3. In happier times. Peter Ryan and Manning Clark at the
National Press Club, Canberra, 17 April 1980.   6

Figure 4. Dymphna Clark, early 1990s.   32

Figure 5. Robert Manne, editor of *Quadrant* (1990–97), at around
the time the controversy broke out.   34

Figure 6. Michael Cathcart (foreground) and Stuart Macintyre were
both critics of Peter Ryan.   42

Figure 7. Roslyn and Katie Russell, 1981.   91

Figure 8. Paul Keating and John Howard squaring off.   115

Figure 9. John Howard on history, facts and dates, 5 July 2006.   117

Acknowledgements

One reason this book was long in the making is because I had prior commitments, including my share of the work for a couple of coedited volumes. Second, I live in New Zealand, meaning that the archival research was conducted whenever I could get over to Australia for brief smash-and-grab raids in Canberra and Melbourne, and to a lesser extent in Adelaide. I simply could not have got through all the material in the time available before the advent of the digital camera, and it also helped that many of the newspaper sources are available as clippings in the Papers of Peter Ryan and the Papers of Dymphna Clark. Third, my original intention was to write an 8,000-word article for *Australian Historical Studies*, which I hoped would be published in 2018—the silver anniversary of the controversy—but the first draft exceeded 12,500 words. Like Bain Attwood before me, in another contribution to Australia's History Wars,[1] I realised that I had too much material for a journal article, especially for a forensic study of this nature that demanded minutely detailed argument and extensive footnoting. At that point I decided to expand what I had written into a small book, which added to the timeframe as well as to the list of people and institutions requiring acknowledgment.

The first round of applause goes to the staff of the Manuscripts Section, National Library of Australia and their counterparts at the University of Melbourne Archives (especially Jane Beattie, Katie Wood and Sophie Garrett). They continue to show why historians value archivists so much. The staffs of the State Library of South Australia; Special Collections, Barr Smith Library, University of Adelaide (Cheryl Hoskin, Maree Larsen and especially Lee Hayes); and Special Collections, Flinders University are also much appreciated.

---

1   Bain Attwood, *Telling the Truth about Aboriginal History,* Sydney: Allen & Unwin, 2005, p. vii.

At an individual level, I am first and foremost obliged to Sebastian Clark. In his capacity as literary executor, Seb gave permission for me to consult the Papers of Dymphna Clark and to make copies from the Papers of Manning Clark. Having done so much to make this book possible, he then kept well away, never looking over my shoulder and never interfering in what I was doing or thinking. Not all authors are so blessed with a non-interventionist literary executor. I am also grateful to David Stephens who, in a chance encounter in the National Library of Australia, put me in contact with Seb.

For other permissions I am beholden to: Katerina Clark, who allowed me to quote from the transcript of her oral history interview (with Axel Clark) at the National Library of Australia; Stuart Macintyre for permission to consult his papers at the National Library; Louise Adler for permission to consult the Melbourne University Press Archives; and Chris Wallace-Crabbe for allowing me to publish his limerick on Messrs Ryan and Clark.

Michael Silver (Magnet Galleries Melbourne Inc.) and Heide Smith (Heide Smith Photographer) kindly gave permission to reproduce their photographs, as did Peter Nicholson (Rubbery Figures Pty Ltd) to reproduce two of his cartoons. The University of Melbourne Archives also permitted the reproduction of one of the photos in its keeping, whilst the images of the front covers of *Quadrant* for September 1993 and October 1994, depicting Manning Clark and Peter Ryan, respectively, appear with the consent of John Spooner, the artist, and Keith Windschuttle, the editor of *Quadrant*. Alicia Tolley of the Alexander Turnbull Library facilitated my obtaining images of the two *Quadrant* front covers.

Along the journey, colleagues commented in earlier drafts and were helpful in other respects. The present book is much improved from its earlier incarnations as a result of their assistance. Most helpful of all was the advice and encouragement of Frank Bongiorno, Graeme Davison, Stuart Macintyre, Mark McKenna and Roslyn Russell, all of whom commented on earlier versions of this book as well. During the early stages of this project Mark also sent some of his research notes for his own biography of Manning Clark. I must also include Robert Manne in this paragraph; his assistance and courtesy were all the more generous given that we disagree on some matters of interpretation.

A number of others also commented on parts or all of the manuscript: Anna Clark, Katerina Clark, James Cotton, James Curran, Geoffrey Gray, Peter Hempenstall, Brij V. Lal and Clive Moore. For providing 'outsider' perspectives, I am indebted to Russell Campbell, Richard Hill and especially Robert J. Tristram in New Zealand, and to John G. Reid, John C. Weaver and Donald Wright in Canada.

Numerous individuals responded to my enquiries. I am grateful to them all, even when I sometimes wasn't eventually able to use their information: Fay Anderson, James M. Banner, Jr., Carol Bolton, Michael Cathcart, David Day, Brian Dickey, Richard J. Evans, Stewart Firth, Stephen Foster, Maurice French, Deborah Gare, Nicola Gilmore, Ian Hancock, Joanna Kidman, Donato Longo, Brian Matthews, the late Allan Martin, Sylvia Martin, John Mayo, Peter McPhee, the late Ann Moyal, Barry Ninham, John Poynter, Wilfrid Prest, Carol Rasmussen, Michael Roe, Michael Sharkey, Rory Sweetman, Wray Vamplew and Robert Wallace.

Being a departmental visitor in the history department at the University of Adelaide during the first half of 2019 was most helpful. Indispensably, the University of Queensland has supported my dotage with an adjunct position and access to the Fryer Library's electronic resources.

The ANU Press Social Sciences Editorial Board and the referees put my manuscript through an exacting peer-review process, very much to the betterment of the eventual book. Particular thanks here go to Frank Bongiorno, Richard Reid and Marian Sawer. I have also been fortunate in being able to secure the copy-editing services of Carolyn Brewer once again.

My continued association with the ANU Press has been a pleasure. I am specifically grateful to Emily Tinker for shepherding this book through the editorial process, to Elouise Ball for her vigilant second round of copy editing and to Teresa Prowse for the splendid cover.

Bethany Phillips-Peddlesden (Melbourne) and Declan Lawless (Adelaide) and especially Emily Gallagher (Canberra) provided capable research assistance.

My gratitude to you all.

Referencing Conventions

Newspaper articles are cited in full throughout, both on first appearance and subsequently. Other printed sources, whether a book or a journal article are cited in full upon their first appearance in each chapter. Subsequent citations within each chapter appear in abbreviated form.

The reviews of the various volumes of Clark's *A History of Australia* are attributed thus: 'review of Volume 1', 'review of Volume 2', through to 'review of Volume 6'. Except for Volume 1 (that has no dates in the title), the dates of the various volumes are also included.

DOIs have been inserted against the matching publication upon their first appearance in each chapter. They also appear in the Appendices. Unless otherwise stated, the weblinks cited in the footnotes were current as of 28 September 2021.

The *dramatis personae* in this book, both great and small, have been briefly introduced upon their first mention. If required, additional information on most can be accessed online in either/or the *Australian Dictionary of Biography*,[1] *Obituaries Australia*,[2] *People Australia*[3] and *Wikipedia*.[4]

---

1 *Australian Dictionary of Biography*, National Centre of Biography, Canberra: The Australian National University, available at: adb.anu.edu.au/.
2 *Obituaries Australia*, National Centre of Biography, Canberra: The Australian National University, available at: oa.anu.edu.au/.
3 *People Australia,* available at: peopleaustralia.anu.edu.au/.
4 *Wikipedia,* available at: en.wikipedia.org/wiki/Main_Page.

Foreword

Doug Munro: A Very Short Introduction

> Tuvaluans also created a documentary record. According to one naval captain, they were such inveterate letter writers and pestered so much for stationery that his ship almost ran out of ink.[1]

It began with a letter postmarked Wellington, New Zealand. Fifteen years later, I count its sender among my good friends, even if we are separated by a large continent and an even larger ocean. But readers of this book may be asking, 'Who is Doug Munro?' and it's a fair enough question. He is a New Zealander whose original specialisation was Pacific Islands history and who taught for nine years at the University of the South Pacific in Fiji. Although his two degrees were awarded by Australian universities (Flinders and Macquarie), and although he lived in Australia for some 20 years, he has published little on Australian history. He would be the last to describe himself as an historian of Australia. Yet, like the letter I received in 2007, he has seemingly come out of nowhere to write a wonderful book on an aspect of Australia's History Wars.

Like the late nineteenth-century Tuvaluans, the subject of his doctoral thesis, Doug is an inveterate missive writer. Every couple of weeks, we exchange emails about the books we have read, the research projects we are trying to get across the finish line, and the absurdity of politics and politicians, both New Zealand and Canadian. Of course, our exchanges are not entirely scholarly: the occasional meme has been known to travel 15,000 kilometres from Wellington to Fredericton and vice versa, as have photographs of Belle, Doug's much-loved Maltese Terrier, and Bruce,

---

1   Doug Munro, 'On Being a Historian of Tuvalu: Further Thoughts on Methodology and Mindset', *History in Africa: A Journal of Debates, Methods, and Source Analysis,* vol. 26, 1999, pp. 218–36, specifically p. 225, doi.org/10.2307/3172142.

my new Labrador Retriever. Academic friendships may start with what matters most to us as scholars—books, ideas and, for historians, archival discoveries that range from the everyday to the jackpot—but they quickly move into what matters most to us as people—the comings and goings of our kids, the fortunes and misfortunes of mutual friends, our health and our partner's health.

Fifteen years ago, I was a junior scholar, insecure in my research and writing. Doug's letter, coming when it did and coming as it did, completely out of the blue, meant a lot: a senior scholar, with a lot on his plate, had taken the time to send me some material relevant to my own research. For the next couple of years, I took more than I gave, seeking his criticism, incorporating his frank advice, and needing his genuine encouragement. It's now my turn to return the favour to a fine historian, biographer and friend.

> An abiding memory is wading through miles of microfilms looking for nuggets—very much like a gold miner.[2]

Doug's scholarship moves widely across both time and space, from the Pacific Islands in the nineteenth century to activist-historians in North America in the twentieth century, and from indentured labourers who appear as fragments in a larger archive to great historians who appear larger than life in books, articles and countless archival boxes. The Manning Clark papers alone measure a staggering 30.3 metres. At each stop, Doug immerses himself in his subject, wades through miles of material and emerges with a manuscript that invariably contains something original, or golden, either a new set of facts or a new interpretation. In a way, he reminds me a bit of Canadian historian Ramsay Cook, who once described himself as a grasshopper: because he didn't like staying in one place for extended periods of time, he jumped from one topic to the next, exploring it long enough to write an article or a book, before moving on.

In his doctoral work, completed at Macquarie University in 1983, Doug studied Tuvalu and its long encounter with European traders, missionaries and colonial officials across the nineteenth century, or in his words, its long

---

2 Munro, 'On Being a Historian of Tuvalu', p. 226.

encounter with 'commerce, the cross, and the flag'.[3] From 1984 the focus of his research was indentured labour and unfree labour generally, although he occasionally returned to missionary activity and colonial rule. Caught up in what have been called the 'messy entanglements' of Pacific history, he published a remarkable run of 20-plus articles.[4] (Parenthetically, Doug doesn't like the phrase 'messy entanglements' because it implies that the past is indecipherable when it isn't. Personally, I like it because it speaks to the complexity and contingency of history. I suspect it's a generational thing or a grad school thing. After all, Doug is a generation ahead of me and was trained in the Canberra-school tradition of empiricism.) In between his work on indentured labourers and Polynesian pastors, Doug co-authored a fascinating article—frankly, there is no other word for it—on the frequency and intensity of tropical storms in Tuvalu: that its findings may be helpful to the identification of 'temporal trends and variations in low latitude tropical cyclone frequencies over the long term' eerily anticipates the environmental historian's imperative to understand yesterday's weather in order to understand the impact of climate change on today's weather.[5]

Even before Doug left the University of the South Pacific and returned to New Zealand in 2000, he was switching lanes and developing an interest in biography—notably his biographical work on other Pacific historians, culminating in a book on five of his compatriots, *The Ivory Tower and Beyond*.[6] Another research interest was suicide in twentieth-century New Zealand, by any definition an intellectually and emotionally draining subject. Historians dig where they stand and Doug stood in Wellington, giving him easy access to Archives New Zealand: using routinely generated sources—in this case, state coronial inquests—he and his Canadian co-author studied people at their lowest, who were dealing with any number of challenges, from physical and mental illness to financial difficulty, and from marital breakdown to alcohol abuse.

---

3   Doug Munro, 'The Lagoon Islands: A History of Tuvalu, 1820–1908', PhD thesis, Macquarie University, 1983, p. ii, available at: digilib.library.usp.ac.fj/gsdl/collect/usplibr1/index/assoc/HASH01e1.dir/doc.pdf.
4   See Doug Munro, 'Labour Trade Studies: What and Where?' in Alaima Talu and Max Quanchi (eds), *Messy Entanglements: The Papers of the 10th Pacific History Association Conference, Tarawa, Kiribati,* Brisbane: Pacific History Association, 1995, pp. 131–39.
5   R.F. McLean and Doug Munro, 'Late 19th Century Tropical Storms and Hurricanes in Tuvalu', *South Pacific Journal of Natural Science,* vol. 11, 1991, pp. 203–19, specifically p. 216, available at: uspaquatic.library.usp.ac.fj/gsdl/collect/spjnas/index/assoc/HASH0199.dir/doc.pdf.
6   Doug Munro, *The Ivory Tower and Beyond: Participant Historians of the Pacific,* Newcastle-upon Tyne: Cambridge Scholars Publishing, 2009.

The end result was a series of articles on suicide in New Zealand that are both insightful and humane, that treat a difficult subject—a 'sequence of trials and sorrows'[7]—with equal parts analysis and empathy.

But in the main, Doug focused his scholarly energy on the relationship between historians and historical writing in the Pacific Islands, his original stomping ground, but also in Australia, Great Britain, Canada, and the United States, with a special interest in biographies of historians and academic controversies. His output has been deep, wide and prolific: books, edited volumes, interviews and a special issue of the *Journal of Historical Biography* (2014), 'Telling Academic Lives'. It's also been very good, and the reviewers have been generous, even effusive. Peter Hempenstall, for example, singled out Munro's 'indefatigability as a researcher', adding that the endnotes to *The Ivory Tower and Beyond* are alone 'worth the price of admission'.[8]

Doug's research may be worth the price of admission, but his writing is the show. Again, the reviewers have been kind, describing his prose as 'clear', 'smooth flowing' and even 'elegant'.[9] Although he once called himself a 'grubber with an ability to find things' in the archives,[10] Doug understands that the grubbiness of research must be polished with jargon-free writing that aspires to tell a well-structured story.

> Originality takes many forms.[11]

One form of originality is a new take on an old story, in this instance the story of Peter Ryan's 1993 assault against the scholarship and reputation of Manning Clark, the recently deceased author of a renowned six-volume history of Australia. That an unapologetic and unrepentant Ryan had been Clark's publisher at Melbourne University Press makes the story that

---

7   John C. Weaver and Doug Munro, 'Country Living, Country Dying: Rural Suicides in New Zealand, 1900–1950', *Journal of Social History*, vol. 42, no. 4, 2009, pp. 933–61, specifically p. 943, doi.org/10.1353/jsh.0.0186.
8   Peter Hempenstall, review of *The Ivory Tower and Beyond: Participant Historians of the Pacific*, in *Journal of the Pacific*, vol. 45, no. 2, 2013, pp. 284–86, specifically p. 285, doi.org/10.1080/00223344.2010.501703.
9   Arthur Crook, review of *J.C. Beaglehole: Public Intellectual, Critical Conscience*, in *Australian Journal of Politics and History*, vol. 60, no. 1, 2014, p. 145, doi.org/10.1111/ajph.12050; D.K. Fieldhouse, review of *J.C. Beaglehole: Public Intellectual, Critical Conscience*, in *Journal of Historical Biography*, vol. 12, 2012, pp. 118–20, specifically p. 119, available at: www.ufv.ca/jhb/Volume_12/Volume_12_Fieldhouse.pdf; Jaume Aurell, review of *Clio's Lives: Biographies and Autobiographies of Historians*, in *Biography*, vol 42, no. 2, 2019, pp. 421–26, specifically p. 421, doi.org/10.1353/bio.2019.0045.
10 Munro, 'On Being a Historian of Tuvalu', p. 227.
11 Munro, 'On Being a Historian of Tuvalu', p. 232.

much more complicated. Why did he, in his words, take 'an overdue axe' to 'the stalk of a tall poppy'? To answer that question, Doug went to the archives in Canberra, Melbourne and Adelaide where he spent long hours in reading rooms, scurrying for answers. To call Doug an 'archive rat' is not an insult. It's a compliment from one historian to another. Indeed, the research sustaining *History Wars* is remarkable, or 'forensic', to use Doug's word: no stone was left unturned, no file was left unopened and no commentary was left unread. Yet why should anyone care about Ryan's admittedly bizarre attack against his leading author and close friend? Or, as Doug asks, 'what does a controversy that basically lasted a fortnight as a media and talkback radio event mean to us almost thirty years later?'

As the title indicates, it speaks to Australia's ongoing History Wars, which are nasty and brutish but never short because they are fought over long stretches of time on multiple fronts: settler colonialism, reconciliation, immigration, multiculturalism, statues, holidays, museum exhibits and school curricula. Ultimately, they are fought over national identity and national symbols and that fight is visceral. For example, when a Bermagui cafe owner displayed a sign on Australia Day in 2016 saying, 'Yes, we're open on National Dickhead Day', he received death threats.[12] And when some Australians vandalised statues of James Cook, other Australians asked: what's wrong with celebrating the man who, in 1770, raised a flag and claimed British sovereignty over what became Australia? But Cook's ceremony of possession—which historian Mark McKenna brilliantly called 'nothing less than a form of sorcery'[13]—was also a ceremony of dispossession that marked devastating consequences for Aboriginal peoples. All of this is to say that the Ryan–Clark controversy is about more than Peter Ryan and Manning Clark. Ultimately, it's about Australia's national identit(ies) and conversations about national identity are necessarily fraught and never easy: Canada came within a few thousand votes of breaking up in 1995 over its identity question.

The Ryan–Clark controversy also speaks to the place of Manning Clark in Australia's national imagination. Had Ryan taken his axe to another historian, it's unlikely that we would be still talking about it 30 years later. But Clark wasn't just any historian. He was the author and keeper of

---

12 Paul Daley, 'Australia Day is "dickhead day": year-long visceral backlash over chalkboard message', *Guardian*, 25 January 2017, available at: www.theguardian.com/australia-news/2017/jan/25/australia-day-is-dickhead-day-year-long-visceral-backlash-over-chalkboard-message.
13 Mark McKenna, 'Crown', in Melissa Harper and Richard White (eds), *Symbols of Australia*, Sydney: UNSW Press, 2010, pp. 30–37, specifically p. 35.

Australia's national story, however imperfect his scholarship and however blinkered that story. Few, if any, historians in the Anglo-American world have occupied the space that Clark occupied by dint of will, force of personality and felicity of pen. Canada's Donald Creighton (b.1902)? Maybe. But not even Creighton, for all his gifts, enjoyed the same prominence; when he died in 1979, he had been already written off as a caricature, as yesterday's man unable to speak either to the past or the present. Not so Manning Clark: 'In death as in life, [he] has retained the capacity to disturb and astound his fellow Australians'.[14]

I was reminded of Clark's tenacious and complicated place in Australia's national imagination in 2015 when Doug—along with a Canadian colleague, curiously enough—invited me to a conference on biographies of historians at ANU.[15] Preparing for my first trip to Australia, I made a list of novels: Patrick White's *Voss,* Kate Grenville's *The Secret River,* Richard Flanagan's *The Narrow Road to the Deep North* and Peter Carey's *Amnesia*. Each in its own way affected me. But I was especially struck by the history they drew on and the history they tried to make sense of. To quote William Faulkner, 'The past is never dead. In fact, it isn't even past'.[16]

In the opening scenes of *Amnesia,* the main character—a flawed, shambolic, down-on-his-luck journalist named Felix Moore—is finally given the boot by his long-suffering wife. Tracking him down at a local watering hole—a dive, really—she summarily presents him with a plastic bag containing, he says, 'a mobile phone, a charger, a framed photo of my daughters, and my complete signed set, all six volumes, of Manning Clark's much loved *History of Australia*'. Without a nickel to his name and his credit cards maxed out, Felix is forced to sell his 'treasured Manning Clarks' to a book dealer on Sydney's Oxford Street.[17] With $200 in his pocket, he is able to move on with his life, even if things don't go according to plan.

---

14 Stephen Holt, *A Short History of Manning Clark,* Sydney: Allen & Unwin, 1991, p. 231.
15 See Doug Munro and John Reid (eds), *Clio's Lives: Biographies and Autobiographies of Historians,* Canberra: ANU Press, 2017, doi.org/10.22459/CL.10.2017.
16 William Faulkner, *Requiem for a Nun,* Act 1, Scene III, Vintage Books, 1951.
17 Peter Carey, *Amnesia,* London: Penguin Random House, 2014, pp. 15–17.

It's a clever literary trick: selling Clark's *History* both saves Felix in the immediate term and frees him in the medium term, allowing him to explore Australia's complicated past unburdened by the physical and symbolic weight of Clark's *History*. And that's when it dawned on me, on Manly Beach, of all places: 'Manning Clark is never dead. In fact, he isn't even Manning Clark'. He's a blank slate on which Australians, including Peter Ryan, can write what they want, making the Ryan–Clark controversy a text to be analysed and *History Wars* an important contribution to Australia's national conversation.

Donald Wright
University of New Brunswick

Figure 1. Caricature of Manning Clark on the front cover of *Quadrant*, September 1993.

Source. © John Spooner (artist) and *Quadrant* 1993; reproduced with the permission of John Spooner and Keith Windschuttle, editor of *Quadrant*. Image provided by the Alexander Turnbull Library, Wellington, NZ.

FOREWORD

Figure 2. Peter Ryan—drawn from life—on the front cover of *Quadrant*, October 1994.

Source. © John Spooner (artist) and *Quadrant* 1994; reproduced with the permission of John Spooner and Keith Windschuttle, editor of *Quadrant*. Image provided by the Alexander Turnbull Library, Wellington, NZ.

Prologue

> In death as in life, Manning Clark has retained the capacity to disturb and astound his fellow Australians. He continues to generate conflict.
>
> Stephen Holt (1999)[1]

> Clark has always boldly accepted the view that history-writing is ultimately an imaginative art—or so his practice suggests. Through it, Clark declares his own vision of spiritual purpose, and of the dilemmas inherent in the process of living.
>
> A.A. Phillips (1978)[2]

In 1993, Peter Ryan (1923–2015), the former director of Melbourne University Press (hereafter MUP), launched an out-of-the-blue attack on the work and character of his best-selling author Manning Clark (1915–1991), who had died two-and-a-half years earlier. The assault took place in the September 1993 issue of the conservative monthly journal *Quadrant,* and it caused quite a stir.[3] The catalyst was one of the Wednesday lunchtime gatherings involving Robert Manne, a political scientist and editor of *Quadrant,* and a group of colleagues at La Trobe University. At one of these meetings—on 8 May 1991 to be exact—Ryan was in attendance and he asked whether *Quadrant* would be interested in an essay on Clark. As Manne recalled: 'The subject of Clark had clearly been weighing heavily on his mind. He spoke of his intention to write an

---

[1] Stephen Holt, *A Short History of Manning Clark,* Sydney: Allen & Unwin, 1999, p. 231.
[2] A.A. Phillips, 'The Unlucky Countryman: Manning Clark's Lawson', *Meanjin Quarterly,* vol. 37, July 1978, pp. 257–61, specifically p. 257.
[3] Ryan's attack on Clark and his replies to critics were spread over three issues of *Quadrant:* Peter Ryan, 'Manning Clark', *Quadrant,* vol. 37, no. 9, September 1993, pp. 9–22; Ryan, 'A Reply to my Critics', *Quadrant,* vol. 37, no. 10, October 1993, pp. 11–14; Ryan, 'The Charge of the Lightweight Brigade', *Quadrant,* vol. 38, no. 10, October 1994, pp. 10–14. The three articles were republished in his *Lines of Fire: Manning Clark & Other Writings,* ed. A.K. Macdougall, Binalong, NSW: Clarion Editions, 1997, pp. 179–234. The page references throughout are to the *Lines of Fire* versions.

essay about his old friend; it would not be flattering'. In full knowledge that severe criticism would follow, Ryan was determined that the job 'had to be done'.[4] Clark died a fortnight later and the proposed essay went into abeyance, only for Ryan to resurrect the idea in mid-1993. Manne was still interested, on the grounds that a 'serious discussion' of Clark's *History* that showed 'the interconnection between character and work' was overdue; he hoped that '"Quadrant" might become the forum for a lively debate about the status of Clark's "History"'.[5] Ryan duly delivered in August 1993 and his essay was promptly published.

Ryan started in uncompromising fashion: 'This essay is an overdue axe laid to the stalk of a tall poppy'.[6] In a full-throated assault on Clark as both a person and an historian, Ryan catalogued his victim's personal faults and indiscretions—the drinking sprees of his earlier days, his neediness, 'his propensity to strike an attitude',[7] his 'humbug',[8] his unworthy criticisms of others, his indictable offences as an historian and his delinquencies as an MUP author. He then wades into Clark's six-volume *A History of Australia* as having the 'insubstantiality of thistledown', of being 'a construct spun from fairy floss'[9] and adding for good measure that 'Clark's literary style was bad to the point of embarrassment'.[10] Ryan also makes the extraordinary statement, with all the zeal of the repentant sinner, that:

> Of the many things in my life upon which I must look back with shame, the chiefest is that of having been the publisher of Clark's *History of Australia,* and of having given him that support and encouragement which an author expects of his publisher.[11]

He goes on to describe the *History* as 'largely an imposition on Australian credulity—more plainly, a fraud'. The author, Ryan went on to assure his readers, was 'partly a mountebank',[12] and he berated the Australian historical profession for its dereliction in failing to expose the sheer

---

4   Robert Manne, 'A holy cow called history', *Age,* 1 September 1993, p. 16; Manne, email to author, 10 March 2018.
5   Manne, 'A holy cow called history', *Age,* 1 September 1993, p. 16; Cameron Forbes, 'The men who wrinkled history's page', *Weekend Australian*, 28–29 August 1993, p. 4.
6   Ryan, 'Manning Clark', p. 179.
7   Ryan, 'Manning Clark', p. 188.
8   Ryan, 'Manning Clark', pp. 182, 202.
9   Ryan, 'Manning Clark', p. 180.
10   Ryan, 'Manning Clark', p. 212.
11   Ryan, 'Manning Clark', p. 181.
12   Ryan, 'Manning Clark', pp. 200–1.

awfulness of Clark's work. He acknowledged that Clark's *History* was 'born ... of a weighty and even noble vision';[13] apart from that it was without redeeming feature.

Ryan's initial attack in the September 1993 issue of *Quadrant* caused immediate uproar, with Clark's family and friends in high dudgeon. Ryan had never publicly declared his dissatisfaction with his author or the *History* in the 25 years (from 1962 until 1987) that he had published the remaining five volumes of the *History*, and neither did he convey to Clark his dissatisfactions at any point during their lengthy professional relationship.[14] To the contrary, he encouraged Clark every step of the way as well as vigorously promoting the *History* and praising its author to the skies. But now Ryan was telling the world that the *History* contained 'over a million printed English words, probably unrivalled in their power to combine the non sequitur with the anti-climax, and to wring the last drops from a series of foregone conclusions'.[15] The unforeseen posthumous attack, and its ferocity, caused reeling and revelling, depending on what side of the political fence one stood. More than 25 years later, the episode still resonates.

Even so, the sceptic is entitled to ask: what does a controversy that basically lasted a fortnight as a media and talkback radio event mean to us almost 30 years later? When responding to his critics, following the publication of his first *Quadrant* article on Clark, Ryan observed that their reactions demonstrated that Australia was still 'a very provincial place'.[16] The implication is that the 'Clark controversy' or the 'Ryan affair', as it is variously called, was just another storm in a teacup, involving small-minded people indulging their bitchiness in ways that had no possible significance for those with a broader perspective on the world. To the contrary, the Ryan–Clark imbroglio is noteworthy because it extended well into the public realm, to the extent of being debated in Britain. Memorable in itself, the controversy also matters because it exposed fault lines in the ongoing Australia History Wars. The issues laid bare

---

13 Ryan, 'Manning Clark', for quotation see p. 180, also p. 205.
14 Clark's project is comprised of: *A History of Australia*. Volume 1: *From the Earliest Times to the Age of Macquarie* (1962); Volume 2: *New South Wales and Van Diemen's Land, 1822–1838* (1968); Volume 3: *The Beginning of an Australian Civilisation, 1824–1851* (1973); Volume 4: *The Earth Abideth for Ever, 1851–1888* (1978); Volume 5: *The People Make Laws, 1890–1915 (1981);* Volume 6: *'The old dead tree and the young tree green', 1916–1935* (1987), all published by MUP.
15 Ryan, 'Manning Clark', p. 214.
16 Ryan, 'A Reply to my Critics', p. 214.

have not gone away. As if to underline the extent of ongoing interest in the Ryan–Clark controversy, a somewhat hagiographic short biography of Peter Ryan (*Ryan's Luck*) appeared in November 2020, written by his friend Peter Tidey, in which the controversy is discussed at some length.[17] Moreover, in excess of half the first review of *Ryan's Luck,* which appeared the following month in *Quadrant,* is taken up by discussion of Clark and/or the controversy.[18] Both biographer and reviewer accept Ryan's version of events, which is repudiated in the present book.[19]

* * *

Ryan said that a given author 'is of but passing interest'. What matters is the subject—the person or thing that is being discussed.[20] Nonetheless, the genesis of the present book should be explained and the reader is entitled to know why (and how) I embarked on a study of this sort when my interest in the Ryan–Clark controversy was so belated. I barely noticed the imbroglio when it erupted and only got around to reading Ryan's first *Quadrant* article in 1999. I was teaching at the University of the South Pacific for much of the 1990s and my concerns lay elsewhere. Gradually, I became less interested in Pacific Islands history—I left Fiji at the beginning of 2000—and my research and writing increasingly turned to biography, and more specifically to 'telling academic lives', particularly in Australia.

Ryan gradually worked himself into the picture. I had been aware from at least the early 1970s that Ryan was a long-serving director of MUP, and I was—and remain—mightily impressed with his wartime narrative *Fear Drive My Feet*.[21] In 1997, I referred to it as 'the incomparable personal

---

17   John Tidey, *Ryan's Luck: A Life of Peter Ryan MM,* Melbourne: Arcadia, 2020, pp. 44, 68, 104–11.
18   Robert Murray, 'The Punch and Sparkle of Peter Ryan', review of *Ryan's Luck,* by John Tidey, *Quadrant,* vol. 64, no. 12, December 2020, pp. 91–93.
19   Every so often down the years, a Ryan supporter has come out in sturdy defence of his attacks on Manning Clark, endorsing Ryan's depiction of what happened—e.g. Andrew Bolt, 'The thought deadening legacy of Manning Clark', 11 February 2007, *Herald-Sun* (Melbourne), available at: blogs.news.com.au/heraldsun/andrewbolt/index.php/heraldsun/comments/the_thought_deadening_legacy_of_manning_clark/P20/ (viewed on 3 September 2015 but site discontinued); Peter Coleman, 'Australian notes', *Spectator Australia,* 15 January 2011, www.spectator.co.uk/australia/6613193/australiannotes-67/ (viewed on 1 September 2014 but site discontinued).
20   Ryan, 'Manning Clark', p. 183.
21   Peter Ryan, *Fear Drive My Feet,* Sydney: Angus & Robertson, 1959, and subsequent editions. Excerpts republished in his *Lines of Fire,* pp. 19–38. In my view, *Fear Drive My Feet* rivals Eric Feldt's *The Coast Watchers,* Melbourne: Oxford University Press, 1946. That's how good it is.

account of the New Guinea campaign by Peter Ryan'.[22] On the other hand I was becoming less enamoured of Ryan as a public commentator, remarking in 2007 that he was 'adding his mite to the vulgarisation of public discourse in Australia'.[23] We 'crossed paths' again in 2012 when I reviewed Mark McKenna's biography of Clark, this time observing that 'there was much truth in Ryan's allegations [against Clark] … but his tone and his very motivations were just cause for offence'.[24] I also raised the obvious points: why did Ryan continue to publish a multivolume work that he considered substandard, and why did he not tackle Clark about these perceived shortcomings at any point in their 25-year professional relationship? (He never adequately answered these questions, even when pressed to do so.)

Over the next 18 months, I became increasingly aware that Ryan's version of events didn't stack up. I was also struck by the extent to which he personalised and politicised everything, while in the same breath accusing his critics from the 'loquacious Left' of being emotional and ideological. A related problem, as I saw it, was Ryan's continuing hostilities despite saying, in 1994, that he hoped 'never to write another word about Manning Clark, who has occupied much time during which I would have preferred to be thinking about something else'.[25] Yet he kept on attacking Clark in print. There was also Ryan's allegation that Clark's *History* was waved through by academic reviewers down the years. Indeed, a central plank in Ryan's argument is his assertion that the Australian historical profession was a halfway house between a protection racket and a sheltered workshop whereby a miscreant author was shielded against valid criticism. Yet Clark had plenty of critics within the historical profession, and Ryan was in a position to know this.

In light of these misgivings I decided, in January 2014, to re-examine the Ryan–Clark affair and to embark on a forensic re-evaluation. Two broad conclusions quickly became apparent. First Ryan's criticisms of Clark's *History* were wholly unoriginal. Second, much of what Ryan says is

---

22   Doug Munro, 'The Making of *Ai Matai*: A Cautionary Tale in Fijian Historiography and Publishing', *Pacific Studies,* vol. 20, no. 3, 1997, pp. 61–79, specifically p. 75 n.10.
23   Doug Munro, review of *Ida Leeson: A Life: Not a Blue-Stocking Lady,* by Sylvia Martin, *Journal of Pacific History,* vol. 42, no. 1, 2007, pp. 125–27, specifically p. 126, doi.org/10.1080/00223340701286958.
24   Doug Munro, review of *An Eye for Eternity: The Life of Manning Clark,* by Mark McKenna, *Reviews in History,* review no. 1253, 17 May 2012, available at: www.history.ac.uk/reviews/review/1253.
25   Ryan, 'The Charge of the Lightweight Brigade', p. 234.

inaccurate. He is not a trustworthy source of information. Whether you call the present study a post-mortem or the exhumation of a grave, it is a minute chapter-and-verse examination of the bases of Ryan's strictures—their inaccuracies, false representations and strategic omissions—as well as a systematisation of the scattered and piecemeal defences offered on behalf of Clark. Hence the need for heavy footnoting.

Years later, Ryan recalled how he was treated in the manner of a leper in biblical times:

> My infection with the socially embarrassing distemper of literary leprosy arose from a long article in *Quadrant* of September 1993. It was only my second contribution to that admirable magazine [it was actually his fifth[26]], and it is interesting now to reflect that it was written with high encouragement from its then Editor, Robert Manne.
>
> That article re-examined the value of the work of historian Manning Clark, who had died a few years earlier. Re-reading it the other day, some seventeen years later, I remained confident that it was written in polite terms, and that all its assertions were backed by cogent evidence. Of course I realised that my conclusions would be widely unacceptable, but I took it for granted that contrary argument would be made within the arena of reasonable evidence and civil language: I never made a bigger mistake in my life.[27]

Ryan's version of events cannot be accepted as a reasonable way of looking at the controversy. Clark could be a sloppy writer as well as being a needy and sometimes uncooperative author. The reader will soon discern that I am no more enamoured of Clark now than I have been in the past, but I believe that Ryan behaved badly. Hence my motivation for writing this book parallels that of David Marr when he decided to embark on a biography of Sir Garfield Barwick (1903–1997)—namely, that Marr was horrified by Barwick's involvement in The Dismissal of the Whitlam Government in 1975, and the abuse of his supposedly politically neutral

---

26 The previous four contributions were: Ryan, 'The Fall and Mr Fairfax', review of *Heralds and Angels: The House of Fairfax, 1841–1990*, by Gavin Souter, *Quadrant*, vol. 35, no. 6, June 1991, pp. 72–74; Ryan, 'Did People Laugh before 1700?', review of *The Oxford Book of Humorous Prose from William Caxton to P.G. Wodehouse*, by Frank Muir, *Quadrant*, vol. 35, no. 12, December 1991, pp. 76–78; Ryan, 'A.D. Hope: A Memoir', *Quadrant*, vol. 36, nos 7–8, July–August 1992, pp. 30–40 (reprinted in his *Lines of Fire*, pp. 153–76); Ryan, 'Hasluck: The Private Man', *Quadrant*, vol. 37, no. 3, March 1993, pp. 21–24 (reprinted in his *Lines of Fire*, pp. 129–37).

27 Peter Ryan, 'My Life as a Leper', *Quadrant*, vol. 55, nos 1–2, January–February 2011, pp. 127–28, specifically p. 127.

role as chief justice of Australia that this entailed. Although the present book deals with a much less momentous event, I too have sought the reasons why Ryan behaved in the manner he did. Or in Marr's words, 'I had to understand how that man could have done what he did. I wanted to work it out for myself and explain it to others'.[28] The urge to write, after all, comes from not knowing and wanting to find out. That was my agenda. There was also the purely professional interest in pursuing a story worth telling and the prospect of venturing into new academic territory.

In the process, I have reached negative conclusions about Ryan after comparing what he wrote in *Quadrant,* and afterwards, with the newspaper coverage at the time. In addition, I consulted several sets of personal papers, his own included, various oral history interviews (in the National Library of Australia), the files relating to Clark's *History* and the minutes of the MUP Board of Management (at the University of Melbourne Archives). Ryan's habitual evasiveness and untruthfulness is striking. Ironically, the most incriminating evidence against Ryan is found in his own papers and in his autobiography, *Final Proof: Memoirs of a Publisher.*[29] In the interests of fairness and accuracy, I have given Ryan every opportunity to put his case by quoting from his writings. Paraphrasing can run the risk of distortion, so his actual wording is used wherever possible. He does write very well, and unambiguously at that. As well as documentary research and a reading of the relevant literature, I spoke to numerous colleagues who well remember the Ryan–Clark controversy. The level of interest in what I was doing somewhat surprised me. Mostly I would raise the subject in casual conversation and the respondents often sang like nightingales. Sometimes I was approached and information was volunteered—whether criticism of the *History,* or negative comments about Ryan, and occasionally positive statements about him. People were also contacted by email. The only formal interview was over the telephone with Michael Cathcart. All in all, I cast a fairly wide net.

I should add that researching and writing this book was not a furtive exercise, whereas prior knowledge of Ryan's attack on Clark had been within a closed circle. I told many colleagues of my plans and progress. I gave forewarning with seminar presentations on the subject at Flinders

---

28   Quoted in Melanie Suzanne Wilson, 'David Marr: A Man of Conviction', Sydney Writers' Festival, 20 May 2015, available at: atthefestival.wordpress.com/2015/05/20/david-marr-a-man-of-conviction/; David Marr, *Barwick,* Sydney: George Allen & Unwin, 1980.
29   Peter Ryan, *Final Proof: Memoirs of a Publisher,* Sydney: Quadrant Books, 2010.

University in 2015 and at the University of Melbourne the following year. I announced my intentions in a couple of publications (freely available on the internet as well as in print), where it is clear that I am no apologist for Clark.[30]

What I did not do was to contact Ryan, although he could have easily found out what I was up to. Initially, I was not far enough into the research to ask the right questions. For example, when I gave my seminar presentation at Flinders University in mid-2015 I had yet to learn about MUP's contractual arrangements with Clark (which Ryan comprehensively misrepresents and which I would never have thought to question). The further I got into the research the more I realised that Ryan was misleading, wrong or just plain downright dishonest in so many matters. There came the point when I decided not to contact him, realising that an interview, or even correspondence, would likely be confrontational and unproductive. It is hard to see what would have been accomplished and I would probably have been accused of harassing a defenceless old man who was in poor health. I am in two minds about how I handled the matter. There is an element of regret in not having at least sent him a letter of enquiry, if only to avoid the admission in this paragraph. It would also have put him on notice. On the other hand, my feeling that nothing good would have resulted from any such letter is seemingly vindicated because I later learned that Ryan was loath to admit that he might be in error.

Writing aversely about the recently deceased (Ryan died in late 2015) carries risks, just as Ryan himself was criticised for the same thing in relation to Clark in 1993. Ryan could not complain, at least in principle, given his statement at the time that '[t]he notion that the dead should stand immune in some sanctuary is a mealy-mouthed cop-out'.[31] Ryan also justified his disclosures on Clark on the grounds that 'the drive of Manning Clark's life was to be a *public* citizen' [emphasis in original],[32]

---

30 Doug Munro, 'The "Intrusion" of Personal Feelings: Biographical Dilemmas', *Flinders Journal of History and Politics*, vol. 30, 2014, pp. 3–20, specifically pp. 11–12, available at: dspace.flinders.edu.au/xmlui/bitstream/handle/2328/36712/FJHP30_2014_01_Monroe.pdf?sequence=1&isAllowed=y; Munro, '"How illuminating it has been": Matthews, McKenna and their Biographies of Manning Clark', in Philip Payton (ed.), *Emigrants & Historians: Essays in Honour of Eric Richards*, Adelaide: Wakefield Press, 2016, pp. 98–131 (text), 169–75 (endnotes), specifically p. 174 n.75, available at: honesthistory.net.au/wp/wp-content/uploads/Munro_MatthewsMcKenna.pdf.
31 Ryan, 'A Reply to my Critics', p. 216.
32 Ryan, 'Manning Clark', p. 189.

which 'had put him on the map'.³³ Indeed, as early as 1974 Clark was described as 'the best *guru* in the business'.³⁴ Ryan was also a public figure, although fairly minor compared with Clark, and of different ilk. He did not give public addresses to the masses. But Ryan still placed himself in the public gaze via the print media and had done so since at least the early 1980s. Like Clark, his public interventions were integral to his being.

What follows is the first systematic and extended attempt to get to the bottom of the Ryan–Clark controversy, and to trace its broader cultural significance. In doing so, I take to heart the sentiment expressed in Ryan's (spurious) claim that 'It is perfectly amazing how seldom one can actually bring a Clark fan to engage on any point of detail in his works'.³⁵ In that spirit, although I could hardly be described as 'a Clark fan', I have gone through Ryan's attack on Clark and the replies to his critics on a pretty much point-by-point basis. I take a leaf out of Ryan's book by confronting him on his own terms—that is to say, by means of an old-fashioned, if you like, empirical approach that tests the evidence and scrutinises Ryan's factual accuracy, or lack thereof, and the validity of his representations of *wie es eigentlich gewesen* (what actually happened, or even what *essentially* happened).

In the process, this book is divided into three sections, each with a different purpose. The two chapters in Part 1 ('Wider Setting'), as the name implies, provide the necessary background on the Ryan–Clark controversy, as well as biographical introductions of Clark and Ryan, and a contextualisation of the History Wars so that readers get their bearings. Part 2 ('Contention and Dissension') is intended as a narrative of the controversy—the reactions to Ryan's initial onslaught in *Quadrant*, Ryan's vigorous counter-reactions, a dissection of his unoriginality when discussing Clark's *History* and, by extension, a qualified rebuttal of Ryan's accusations that Clark was shielded by a complicit historical profession. In these fours chapters, interpretation is embedded within the narrative but they are largely descriptive, establishing what happened and offering explanations for the various outcomes. The trio of chapters in Part 3 ('Ruminations'), by contrast, deal with broader concerns and are thematic and reflective—locating Clark within the context of the Australian

---

33 Ryan, 'Manning Clark', p. 194.
34 Geoffrey Serle, 'One Man's Window on Our Past: Manning Clark's Third Volume', *Meanjin Quarterly*, vol. 33, no. 1, 1974, pp. 86–88, specifically p. 86.
35 Ryan, 'A Reply to my Critics', p. 217.

History Wars; assessing whether his influence on Paul Keating's thinking was as great as alleged at the time (it wasn't); tracing the migration of the Ryan–Clark controversy to England; examining Ryan's motives for his attack on Clark, which are sometimes hard to pin down; assessing the role of *Quadrant* in the controversy and its continued attacks on Clark in the years that followed and the magazine's role in the History Wars generally; and finally a summation of Ryan's culpable and duplicitous representations and what these say about him as a credible witness to history.

Part 1.
Wider Setting

1

Manning Clark and Peter Ryan

> Peter Ryan cried out in the dark,
> 'My greatest success was M. Clark
>   An odd sort of chap
>   Whose writings were crap;
> I published them just for a lark.'
>
> Chris Wallace-Crabbe[1]

During their 25-year professional relationship, from 1962 until 1987, Manning Clark was Australia's best-known and most controversial historian, and Peter Ryan probably became Australia's best-known publisher and certainly the best-known academic publisher.

Clark's career trajectory, like his life itself, was singular, even if he was by no means unusual among Australian historians in being a clergyman's son. His father was Charles Clark (1881–1951) an Anglican Church minister of low-church persuasion who, in the parlance of the time, had aspired above his station in marrying Catherine Hope (1878–1943), of distinctly upper-middle-class background and a descendant of Rev. Samuel Marsden. Clark and his two siblings were born in Sydney, but their father's adultery resulted in the family being shuffled to a vicarage at Phillip Island, near Melbourne. Manning Clark regarded his two years on

---

1   Handwritten copy of untitled limerick in the Macintyre Papers, National Library of Australia (hereafter NLA), MS 9389, Series 1, Box 5, Folder 32 (published with the poet's permission).

the island, when he was between the ages of seven and nine, as the idyllic part of his life that licensed him in later years to describe himself as 'a boy from the bush', when in fact he was a thoroughgoing urbanite.[2]

Much of the information about Clark's early years comes from his autobiography of childhood and coming of age (*The Puzzles of Childhood*), which he wrote in his old age.[3] *Puzzles* is more revealing of Clark the historian than an accurate depiction of the events and relationships described. His brother and sister were scandalised by the book, considering it a travesty of their family life.[4] As Clark's latest biographer puts it:

> His parents appear in *Puzzles* either as characters playing out his own inner conflicts or as mere precursors of his later self ... In *Puzzles,* Clark dramatized his parents' relationship, imagined his way into their minds and hearts, spoke for them and through them, invented thoughts and conversations, and recreated the experience of his early family life as a tragedy. The boy's world was inhabited by two types of human beings: angels and devils. His memories behaved with uncanny poetic licence ... or they conveniently served to explain what the old man had become ('my mother tells me one day I will be a famous man'). The whole narrative was infused with a moody, eternal melancholy ... descending on the reader like a heavy fog.[5]

In this, perhaps, we can discern Clark's tendency in the *History* to base his narratives around a series of personality clashes.

Charles and Catherine did not have a particularly happy marriage but the temptation to see the siblings as being overly defensive is dispelled when one realises that contemporaries at the prestigious Melbourne Grammar School, where Clark was enrolled in 1928, considered that the allegations in *Puzzles* of bullying were greatly exaggerated and that the book misrepresents the culture of the school beyond recognition.[6] Being an accomplished cricketer and a precocious student eased his

---

2   Stephen Holt, *A Short History of Manning Clark,* Sydney: Allen & Unwin, 1999, p. 9.
3   Manning Clark, *The Puzzles of Childhood,* Melbourne: Viking, 1989; republished by Penguin Books Australia, 1990.
4   Peter Ryan interviewed by John Farquarson, 10–11 October 2000 (p. 37 of transcript), NLA, ORAL TRC 4631; Ryan, notes of telephone conversation with A.G.L. Shaw, 4 October 1993, Ryan Papers, NLA, MS 9897, Series 6, Box 10, Folder 4; Mark McKenna, *An Eye for Eternity: The Life of Manning Clark,* Melbourne: Miegunyah Press, 2011, p. 61.
5   McKenna, *An Eye for Eternity,* pp. 59–60.
6   Brian Matthews, *Manning Clark: A Life,* Sydney: Allen & Unwin, 2008, p. 17; McKenna, *An Eye for Eternity,* pp. 93, 721 n.3.

path; he was dux equal in 1933. Rather than being a reliable account of his earlier life, *Puzzles* opens a window on the historian that Clark had become—prone to distortion, needing to be noticed and striving for effect, with his spiritual musings and ethereal turns of phrase imparting an aura of profundity.

Academic success followed him to the University of Melbourne where he caught the eye of the recently appointed professor of history, R.M. (Max) Crawford (1906–1991). At that time the usual high road to success was a scholarship to Oxbridge to complete a second degree, and Clark was the first of Crawford's bright young men to be sent to Oxford University (usually to Balliol College where Crawford himself had studied).[7] Clark sallied forth to Balliol in 1938, accompanied by his fiancée, Dymphna Lodewyckx (1916–2000), an accomplished linguist, who was set for postgraduate study of her own in Germany. With World War II in progress, Clark (by then married to Dymphna) insisted on their returning to Australia, in 1940, despite their studies being incomplete. Unable to secure a university job, he spent a frustrating four years teaching at Geelong Grammar School and trying to write up an MA thesis on Alexis de Tocqueville on the side.[8] Salvation came in 1944 with a temporary lectureship in political science at the University of Melbourne, and the following year he secured a permanent position in the department of history. He was doubly fortunate in being able to teach a full-year course in Australian history, which his students, Peter Ryan included, recall with yearning: 'The man could teach as naturally as a thrush could sing', was Ryan's verdict.[9] Clark liked to think that 'the historical map of Australia', when he started teaching at the University of Melbourne, 'was almost a blank' and that he 'had to set out on a journey without

---

7   Fay Anderson, *An Historian's Life: Max Crawford and the Politics of Academic Freedom*, Melbourne; Melbourne University Press (hereafter MUP), 2005, pp. 226–27; John Poynter, '"Wot Larks To Be Abroad": The History Department, 1937–71', in Fay Anderson and Stuart Macintyre (eds), *The Life of the Past: The Discipline of History at the University of Melbourne, 1855–2005*, Melbourne: Department of History, University of Melbourne, 2006, pp. 39–91, specifically pp. 57–59.
8   Posthumously published as Manning Clark, *The Ideal of Alexis de Tocqueville*, ed. Dymphna Clark, David Headon and John Williams, Melbourne: MUP, 2000.
9   Peter Ryan, 'Manning Clark', in his *Lines of Fire:Manning Clark & Other Writings*, ed. A.K. Macdougall, Binalong, NSW: Clarion Editions, 1997, pp. 179–214, specifically p. 185. Other memories are recalled in John Thompson, *The Patrician and the Bloke: Geoffrey Serle and the Making of Australian History*, Canberra: Pandanus Books, 2006, pp. 134–37; Geoffrey Blainey, *Before I Forget: An Early Memoir*, Melbourne: Hamish Hamilton, 2019, pp. 154–56; Hugh Stretton to Clark, 7 August 1987, Manning Clark Papers, NLA, MS 7550, Series 18, Box 158, Folder 27.

maps'.[10] A little earlier, in 1938, he went so far as to say that Australian history had been 'betrayed' by its practitioners.[11] He was doing less than justice to his predecessors. Rather, he stood on their shoulders and they provided fodder for his earlier lectures. That the secondary literature was not extensive had the indirect advantage of Clark requiring his honours students to engage in archival research.

Figure 3. In happier times. Peter Ryan and Manning Clark at the National Press Club, Canberra, 17 April 1980.
Source. University of Melbourne Archives, 1993.0063.00001. Reproduced with permission.

Such was the state of the academic job market that Clark was appointed, in 1949, professor of history at Canberra University College, a satellite of the University of Melbourne. He would not have secured a lectureship when judged by today's standards—no PhD, no academic publications and the first volume of *Select Documents in Australian History* (1950) still

---

10   Quoted in McKenna, *An Eye for Eternity*, p. 250. Actually, the first such course in Australian history was mounted 20 years earlier, at the University of Melbourne no less. See Stuart Macintyre, *A History for a Nation: Ernest Scott and the Making of Australian History*, Melbourne: MUP, 1994, p. 103.
11   McKenna, *An Eye for Eternity*, p. 145.

with the publisher. He and Dymphna would spend the rest of their lives in the nation's capital, and from that base he wrote his epic six-volume *A History of Australia*.

* * *

Clark's great ambition was 'to tell Australia's story', but without being constrained by the canons of an increasingly professionalised, university-based discipline. Telling Australia's story was a major commitment, whose rationale and journey are beautifully delineated by Monash University historian John Rickard:

> Manning Clark, Patrick White and Sidney Nolan belong to a generation that, growing up in the shadow of cultural dependency, felt a burning need to imagine myths and monuments. So White despatched 'Voss' on his spiritual journey ('I am compelled into this country'), while Nolan transformed a bushranger into a surreal symbol of the landscape. Clark, who pioneered the teaching of Australian history, chose nothing less than to write 'the whole story' of his country, a history that 'was going to tell the reader something about life'.
>
> He first put pen to paper in 1956—the time of the Melbourne Olympics, the birth of 'Quadrant' and the debut of Edna Everage. The setting was ironically—yet perhaps appropriately—Oxford, for the telling of this story was in a sense the voyage of 'an Austral Briton' from the Old World to the New. Although he knew some of 'the great themes' he wanted to proclaim, the shape of the whole 'History' remained problematic and he was uncertain where it might end. It became part of his life, and its character and import changed as Clark himself underwent a transformation from history professor to cultural statesman. The sixth and last volume, published in 1987, ground to a halt in 1935, a time when Clark had been a student at Melbourne University. It might have been poetic symmetry to have brought it up to 1956, to that very moment when he wrote the first sentence: 'Civilisation did not begin in Australia until the last quarter of the eighteenth century'.[12]

---

12   John Rickard, 'Manning abridged', *Age Weekend Supplement,* 13 November 1993, p. 8.

Far from being in the thrall of Rankean scholarship, Clark aspired to write grand narrative history in the manner of the nineteenth-century masters and in a way, moreover, that would reflect glory upon himself. As early as 1938, at a mere 23 years of age, he told Dymphna that he felt certain that he could 'write something some day on Australian history' and that he would approach the task with insight and originality. He went on to say:

> I believe quite passionately that Australia is a 'weird' country and that its weirdness has never been portrayed before except in landscape painting. Australia is virgin soil in this respect & I feel something can be done about it.[13]

Full marks for the audacious ambition to supersede what had gone before and a vision of how to go about it. But his reasoning at another level might have set alarm bells ringing when he confided to his notebooks, in 1943:

> The confession must be made, my motive is to impress, vulgarly, to play to the gallery. It will satisfy my ego to produce a work which will bring publicity to me.[14]

Historian Carl Bridge nicely captures how this aspiration, and its accompanying clichés and pat phrases, worked in practice:

> Clark wrote his books in a language taken from the Bible, the *Book of Common Prayer,* and bits of Ibsen, Carlyle, Gibbon, Tolstoy, Newman, Marx, Macaulay, Dickens, Hardy, Henry James, Lawson and, above all, Dostoevsky—'I want to be there when everyone suddenly understands what it has all been for'. This is apocalyptic stuff. A search for divine truths and flaws in the clay. All humanity is divide[d] up into suffering virgins, Magdalens, forgiving Christs, 'banquet of life' men, and 'measurers', 'straighteners' or 'men in black coats'. He invented or stole a whole quasi-mythical terminology to describe his Australia—for instance, bourgeois society is 'Yarraside' or 'the six-toed sloth of British philistinism'; the Australian republic is the 'Young Tree Green' and the British Empire is the 'Old Dead Tree'. Is this history or is it myth?[15]

---

13 Quoted in McKenna, *An Eye for Eternity,* pp. 145–46.
14 Quoted in McKenna, *An Eye for Eternity,* p. 221.
15 Carl Bridge, 'Manning Clark and the Ratbag Tradition', *Journal of Australian Studies,* vol. 21, nos 54–55, 1997, pp. 91–95, specifically p. 92, doi.org/10.1080/14443059709387341.

Clark, in other words, mirrored the great nineteenth-century historians by writing character-driven narratives on an epic canvas, not according to 'scientific' precepts of the discipline but rather in the literary tradition of Gibbon and Carlyle. They, in turn, were criticised by their contemporary J.R. Seeley for turning history into a 'department of *belles-lettres*' that had scant regard for the truth—a charge that would be applied to Clark by some of his own contemporaries.[16]

In short, Clark was a throwback from a previous age; the one difference was that the romantic idealisation of heroes was not part of his repertoire. Academically he was a generalist in an age of increasing specialisation, writing history on an expansive canvas, increasingly doing so for a public rather than an academic audience. In fact, he wrote only two journal articles involving original research.[17] Aesthetically, Clark saw history as a branch of literature and, as preparation and inspiration for each volume of the *History*, he steeped himself in the literary classics—above all those of the Russian novelist Fyodor Dostoevsky (1821–1888)—and the historians of classical antiquity, as well as in classical music and the landscape.[18] Politically, and again like many of the nineteenth-century English and American historians, he cast himself in the role of public moralist, claiming 'the right to judge [his] society as a whole and to prescribe the best way of resolving its most perplexing dilemmas and conflicts'.[19]

University of Sydney historian Hazel King (1908–1997) favourably summed up Clark's intentions, at the same time gently indicating some of its pitfalls and limitations:

---

16   Deborah Wormell, *Sir John Seeley and the Uses of History*, Cambridge: Cambridge University Press, 1980, p. 126.
17   M. Clark, 'The Origins of the Convicts Transported to Eastern Australia, 1787–1852: Part I', *Historical Studies, Australia and New Zealand*, vol. 7, no. 26, 1956, pp. 121–35, doi.org/10.1080/10314615608595051; Clark, 'The Origins of the Convicts Transported to Eastern Australia, 1787–1852: Part II', *Historical Studies, Australia and New Zealand*, vol. 7, no. 27, 1956, pp. 314–27, doi.org/10.1080/10314615608595070; Clark, 'The Choice of Botany Bay', *Historical Studies, Australia and New Zealand*, vol. 9, no. 35, 1960, pp. 221–32, doi.org/10.1080/10314616008595173.
18   Manning Clark, *A Historian's Apprenticeship*, Melbourne: MUP, 1992, pp. 77–79.
19   Wormell, *Sir John Seeley and the Uses of History*, p. 179; see also Sean R. Busick, *A Sober Desire for History: William Gilmore Simms as Historian*, Columbia: University of South Carolina Press, 2005, pp. 18–19. The literary and intellectual influences bearing on Clark are discussed by his daughter Katerina Clark, 'Manning Clark and Russia: A Memoir', in Stuart Macintyre and Sheila Fitzpatrick (eds), *Against the Grain: Brian Fitzpatrick and Manning Clark in Australian History and Politics*, Melbourne: MUP, 2007, pp. 258–70.

> For those who, like Bury, believe that history is 'a science, no more and no less', Professor Clark's *History of Australia* will have no appeal for it is above all literary history, a work of art rather than of science. But those who believe that there is not one way but many ways by which historians can lead us to a better understanding of the past, will acclaim it. For as the artist makes us aware of a world which we had looked at, but never before seen, so Professor Clark, with his highly individual vision, illumines areas of the past which before were obscure. It does not, of course, follow from this that we will agree with all that he shows us, any more than we may be wholly in sympathy with the vision of the artist. But both have deepened our understanding ...
>
> ... But while we may not agree with all that Professor Clark has to say, and while a few inaccuracies and omissions could be pointed to, his book remains a *tour de force*, a great achievement. It is not, nor does it claim to be, 'the' history of Australia, but rather 'a' history of Australia—a personal view of our past as seen by a discerning and perceptive historian. It cannot fail to contribute much to our understanding of the period with which it deals.[20]

* * *

The singular writer was matched by an equally singular personality. A controversial and often polarising figure, Clark was inspiring to some and infuriating to others. His ability to ruffle feathers was legend. In a moment of real frustration, Max Crawford made the observation that 'there is a lot to be said for plain blokes who have never read a line of Dostoyevsky'.[21] It is little wonder, during the paranoia of the Cold War years, that he was widely regarded as a 'closet red' and attracted unfriendly attention from ASIO (the Australian Security Intelligence Organisation). Given his own experiences and of others whom he knew about, Clark was untoward in reminiscing that people blamed ASIO for 'their failure to be appointed to positions to which they believed their talents and their industry entitled them' rather than acknowledging their

---

20   Hazel King, review of Volume 2 (1822–1838), *Journal of Religious History*, vol. 5, no. 2, 1968, pp. 180–82, doi.org/10.1111/j.1467-9809.1968.tb00502.x. King was an authority of the history of early colonial New South Wales. She wrote biographies of Governor Richard Bourke and Elizabeth Macarthur, and became the first female President of the Council of the Royal Australian Historical Society, 1982–85.
21   Quoted in Anderson, *An Historian's Life*, p. 283.

own deficiencies.²² In reality, ASIO's harassment and incursions into academic freedom were pervasive, including Clark's house being put under observation.²³ Moreover, Australian universities were disinclined to confront the organisation in defence of their own staff members.²⁴

The other protagonist in this story, Peter Ryan, was close to the mark in observing:

> through most of his life, Manning's politics kept him in and out of hot water; he made sure of this, because although some of the resultant controversies were painful and distracting from his work, he found the lure of the accompanying publicity irresistible.²⁵

Through his writing and his utterances, Clark had always had a public profile and one that became overtly political. He had what has been described as 'an unsurpassed talent for getting up right wing nostrils',²⁶ especially in the wake of The Dismissal when he increasingly embraced the role of a pro-Labor intellectual and publicist. His political repositioning is important in the context of the present study.

Humphrey McQueen, a radical historian whom Clark had appointed senior tutor in his department, wondered how someone so mild-mannered could arouse such ire.²⁷ It was the content of Clark's messages rather than his dulcet tones that was the provocation. The hostile response from the political right was heightened, precisely because the conservatives had no comparable 'guru' (or 'cultural statesman', if you prefer). Clark was

---

22   Manning Clark, *The Quest for Grace*, Ringwood: Penguin, 1991, p. 178. Yet on p. 204 he bemoans being relieved of teaching a course to diplomatic cadets in the Department of External Affairs, in which ASIO played a part, although he found this uninspiring work.
23   Fiona Capp, *Writers Defiled: Security Surveillance of Australian Authors and Intellectuals, 1920–1960*, Melbourne: McPhee Gribble, 1993, pp. 95–101; Roger Douglas, 'Brian Fitzpatrick, Manning Clark and ASIO', in Macintyre and Fitzpatrick, *Against the Grain*, pp. 170–90; Matthews, *Manning Clark*, p. 137; McKenna, *An Eye for Eternity*, pp. 394–95.
24   Jude van Konkelenberg, 'Australia's Cold War University: The Relationship between the Australian National University's Research School of Pacific Studies and the Federal Government, 1946–1975', PhD thesis, University of Adelaide, 2009, available at: digital.library.adelaide.edu.au/dspace/handle/2440/63714; Geoffrey Gray, '"A great deal of mischief can be done": Peter Worsley, the Australian National University, the Cold War and Academic Freedom, 1952–1954', *Journal of the Royal Australian Historical Society*, vol. 101, no. 1, 2015, pp. 25–44; Anderson, *An Historian's Life*, pp. 234–40.
25   Peter Ryan, 'Hollow Man of Yesterday', review of *Manning Clark: A Life*, by Brian Matthews, *Quadrant*, vol. 53, nos 1–2, January–February 2009, pp. 127–28, specifically p. 128.
26   Stephen Foster and Margaret M. Varghese, *The Making of The Australian National University, 1946–1996*, Sydney: Allen & Unwin, 1996, p. 288.
27   Humphrey McQueen, *Suspect History: Manning Clark and the Future of Australia's Past*, Adelaide: Wakefield Press, 1997, p. 124.

so much identified with the left's cultural dominance, and (incorrectly) seen by many as the evil genius behind Prime Minister Paul Keating's push for republican nationalism in the early 1990s, that he had to be brought down to discredit the cause he espoused (discussed in Chapter 7). As Macquarie University historian Portia Robinson pointed out, there were correlations between Clark's perceived influence and the abuse that his ghost had continued to encounter—hardly a novel proposition but apposite in the circumstances.[28]

* * *

Peter Ryan came from a different background. Born and brought up in Melbourne his childhood was not altogether happy. His schooling was marred by undiagnosed near-sightedness, and his consequent ineptitude at cricket and football ('I could scarcely see a ball before it hit me') resulted in an abiding distaste for sport of any kind, or so he said.[29] As with Manning Clark, Ryan's description of childhood events is a forewarning of an unreliability with mere facts. Rather, he was a strong swimmer and was in his school's top football team.[30] His father died when he was 13, leaving him with a 'lasting sadness' that contributed to a grim outlook on life. Leaving school at age 16, Ryan was successively a clerk within the Commonwealth Railways and the Crown Law Office; the latter position, as his biographer notes, 'was a step closer to his ambition to become a lawyer'.[31] He then, in 1941, enlisted for military service and served with distinction behind enemy lines in intelligence-gathering operations in the Papua New Guinea theatre. His wartime memoir, *Fear Drive My Feet,* is rightly regarded as a classic as well as being testimony to an enduring affection for the place and its people.[32]

Ryan took pride in his war record and his Military Medal and, not least, being part of the remarkable Directorate of Research and Civil Affairs (DORCA), which he joined in 1944. DORCA was one-of-a-kind. It was a shadowy, mysterious and raffish think tank within the Australian Army that was involved in what might be described as 'special duties of a secret

---

28   Portia Robinson, 'The abuse continues' (letter), *Sydney Morning Herald,* 3 September 1993, p. 10. Clark had been supportive of Robinson when her book, *The Women of Botany Bay* (1988), came under attack.
29   Peter Ryan, 'Short Sight, Sharp Vision' (1971), in his *Lines of Fire,* pp. 51–55.
30   John Tidey, *Ryan's Luck: A Life of Peter Ryan MM,* Melbourne: Arcadia, 2020, p. 7.
31   Tidey, *Ryan's Luck,* p. 11.
32   Peter Ryan, *Fear Drive My Feet,* Sydney: Angus & Robertson, 1959.

nature' concerning policymaking for the war effort and for postwar reconstruction.[33] Ryan's two years in DORCA were a pivotal part of his life—he was a young man elevated beyond his wildest dreams and mixing with an intellectual elite who saw a new future for postwar Australia—but the fact remains that Ryan was a minor figure in the scheme of things. He looked back on DORCA with a lifelong affection and he lived long enough to bask in its glory. He wrote himself into the record with his writings on DORCA and subsequent researchers came knocking on his door for information about the outfit. He was a source of detail and anecdotes but not an historical actor of any significance.[34]

Ryan's literary background indeed had substance. He had received every encouragement as a child to read good books, and at high school he had, in the words of his English teacher, displayed 'a marked gift for literary expression', which carried over into adult life.[35] The book-lined shelves in his home bear testimony to his literary interests and he spoke unaffectedly of his 'love of books and reading, which every year becomes a more consuming passion and which, like Gibbon, I would not exchange for all the treasures of India'.[36] Ryan not only loved books but was a highly accomplished writer with a feel for language. And he valued his literary associations, which started with being an eager onlooker when two of his comrades at DORCA perpetrated the Ern Malley literary hoax—whereby the *literato* Max Harris (1921–1995), who championed modernist poetry, was fooled into publishing the nonsense poetry of a fictitious dead poet that the two hoaxsters had concocted during the course of an afternoon, thus achieving their twin objectives that modernist poetry and its sponsor be held up to ridicule.[37] His literary crowd included Cyril Pearl

---

33 Graeme Sligo, *The Backroom Boys: Alf Conlon and Army's Directorate of Research and Civil Affairs, 1942–46,* Sydney: Big Sky Publishing, 2012.
34 Almost all the numerous references to Ryan in Sligo, *The Backroom Boys,* pertain not to what he did, which was to provide instruction in Pidgin, but to his recollections of DORCA. See also Ian Howie-Willis, *A Medical Emergency: Major-General 'Ginger' Burston and the Army Medical Service in World War II,* Sydney: Blue Sky Publishing, 2012, pp. 396–97. Ryan's various writings on DORCA include: 'Alf Conlon', in John Thompson (ed.), *Five to Remember,* Melbourne: Landsdown Press, 1964, pp. 113–15; 'Conlon, Alfred Austin (Alf) (1908–1961)', *Australian Dictionary of Biography,* The Australian National University, available at: adb.anu.edu.au/biography/conlon-alfred-austin-alf-9804, published first in hardcopy 1993; and *Brief Lives,* Sydney: Duffy & Snellgrove, 2004, pp. 28–61 (Alf Conlon), 139–52 (Ida Leeson).
35 Tidey, *Ryan's Luck,* p. 8, for quotation see p. 10, also pp. 123–26.
36 Ryan, 'Short Sight, Sharp Vision', in his *Lines of Fire,* for quotation see p. 54, also pp. 98–101.
37 Michael Heyward, *The Ern Malley Affair,* Brisbane: University of Queensland Press, 1993; Cassandra Pybus, *The Devil and James McAuley,* Brisbane: University of Queensland Press, 1999, pp. 39–44.

(1904–1987), Paul Hasluck (1905–1993) and A.D. Hope (1907–2000); he also placed importance on rubbing shoulders with luminaries such as political scientist W. Macmahon Ball (1901–1986) and the renowned virologist Macfarlane Burnet (1901–1986).[38] But the combination of knockabout, self-made man and *literato* is only half the picture. He also liked to present himself as a gentleman of the old school with extended lunches, his rural property and communion with nature, horse riding and, endearingly, when he became director of MUP, successive border collies curled up in front of his office fireplace.[39]

But that is well in the future. After being demobbed, Ryan enrolled at the University of Melbourne on a Commonwealth Reconstruction Training Scheme scholarship; he studied law in his first year and then switched to history, where he first encountered Manning Clark.[40] He was active in student politics as an office-bearing member of the university's Labour Club[41] as well as standing for the Victorian State Parliament. Finishing his studies with an honours degree in history, he embarked on a series of jobs including

> public servant ... bush timberworker; publisher of comic books and other rubbish; ten years in advertising and public relations; and a hopeless effort to scratch a living as a freelance journalist.[42]

Then, in 1962, he unexpectedly became director of MUP upon the recommendation of Macmahon Ball, the professor of political science at the University of Melbourne and chair of the MUP Board of Management. It came about when Creighton Burns (1925–2008), a senior lecturer in Ball's department, casually suggested that Ryan was his man.[43] Given Ryan's background in advertising and public relations, it was a surprise appointment. It was also an inspired decision to the extent that Ryan's

---

38 Ryan, *Brief Lives*, pp. 5–23 (Pearl), 62–73 (Burnet), 91–104 (Hasluck), 116–32 (Ball), 158–85 (Hope); and *Lines of Fire*, pp. 129–37 (Hasluck), 141–76 (Ball).
39 Peter Ryan, 'The Art and Craft of the Luncheon', *Quadrant*, vol. 52, nos 1–2, January–February 2008, pp. 127–28; Ryan, 'Winter Firewood' (1988), in his *Lines of Fire*, pp. 236–55; Ryan, 'Animals and Us', *Quadrant*, vol. 50, no. 3, March 2006, pp. 95–96; Ryan, *Final Proof: Memoirs of a Publisher*, Sydney: Quadrant Books, 2010, pp. 142–45, 194–95; Rowan Callick, 'A literary man of action' (obituary), *Australian*, 17 December 2015, p. 11, available at: oa.anu.edu.au/obituary/ryan-peter-25437.
40 Tidey, *Ryan's Luck*, pp. 43, 97.
41 John McLaren, *Free Radicals of the Left in Postwar Melbourne*, Melbourne: Australian Scholarly Publishing, 2003, pp. 60–61; Peter Ryan, 'End of the Dreamtime' (1986), in his *Lines of Fire*, pp. 101–11, specifically p. 106.
42 Ryan, 'My Life as a Leper', *Quadrant*, vol. 55, nos 1–2, January–February 2011, pp. 127–28, for quotation see p. 127; Tidey *Ryan's Luck*, pp. 46–53.
43 Tidey, *Ryan's Luck*, p. 63.

good management was instrumental in clearing the press's debilitating overdraft and in maintaining a list of considerable merit. A long-serving chair of the MUP Board acknowledged:

> how economically the Director and a handful of trusted colleagues managed the organisation, how meticulously he briefed the Board and its various committees, and how shrewdly he negotiated legal agreements.[44]

At MUP, Ryan joined forces with Manning Clark once again and got Volume 1 of the *History* into the bookshops in 1962, to the betterment of both MUP's and Clark's finances. They had much in common but eventually drifted apart. Clark was not an easy author, and he tested Ryan's patience. Their politics increasingly diverged with Ryan's swing to the right in the 1970s. Neither did Clark's tragic vision of Australian history nor the fluctuating quality of his work appeal to Ryan, although Ryan was exaggeratedly vocal in publicly praising both Clark as a great writer and his *History* as a great work. Another anomaly was Ryan's growing prejudice against academics generally, despite his working in a university setting for 25 years, or perhaps because of it. As a mutual friend lamented to Clark:

> He is a remarkable person, in many respects admirable, but I wish he would not feed the already brightly blazing fire of Aussie anti-intellectualism by constantly selling his own colleagues (for he is an academic too) down the river by describing them (in his excellent & most readable prose) as lazy layabouts.[45]

Thus, a good part of the equation is that two men who had been close, or close enough, had moved in different directions. Strangely, Clark seemed unaware of Ryan's change in political outlook, or the fact that Ryan was the proud custodian of a portrait of Sir John Kerr (1914–91), his former colleague at DORCA and later widely reviled for his role in The Dismissal of the Whitlam government in 1975.[46] As late as 1987, Clark told Ryan:

---

44 John Poynter, 'Peter Ryan the Publisher', *Quadrant*, vol. 60, no. 3, March 2016, pp. 58–59, specifically p. 59.
45 Susan Davies (ed.), *Dear Kathleen, Dear Manning: The Correspondence of Manning Clark and Kathleen Fitzpatrick, 1949–1990*, Melbourne: MUP, 1996, p. 112 (Fitzpatrick to Clark, 25 June 1987).
46 Ryan, *Final Proof,* pp. 195–97; Tidey, *Ryan's Luck,* pp. 98–99; see also Jenny Hocking, *The Palace Letters: The Queen, the Governor-General and the Plot to Dismiss Gough Whitlam,* Melbourne: Scribe Publications, 2020.

> [Paul Keating] is one of the most impressive men I have ever met in my life ... You would enjoy a talk with him. You would understand what he thinks about Australia and how he feels about life.[47]

A more improbable mismatch could hardly be imagined. Indeed, the increasing polarisation of Australian public life with an intensification of the History Wars in the lead-up to the bicentenary celebrations was an important element. It all came together with the sensational attack on Clark in the September 1993 issue of *Quadrant*.

---

47   Roslyn Russell (ed.), *Ever, Manning: Selected Letters of Manning Clark, 1938–1991*, Sydney: Allen & Unwin, 2008, p. 451 (Clark to Ryan, 30 January 1987).

2

The Australian History Wars

> The object of war is to vanquish the enemy. The duty of the scholar is to seek understanding. The importation of military methods into historical scholarship is ruinous to the enterprise. Adversarial intolerance is inimical to the principle of academic freedom. The public discussion of history, on the other hand, serves other purposes: remembrance, entertainment, instruction and argument are among them. Such purposes are poorly served when one dogmatic assertion shouts down another, and character assassination replaces reasoned argument. The History Wars are an ugly side of the Australian present and they debase public life.
>
> Stuart Macintyre and Anna Clark (2004)[1]

> Among the most fundamental responsibilities of the national historian is to seek to influence public consciousness with stories that are both true and engaging, and yet sometimes uncomfortable and unsettling. For those who look to the past for a vindication of their own selfhood or past behaviour, the work of historians committed to honest and painstaking historical enquiry can be threatening … [There is] a familiar attitude: the idea that histories of the national past should be patriotic, tidy and usable.
>
> Frank Bongiorno (2019)[2]

---

1 Stuart Macintyre and Anna Clark, *The History Wars,* 2nd edn, Melbourne: Melbourne University Press (hereafter MUP), 2004, p. 243.
2 Frank Bongiorno, 'Inaugural Professorial Lecture—Is Australian History Still Possible? Australia and the Global Eighties', *ANU Historical Journal II,* vol. 1, 2019, pp. 193–208, specifically p. 205, doi.org/10.22459/ANUHJII.2019.15.

The term 'History Wars' came into currency in 1996 in a book of that title about the controversy following the Smithsonian Institution's proposed exhibition that would feature a refurbished *Enola Gay*, the Boeing B-29 aircraft that dropped an atomic bomb on Hiroshima in 1945. The idea behind the exhibition—to encourage discussion on the morality of dropping nuclear bombs on Japanese cities—aroused fierce opposition from veterans' groups, among others.[3] The controversy also attached a label to something that had been happening, in localised outbursts, even before the professionalisation of the historical discipline. One definition reads:

> History wars are not history but an argument for control of the past as a political resource. They are conducted as a polemical argument and rest on a misunderstanding of the nature of history and historical understanding.[4]

To refine this proposition, History Wars can be divided into three types. There are *internal* History Wars—that is, heated debates between historians in their books and journal articles. All historical writing is revisionist to some extent and only a few reinterpretations result in an internal History War. This happens when 'interpretive differences' transform into 'interpretive battles'[5] involving an ongoing, back-and-forth engagement between the two protagonists. Typically, others will enter the fray in support of one side or another, or perhaps to modify a particular point of view, or else to provide a quite different perspective. Such interpretive battles are largely confined to the academy, an example being whether or not a 'declining sense of Canada as a national entity' and the rising popularity of social history was 'killing' Canadian history. This was 'an intellectual family feud'—a case of Michael Bliss and

---

3   Edward T. Linenthal and Tom Engelhardt (eds), *History Wars: The Enola Gay and Other Battles for the American Past*, New York: Holt Paperbacks, 1996.
4   Stuart Macintyre, 'The History Wars', *Evatt Papers*, vol. 6, no. 3, 29 September 2003, n.p., available at: www.evatt.org.au/post/the-history-wars.
5   The phrases are taken from James M. Banner, Jr., *The Ever-Changing Past: Why All History Is Revisionist History*, New Haven: Yale University Press, 2021, p. 74, doi.org/10.2307/j.ctv1g2496z.

J.L. Granastein versus the rest.[6] Some such disputes can become exceedingly rancorous.[7] So was the Ryan–Clark controversy, but it does not qualify as an internal History War. The Ryan–Clark controversy was not played out in a university setting and neither was it an historiographic battle comparable, say, to the dispute over Keith Windschuttle's interpretation of the Australian frontier wars and the extent of Aboriginal deaths, where archival-based discussion was at the forefront, even while ideology was imbricated in the debate.[8] Peter Ryan's focus was not on the issues raised by the *History*, except to a very limited extent, but on Clark himself, both his personality and whatever political influence he was thought to have had.

The Ryan–Clark controversy, in other words, was an *external* History War, when competing versions of the past are fought out in the public domain, via the media. The stakes were to impose a particular view of the nation's self-image—whether it be seen in an affirmative or in a negative light. In settler societies such as Australia, History Wars have come to be dominated by, although not confined to, the past treatment of Indigenous peoples and whether this constitutes a meritorious or a shameful record, and whether that nation's history can or cannot be regarded as a success story. History Wars, by definition, are confrontational, with one side being accused of disparaging the Australian achievement and the other side seeking acknowledgment of past wrongs to clear the ground for

---

6   Michael Bliss, 'Privatizing the Mind: The Sundering of Canadian History, the Sundering of Canada', *Journal of Canadian Studies/Revue d'études canadiennes*, vol. 26, no. 4, 1991–92, pp. 5–17, doi.org/10.3138/jcs.26.4.5; Bliss, *Writing History: A Professor's Life*, Toronto: Dundern, 2011, pp. 296–300; J.L. Granastein, *Who Killed Canadian History?* Toronto: HarperCollins, 1998; A.B. McKillop, 'Who Killed Canadian History? A View from the Trenches', *Canadian Historical Review*, vol. 80, no. 2, 1999, pp. 269–99, doi.org/10.3138/chr.80.2.269; Bryan D. Palmer, 'Of Silences and Trenches: A Dissident View of Granastein's Meaning', *Canadian Historical Review*, vol. 80, no. 4, 1999, pp. 676–86; Timothy J. Stanley, 'Why I Killed Canadian History: Towards an Anti-racial History in Canada', *Histoire Sociale/Social History*, vol. 33, no. 65, 2000, pp. 79–103. See more generally, William Lamont (ed.), *Historical Controversies and Historians,* London: UCL Press, 1998.
7   For example, Mary Lefkowitz, *History Lesson: A Race Odyssey*, New Haven/London: Yale University Press, 2008.
8   Keith Windschuttle, *The Fabrication of Aboriginal History, Vol. 1: Van Diemen's Land, 1803–1847*, Sydney: Macleay Press, 2002; John Connor, *The Australian Frontier Wars, 1788–1838*, Sydney: UNSW Press, 2002; Robert Manne (ed.), *Whitewash: On Keith Windschuttle's Fabrication of Aboriginal History*, Melbourne: Black Inc., 2003; Bain Attwood and S.G. Foster (eds), *Frontier Conflict: The Australian Experience*, Canberra: National Museum of Australia, 2003; John Dawson, *Washout: On the Academic Response to the Fabrication of Aboriginal History*, Sydney: Macleay Press, 2004; 2nd edn, 2010; Bain Attwood, *Telling the Truth about Aboriginal History*, Sydney: Allen & Unwin, 2005. I am grateful to Graeme Davison and Robert J. Tristram, who separately suggested this line of reasoning.

a better future. In these ways, competing versions of the past become matters of media-driven public controversy. The Ryan–Clark controversy is a clear-cut example of an external History War.

A third type of History War involves *outside attacks on historians,* often by politicians who question their loyalty to the nation and their fitness to teach impressionable minds. Manning Clark himself was subject to such onslaughts as early as 1947, being described in the Parliament of Victoria as either 'a highly overpaid ignoramus or an evilly disposed wrong-headed person', as well as being 'either woefully ignorant of what he is teaching or he is a paid agent of the Communist Party'.[9] Again, an outside attack on a given historian can blur into the other types of History Wars. Historian Geoffrey Blainey's criticisms, in 1984, of the level of Asian migration to Australia contains elements of all three types of History Wars. To the extent that 'the Blainey affair' involved widespread public criticism, from politicians included, it can be regarded as an attack-on-an-historian type of History War. To the extent that Blainey's views were debated within the historical profession, it was an internal History War. The Blainey affair is less obviously an external History War because the issues involved a present-day issue, except that Blainey insisted that he was 'speaking very much as a historian'.[10] The three (often overlapping) categories of History Wars here described are, to an extent, labels of convenience, but they do help disentangle some of the conceptual problems surrounding the term.

Then there is the need to broadly distinguish between History Wars and Culture Wars. The former label seems to derive from the word *Kulturkampf,* to describe the hostilities between the German Catholic Church and an alliance of Lutheran conservatives and anticlerical liberals in the 1870s (or sometimes any conflict between secular and religious authorities), but the term Culture Wars was popularised only in the early

---

9   Mark McKenna, *An Eye for Eternity: The Life of Manning Clark,* Melbourne: Miegunyah Press, 2011, specifically p. 264 for quotation; Stuart Macintyre and Fay Anderson, 'History in the Headlines', in Fay Anderson and Stuart Macintyre (eds), *The Life of the Past: The Discipline of History at the University of Melbourne, 1855–2005,* Melbourne: Department of History, University of Melbourne, 2006, pp. 355–76, specifically p. 362.

10 Andrew Marcus, '1984 or 1901? Immigration and "Some Lessons" of Australian History', in Andrew Marcus and M.C. Ricklefs (eds), *Surrender Australia? Essays in the Study and Uses of History: Geoffrey Blainey and Asian Immigration,* Sydney, Allen & Unwin, 1985, pp. 10–35, specifically p. 10.

1990s by a book of that name by James Davison Hunter.[11] The terms History Wars and Culture Wars are often used interchangeably, but this is to confuse issues. My preference is that a History War is an argument, or series of arguments, about the past in ways that connect the past to the present, whereas Culture Wars are contests over current moral and cultural values and played out over hot-button issues such as abortion, LGBTIQ rights, the right to die and affirmative action. The actual boundaries of History Wars and Culture Wars sometimes converge, but the distinction between the two should nevertheless be kept in mind. An illustrative example of the blurring around the edges is—once again—the Blainey affair. It qualifies as a Culture War in that it impinged on a contemporary concern, except that Blainey insisted that he was speaking as an historian and brought the past into play.

Dispensing with definitions, we can move to the broad contours of the Australian History Wars. In settler societies such as Australia, they revolve around a wide variety of issues—including but not confined to: immigration policy and multiculturalism, the representation of the nation's past in the 1988 bicentennial celebrations, the record of the country's military, the meanings of Australia Day and 'Anzackery', 'frontier conflict' and the interpretation of Aboriginal history, and Indigenous rights and redress. They also include school history syllabi and museum display policy.[12] The History Wars of other countries orbit around different concerns that stem from their own individual histories—including past involvement in slavery; whether one's former colonial empire was a 'good' or a 'bad' thing; whether one need acknowledge accusations of war guilt; and what to do about the Holocaust. There can also be an overlay of sectarianism to complicate existing issues, as in Ireland.

---

11 James Davison Hunter, *Culture Wars: The Struggle to Define America,* New York: Basic Books, 1991; see also Robert Manne, 'A Battle of Philosophies', *Australian Quarterly,* vol. 70, no. 5, 1998, 42–45, specifically p. 42; Christopher Clark and Wolfram Kaiser (eds), *Culture Wars: Secular-Catholic Conflict in Nineteenth-Century Europe,* Cambridge: Cambridge University Press, 2003, doi.org/10.1017/CBO9780511496714.

12 Andrew Bonnell and Martin Crotty, 'An Australian "*Historikerstreit*"?' *Australian Journal of Politics and History,* vol. 50, no. 3, 2004, pp. 425–33, doi.org/10.1111/j.1467-8497.2004.00345.x; Anna Clark, *History's Children: History Wars in the Classroom,* Sydney: NewSouth, 2008, specifically ch. 4 ('A National Curriculum', pp. 89–111); Graeme Davison, 'A Historian in the Museum: The Ethics of Public History', in Stuart Macintyre (ed.), *The Historian's Conscience: Australian Historians on the Ethics of History,* Melbourne: MUP, 2004, pp. 49–63; Amanda Nettelbeck, 'The Australian Frontier in the Museum', *Journal of Social History,* vol. 44, no. 4, 2011, pp. 1115–28, doi.org/10.1353/jsh.2011.0047.

The Atlantic slave trade, war guilt, the Holocaust and religious fervour have little, if anything to do with the Australian History Wars. What is noticeable with the Australian version is that the battleground shifts as one issue loses salience and another gains traction. The bicentenary of 1988 seems a distant memory; the disputes over the content of museum displays have gone away, at least for the moment; and the battles over the content of the school history syllabus have quietened down. Moments of quiescence, however, can give way to a period of intensity. The Australian History Wars spluttered back into life in 2016 when the Sydney *Daily Telegraph* rehashed a story over whether the British 'discovered' or 'invaded' Australia,[13] while the Rhodes Must Fall controversies and the growing prominence of the Change the Date movement ensured continuing controversy over Australia Day.[14] The following year ongoing disputes over demands to remove colonial statues gained impetus after the killing of George Floyd by the Minneapolis police, which in turn led to a resurgence of the Black Lives Matter movement in Australia and beyond.[15] As well, disagreements over the Anzac tradition and meaning of Anzac Day can always be counted upon to trigger yet another conservative campaign against alleged sacrilege from 'what passes for the intelligentsia in Australia'.[16]

Questions of national pride versus national guilt over the nation's past are integral to the Australian History Wars. These were explicitly raised a month before the Ryan–Clark controversy erupted, in 1993, when their mutual friend Geoffrey Blainey coined the term 'the Black-Armband

---

13   Janet Fife-Yeomans, 'Whitewash: UNSW rewrites the history books to state Cook "invaded" Australia', *Daily Telegraph,* 30 March 2016, pp. 1, 4–5.
14   Michelle Grattan, 'Liberals stir the culture war pot but who's listening?', *The Conversation,* 24 January 2019, available at: theconversation.com/grattan-on-friday-liberals-stir-the-culture-war-pot-but-whos-listening-110445.
15   Camron Slessor and Eugene Boisvert, 'Black Lives Matter protests renew push to remove "racist" monuments to colonial figures', *ABC News,* 10 June 2020, available at: www.abc.net.au/news/2020-06-10/black-lives-matter-protests-renew-push-to-remove-statues/12337058.
16   Mervyn F. Bendle, *Anzac & its Enemies: The History War against Australia's National Identity,* Sydney: Quadrant Books, 2015; Miranda Devine, 'Insulting charge of history-lite brigade', *Sunday Telegraph* (Sydney), 18 April 2015, available at: www.dailytelegraph.com.au/news/opinion/miranda-devine-insulting-charge-of-historylite-brigade/news-story/53f9ea213fbdc92d737cf9901a931017. See especially the indictment of Anzackery and the associated 'confected ceremonies that manipulated sentiment' in Stephen Garton, 'Contesting "Anzacery": Marilyn Lake and Envisioning Australian Nationalism', in Joy Damousi and Judith Smart (eds), *Contesting Australian History: Essays in Honour of Marilyn Lake,* Melbourne: Monash University Publishing, 2019, pp. 9–20, specifically pp. 9–12.

view of history'.[17] The label summed up an important strand in Ryan's argument and the Australian History Wars generally—that Clark's *History* had purveyed an excessively negative, guilt-ladened and unpatriotic presentation of Australia's past. This was in line with the conservative reaction in other countries to expressions of national guilt, such as Howard Zinn's (1922–2010) *A People's History of the United States* (1980), which is denounced to this day.[18] Ryan denied that his motivations for attacking Clark were in any way political, but we shall see that this was anything but the case.

Meg Foster provided an excellent analysis of the differences between the 'black armband' view of history and the 'three cheers' view of history. As she wrote:

> The expression 'black armband view of history' has been used to describe a brand of Australian history which its critics argue 'represents a swing of the pendulum from a position that had been too favourable, too self congratulatory', to an opposite extreme that is even more unreal and decidedly jaundiced. Not only, it is said, does the black armband view belittle past achievements, it also encourages a 'guilt industry' and impedes rational thinking on current problems. From this perspective, the black armband view of history is a strand of 'political correctness'—the dominant but erroneous view of how we see ourselves and what we see as worthwhile in our culture. For others, the term is inherently political and a misrepresentation of the work of many serious historians. It is an attempt to appropriate an established symbol of genuine grieving, loss and injustice by those who do not accept, or do not want to accept, that past wrongs must be fully recognised before present problems can be resolved. Both sides accuse each other of attempting to distort history and of taking an extreme view.

---

17 Geoffrey Blainey, 'Drawing up a Balance Sheet of Our History', *Quadrant*, vol. 37, nos 7–8, July–August 1993, pp. 11–15, specifically p. 11, which to some extent was anticipated by a forum on 'The Writing of Australian History' in the *IPA Review*, vol. 42, no. 3, December 1988–February 1989, pp. 49–54, notably the contribution by John Hirst, 'The Blackening of Our Past', specifically pp. 49, 51 and 54. Other critiques of black-armband history in the late 1980s are identified in Norman Abjorensen, 'The History Wars', in Jim George and Kim Huynh (eds), *The Culture Wars: Australian and American Politics in the 21st Century*, Melbourne: Palgrave Macmillan Australia, 2009, pp. 142–58, specifically pp. 147–48.
18 Howard Zinn, *A People's History of the United States: 1492–Present*, London/New York: Longman, 1980 and subsequent editions; Mary Grabar, *Debunking Howard Zinn: Exposing the Fake History that Turned a Generation Against America*, Washington, DC: Regnery History, 2019.

By contrast, the 'Three Cheers' view of history looks at Australia's past as a series of achievements, and emphasises events from history that Australians should apparently be proud of.[19]

* * *

The question remains: in what ways did the Ryan–Clark controversy fit into the ever-changing complexion of the Australian History Wars? These had been rumbling away since at least 1900 when G. Arnold Wood (1865–1928), the history professor at the University of Sydney, came under fire from politicians and sections of the media for his stances during the Boer War.[20] Wood's tribulations have been discussed by Max Crawford, who himself had his loyalty questioned in the 1950s on grounds of pro-Soviet sympathies.[21] By then, in the context of continuing Cold War anxieties, the front widened to include politically unacceptable academics being excluded from university positions.[22] In another permutation, the Australian History Wars received impetus, in early 1992, when the recently installed prime minister, Paul Keating, took the contest in new directions and to new levels of discord by repudiating deference to British heritage and announcing his vision for a republican nationalism, engagement with Asia and Aboriginal reconciliation. Henceforth, a key element in the interpretation of the nation's past would be 'a frontline struggle over identity' and what it meant to be Australian. As journalist Paul Kelly observes:

---

19   Meg Foster, 'Drawing the Historian Back into History: Creativity, Writing, and *The Art of Time Travel*', *Re-Thinking History: The Journal of Theory and Practice*, vol. 22, no. 1, 2018, pp. 137–53, specifically p. 149 n.24, doi.org/10.1080/13642529.2017.1421119.
20   John A. Moses, *Prussian–German Militarism 1914–18 in Australian Perspective: The Thought of George Arnold Wood*, Bern: Peter Lang, 1991, pp. 40–42.
21   R.M. Crawford, *'A Bit of Rebel': The Life and Work of George Arnold Wood*, Sydney: Sydney University Press, 1975, pp. 150–259; Fay Anderson and Stuart Macintyre, 'Crawford as Controversialist', in Stuart Macintyre and Peter McPhee (eds), *Max Crawford's School of History*, Melbourne: History Department, University of Melbourne, 2000, pp. 89–112.
22   Hugh Stretton, 'Brenner and the University of Adelaide', *Vestes*, vol. 4, no. 4, 1961, pp. 5–12, available at: www.aur.org.au/archive/1960s; Hannah Forsyth, 'The Russel Ward Case: Academic Freedom in Australia during the Cold War', *History Australia*, vol. 11, no. 3, 2014, pp. 31–52, doi.org/10.1080/14490854.2014.11668530; Doug Munro, 'George Rudé—Communist Activist and Inactivist', *Working USA*, vol. 19, no. 2, 2016, pp. 147–62, specifically p. 155, doi.org/10.1111/wusa.12234.

> Among Australian historians and academics, there had been differences over history for some years, often branded a culture war. But it was Keating's intervention that implanted this debate in the centre of politics.[23]

Such was the immediate History Wars context of the Ryan–Clark controversy.

Keating credited himself for having 'pressed the starter's pistol on the history wars, no doubt about that'.[24] Actually, he reignited it, in early 1992, when he launched a ferocious attack in parliament on 'betrayals' by Britain (the fall of Singapore and entry into the Common Market) and accusing the Opposition of being stranded in the mindset of the 1950s—that land of lost opportunity and subservience when Robert Menzies kow-towed to Britain.[25] His was a party-political narrative: 'By arguing that the values and tradition of the Labor Party were one and the same with Australia's, Keating was essentially constructing a partisan national identity'.[26]

Keating's attempts to socially engineer a less derivative and more distinctive national identity, and one that acknowledged the wrongs inflicted on Aboriginal people, also resulted in the Australian History Wars being conducted across an ever-broadening front, embracing such issues as republicanism, multiculturalism (and increasing engagement with Asia), untying the apron strings of the British connection, disparagement of the Menzies years, as well as native title and Aboriginal reconciliation. Ryan, whose allegiances by then were firmly with the political right, found much that was 'unpalatable' with Keating.[27] Clark was the opposite and, moreover was perceived as a cheerleader and a sort of brains trust upon whom Keating drew for ideas and inspiration.[28] In the process, the largely left-leaning historical profession came under attack from politicians and

---

23   Paul Kelly, *The March of Patriots: The Struggle for Modern Australia*, Melbourne: MUP, 2009, p. 632 n.1. Here is an example of the term 'Culture War' being used when it would be better to say 'History War'.
24   Quoted in Kelly, *The March of Patriots*, p. 65.
25   *Hansard* (House of Representatives), 27 February 1992, pp. 373–74; Macintyre and Clark, *The History Wars*, pp. 124–25.
26   Anna Clark, 'Politicians using History', *Australian Journal of Politics and History*, vol. 56, no. 1, 2010, pp. 120–31, specifically p. 125, doi.org/10.1111/j.1467-8497.2010.01545.x.
27   John Tidey, *Ryan's Luck: A Life of Peter Ryan MM*, Melbourne: Arcadia, 2020, pp. 102–3.
28   Mark McKenna, '"I wonder whether I belong": Manning Clark and the Politics of Australian History 1970–2000', *Australian Historical Studies*, vol. 34, no. 122, 2003, pp. 364–83, doi.org/10.1080/10314610308596260.

large sections of the media, whose rhetoric 'posits the university as a site of disloyalty, self-indulgence, wilful obscurity, enforced conformism and intolerance'.[29]

As such, the History Wars were a series of arguments that both reflected and brought out drastically different views of Australia as a society.[30] These differences in outlook might have influenced historiographies in other settler societies. What is more certain is the renewal of the right-wing challenge to values that seemed in the late twentieth century to have become settled orthodoxies following the end of the Cold War. It created a sea change—or what some might see as the depressing effect of the resurgence of the right and the retreat of the left in the Reagan–Thatcher years. Seen in that light, the Ryan–Clark controversy was an early indicator that all was not as it seemed, and it exemplified the points at issue among opposing conceptions of Australian identity and Australian-ness itself.[31]

---

29 Stuart Macintyre, 'The History Wars and the History Profession', *History Now* (Christchurch), vol. 11, nos 1–2, 2005, pp. 31–36, specifically p. 33. An account by the quarry of a press campaign is: Lyndall Ryan, 'Reflections by a Target of a Media Witch Hunt', *History Australia*, vol. 1, no. 1, 2003, pp. 105–9, doi.org/10.1080/14490854.2003.11828260.
30 See Bain Attwood, 'Denial in a Settler Society: The Australian Case', *History Workshop Journal*, vol. 84, 2017, pp. 24–43, doi.org/10.1093/hwj/dbx029.
31 I am grateful to John G. Reid for these suggestions.

Part 2.
Contention and Dissension

3

Criticisms, Reaction and Counter-Reaction

> It is not so much that Ryan damages our sense of Manning the man as that he strives so spiritedly to do so.
>
> Peter Craven (1994)[1]

> Today you cast the pebble[,] tomorrow comes the ripple.
>
> Dymphna Clark (1960)[2]

Nearing the end of their 25-year professional relationship, when making the final revisions to his final volume of *A History of Australia,* Manning Clark wrote to Peter Ryan in heartfelt terms, thanking him 'for all you have done. No words of mine could ever do justice of my debt to you. But I will try to say something'. To which Ryan responded:

> As to 'thanks'—in the first place, as far as I'm concerned, they are not needed, and would embarrass me. I did nothing beyond what a publisher ought to have done; but may I say, just between us, it *has* been my amazing good fortune to have been associated with such a project, and to have it span virtually my entire time at MUP.[3]

---

[1] Peter Craven, 'The Ryan Affair', in Carl Bridge (ed.), *Manning Clark: Essays in his Place in History,* Melbourne: Melbourne University Press (hereafter MUP), 1994, pp. 165–87, 224, specifically p. 172.
[2] Quoted in Mark McKenna, *An Eye for Eternity: The Life of Manning Clark,* Melbourne: Miegunyah Press, 2011, p. 409.
[3] Clark to Ryan, 9 January 1987, and Ryan to Clark, 13 January 1987, Records of Melbourne University Press (hereafter MUP Records), 2003.0129, Unit 21 (vol. 6).

When Ryan reversed the favour eight years later, in the September 1993 issue of *Quadrant,* he unveiled Clark as a charlatan, a poseur and a dreadful mistake as a human being, whilst the epic six-volume *A History of Australia* was condemned as being sloppy, appallingly written and pernicious. The timing of Ryan's attack was as important as the content given the highly politicised atmosphere of 1993. The Australia's History Wars were in full swing with issues of republicanism and Aboriginal reconciliation at the forefront of debate. Clark had spoken forcefully in the affirmative in both matters. Another site of the History Wars controversy, in which Clark was also prominent, was the view that the European settlement of Australia was a shameful business, especially in the displacement and subsequent treatment of the Indigenous population. Others begged to differ, asserting that Australia had a history to be proud of. Only a month earlier, Geoffrey Blainey's Latham Lecture had been published in *Quadrant,* where Clark's *History* was identified as the principal propagator of 'black-armband' depictions of Australian history, in opposition to what he described as the 'three-cheers' school of history.[4]

* * *

Ryan's attack on Clark gained immediate traction in the daily press, starting with the Melbourne *Age* running a brief front-page story on 27 September 1993.[5] There was a prompt and mostly angry reaction. The Clark family was shocked and Manning's widow Dymphna issued a media statement in which she described Ryan's article as a 'cantankerous piece', whilst acknowledging her gratitude for his work as Manning's publisher. Otherwise, she was content to leave her late husband's work to 'speak for itself'.[6] Although praised for her dignity under fire, she

---

[4] Geoffrey Blainey, 'Drawing up a Balance Sheet of Our History', *Quadrant,* vol. 37, nos 7–8, July–August 1993, pp. 10–15. Detailed discussions of black-armband history are: Mark McKenna, *Different Perspectives on Black Armband History,* Canberra: Department of the Parliamentary Library, 1997, available at: www.aph.gov.au/About_Parliament/Parliamentary_Departments/Parliamentary_Library/pubs/rp/RP9798/98RP05; Anna Clark, 'History in Black and White: A Critical Analysis of the Black Armband Debate', *Journal of Australian Studies,* vol. 26, no. 75, 2002, pp. 1–11 (text), 174–76 (notes), doi.org/10.1080/14443050209387797.

[5] Louise Carbines, 'Publisher pays out on Manning Clark "fairy floss"', *Age,* 26 August 1993, p. 1; Carbines, 'Manning Clark's publisher wishes he wasn't', *Sydney Morning Herald,* 26 August 1993, p. 3; Lisa Clauden, 'Publisher ridicules Manning Clark work', *Advertiser* (Adelaide), 27 August 1993, p. 5.

[6] Robert Hefner, 'Publisher's outburst on Clark is no surprise, says widow', *Canberra Times,* 27 August 1993, pp. 1–2; Margaret Easterbrook, 'Clark's widow to let the History speak for itself', *Age,* 27 August 1993, p. 1; Cameron Forbes, 'Manning's widow turns the other cheek', *Australian,* 27 August 1993, p. 1; 'Widow defends historian', *Sydney Morning Herald,* 27 August 1993, p. 2. The media release is in the Dymphna Clark Papers, National Library of Australia (hereafter NLA), MS 9873, Series 10, Box 35, Folder 1.

was in fact deeply hurt by what she described as Ryan's 'brazen malice'.⁷ The extent of the pain was conveyed to me by her historian friends Ann Moyal and Roslyn Russell, with the latter confirming Dymphna's 'anguish … and her extreme disappointment in a man whose company she had always enjoyed'.⁸ Three years later her sense of hurt was still palpable. When asked by an interviewer whether she was surprised by Ryan's article, Dymphna replied, 'Well of course, how could you possibly expect anything like that? You've read it, have[n't] you? I've only read it once and I'm not going to read it again'.⁹

The Ryan onslaught had the additional effect of making Dymphna increasingly touchy about criticism of her late husband's oeuvre and she reacted with uncharacteristic asperity to a thoughtful newspaper review (of the abridged edition of the *History*). It was written by Monash University historian John Rickard, who stated that the *History* was less than a masterpiece and that 'many of [Clark's] former students had feelings of extraordinary ambivalence towards the work of their mentor'. As well, the tone of Rickard's reaction to Ryan's outburst was more resigned than angry. On her copy of Rickard's review, Dymphna scribbled the Manningesque comment: 'This Rickard tries to run with the hare & hunt with the hounds. Woe unto you scribes & Pharisees, hypocrites!'¹⁰

We are witnessing a familiar enough spectacle—the transformation of an historian's widow from his most incisive critic to defender of the shrine. The irony is that in earlier days Dymphna had rather enjoyed Ryan's character assassinations when she and Manning lunched with him in Melbourne: 'He was absolutely undressing [people] and drawing and quartering them, and terribly, terribly funny'—and now her late husband was on the receiving end.¹¹

---

7   Dymphna Clark to Lyndall Ryan, 16 September 1993, Dymphna Clark Papers, NLA, MS 9873, Series 10, Box 35, Folder 2.
8   Roslyn Russell, email to author, 30 August 2016; also Ann Moyal, discussion with author, Canberra, 11 June 2015; Gia Metherell, 'Skirmishes in cultured halls', *Canberra Times,* 14 June 1997 p. C3 (for Humphrey McQueen's comments at the time); Katerina and Axel Clark, interviewed by Susan Marsden, 19 June 2001, NLA, ORAL TRC 4770, p. 55 of transcript.
9   Dymphna Clark, interviewed by Heather Rusden, 13 February 1997 (starting at 73.38 minutes), NLA, ORAL TRC 3548, available at: nla.gov.au/nla.obj-217338911/listen.
10   John Rickard, 'Manning abridged', *Age Weekend Supplement,* 13 November 1993, p. 8 (the newspaper clipping of the review containing Dymphna's remarks is in the Dymphna Clark Papers, NLA, MS 9873, Series 9, Box 35, Folder 16). A round-up of academic historians' opinions of the *History* at the time of the controversy is provided by Fiona Curruthers, 'Rise and fall of Australian history', *Australian,* 1 September 1993, p. 15.
11   Dymphna Clark, interviewed by Heather Rusden, 13 February 1997 (starting 70.50 minutes), NLA, ORAL TRC 3548, available at: nla.gov.au/nla.obj-217338911/listen.

Figure 4. Dymphna Clark, early 1990s.
Although distressed by Peter Ryan's attack on her late husband, Dymphna maintained her dignity under fire.
Source. © Heide Smith Photographer 1990s (heidesmith.com/). Reproduced with her permission.

In the immediate aftermath of Ryan's attack Dymphna received numerous letters of support, containing such phrases as 'disgusting personal attack', 'despicable', 'obscene', 'contemptible', 'how outraged I am'.[12] In contrast to Dymphna, her son Andrew, a senior journalist, made no attempt

---

12   See also 'Corrie' to Axel Clark, 28 August 1993, Axel Clark Papers, NLA, MS Acc11.079, Box 17, Folder 2.

to play down the situation, correctly pointing out that Ryan's previous comments about his father's work 'bore no relation to the "Quadrant" attack', meaning that:

> Only two conclusions are possible—either Mr Ryan is a hypocrite, or a bitter jealous, old man. In any event, as my father passed away more than two years ago and Mr Ryan had plenty of time to make comments while he was alive, I regard this as the outburst of an opportunistic, cowardly and graceless man.[13]

* * *

The Ryan affair was described by literary journalist Peter Craven as a *succès de scandale*, and he more than implied that the instigator of the newspaper campaign was *Quadrant*'s editor, Robert Manne, whose 'skill at making rapid interventions into the media … give him an influence disproportionate to the marginality of his political position'—an assertion rightly disputed by Manne.[14] It was neither conspiracy nor undue influence at play but journalistic opportunity and the sober reality of *Quadrant*'s finances. The journal, which published 10 issues per year, operated 'very sparingly'. One source of income was donations from mining companies, which Manne declined after Ray Evans of Western Mining tried to interfere with content. To maintain the cash flow, *Quadrant* routinely sought to have its articles partly or wholly re-printed in newspapers, primarily the *Australian*.[15] The daily press got hold of the story, when Michael Gawenda, deputy editor of the *Age*, happened to see an advance copy of Ryan's article, resulting in the scrappy front-page story in that newspaper on 27 August 1993. The story quickly assumed a life of its own with the *Weekend Australian* republishing the entire Ryan article two days later.[16] To maintain the momentum, and to turn what it described as the country's 'greatest literary brawl' into a self-fulfilling prophecy, the *Australian* advance-published the gist of Ryan's second *Quadrant* piece the following weekend.[17]

---

13   Quoted in Margaret Easterbrook, 'Clark's widow to let the History speak for itself', *Age*, 27 August 1993, p. 1.
14   Craven, The Ryan Affair', 167; Robert Manne, 'The Puzzles of Manning Clark: Postscript', *Quadrant*, vol. 38, no. 11, November 1994, pp. 2–3, specifically p. 3.
15   Robert Manne, 'A holy cow called history', *Age*, 1 September 1993, p. 16; Manne, email to author, 14 September 2014 and comment on an earlier version of this book, 13 March 2019. *Quadrant* did have the advantage, over other literary and political commentary magazines, at least before 1981, of having newsagent distribution through Gordon & Gooch magazines. This, and other aspects of *Quadrant*'s finances, are discussed by Phillip Edmonds, *Tilting at Windmills: The Literary Magazine in Australia, 1968–2012*, Adelaide: University of Adelaide Press, 2015, pp. 46, 95–96, 100, 109–10, 137, doi.org/10.20851/windmills.
16   Peter Ryan, 'Why Clark's history is bunk', *Weekend Australian*, 28–29 August 1993, pp. 21–22.
17   Peter Ryan, 'The history men', *Weekend Australian*, 4–5 September 1993, p. 21.

Figure 5. Robert Manne, editor of *Quadrant* (1990–97), at around the time the controversy broke out.

Source. Provided by Robert Manne (photographer unknown) and reproduced with the subject's permission.

It was Ryan's supposed authority as Clark's publisher and his strictures appearing in the *Australian*, with its national circulation, that did such damage to Clark's reputation and caused the controversy to reach the heights it did. Manne was most surprised by the strength of the reaction. After all, he had published a severe attack on Clark two years earlier by his (Clark's) former student John Barrett (1931–1997), which had barely caused a public ripple.[18] As it happened, the September 1993 issue of *Quadrant* sold out in days and Manne regretted not having had more copies printed.

The *Australian* and *Quadrant* both gave ample space to Ryan's critics. Michael Cathcart, who had just published a one-volume abridgement of Clark's *History*, deplored Ryan's 'lack of grace' and the deterioration of national debate that it represented.[19] Fuelling the controversy was the feeling that Ryan's article represented the betrayal of a friendship. Clark's recent biographers have largely confirmed Ryan's portrayal of Clark's flaws and foibles, but without depicting Clark as a charlatan in the ways Ryan did; their access to Clark's darker side was made possible by the lifting of the embargo on Clark's diaries in the National Library of Australia in 2000. As Ann Moyal points out, Clark's diaries:

> Brought a new and confounding figure into view. Scribbled at night over half a century and yielding up their secrets of self-loathing and doubt, they tore at the chords of love in marriage, an ongoing litany of distrust, betrayal and disappointment. Here was a side of Manning Clark which close friends, myself included, neither recognised nor knew.[20]

But this was not part of the equation in 1993. Rather, Ryan's 'tittle-tattle', as Humphrey McQueen described it,[21] caused offence because it was gratuitous and irrelevant to the matter at hand.

---

18 John Barrett, 'Manning Clark: The Historian', *Quadrant*, vol. 35, nos 7–8, July–August 1991, pp. 7–8.
19 Michael Cathcart, 'The sage under siege', *Age*, 27 August 1993, p. 13 (and Cathcart, 'Clark's legacy undimmed', *Sydney Morning Herald*, 27 August 1993, p. 11). See also *Manning Clark's History of Australia*, abridged by Michael Cathcart, Melbourne: MUP, 1993; Peter Corrigan, 'Brave new worlds', *Age*, 16 October 1993 (by-line column), p. 11.
20 Ann Moyal, *A Woman of Influence: Science, Men & History*, Perth: UWA Publishing, 2014, p. 62. Moyal (1926–2019) was by that time a Canberra-based independent scholar after having worked in several Australian universities, notably as an historian of science. She founded the Independent Scholars Association of Australia in 1995. Her earlier autobiography is *Breakfast with Beaverbrook: Memoirs of an Independent Woman*, Sydney: Hale & Iremonger, 1995.
21 Humphrey McQueen, *Suspect History: Manning Clark and the Future of Australia's Past*, Adelaide: Wakefield Press, 1997, p. 166.

Questions of professional ethics were also in the mix; namely, 'the breach of propriety when a publisher turns publicly on an author with whom he has worked and from whom he has benefited'.²² The arguments are similar to those levelled a decade later against Herbert Breslin's unflattering account of Luciano Pavarotti, which was seen as a tasteless betrayal of a manager–client relationship.²³ Others, again, discerned an element of embittered attention seeking, while historian Ken Inglis (1929–2017), who had a long association with both Clark and Ryan, was distressed by the posthumous vilification.²⁴ As another of Ryan's detractors pointed out:

> Of the many things in his life upon which Ryan must look back with shame, the 'chiefest' should be his Clark essay. With an editor like Ryan, a writer doesn't need critics or enemies.²⁵

Yet another thread in the argument was that Ryan not only lacked compassion, but also that his rebuttal of the *History* was unhelpful in resolving 'the serious issue of how this country will determine what will stand as the truth of its history'.²⁶

Robert Manne moved quickly to restore order, explaining that taking a hatchet to a corpse had not been the intention.²⁷ Rather, Ryan had proposed his critique in 1991 but Clark died a fortnight later and the project was put on hold. As for speaking ill of the dead, Manne went

---

22 For example, Stuart Macintyre, 'Clark's work sure to outlive its detractors', *Age*, 28 August 1993, for quotation see p. 17; Peter Craven, 'Publisher damned by attack on Clark', *Australian*, 1 September 1993, pp. 15, 19; Christopher Bantick, 'Clark's place in historical discourse', *Australian*, 8 September 1993, p. 22; Robert Hefner, 'Bound to quality: a tribute to a local printer', *Canberra Times*, 7 November 1993, p. 3; John Bangsund, 'Peter Ryan and the Phoney Debate', *Society of Editors Newsletter* (Melbourne), vol. 32, no. 2, September 1993, p. 3. For a send-up of Ryan's first *Quadrant* article, see Phillip Adams, 'God brought to book at last', *Weekend Australian Review*, 18–19 September 1993, p. 2.
23 Herbert Breslin and Anne Midgette, *The King and I: The Uncensored Tale of Luciano Pavarotti's Rise to Fame by His Manager, Friend and Sometime Adversary*, New York: Doubleday, 2004; Matt Dobkin, 'My Big Fat Obnoxious Opera-Singing Client', 14 October 2004, *New York Magazine*, n.p., available at: nymag.com/nymetro/news/people/features/10106/index1.html.
24 Don Watson, 'Peter Ryan: A Voice from the Great Back Paddock of Australian Grumps', in ('Symposium Defending Manning Clark'), *Evatt Papers*, vol. 1, no. 2, 1993, pp. 21–24, specifically p. 21; Ken Inglis, quoted in Catherine Armitage, 'Clark no fraud, say academics', *Sydney Morning Herald*, 27 August 1993, p. 2. One of the greats of Australian history, Inglis's varied career is traced in Peter Browne and Seumas Spark (eds), *'I Wonder': The Life and Work of Ken Inglis*, Melbourne: Monash University Publishing, 2020.
25 Andrew Field, 'Clark's editor: a paragon of infidelity' (by-line column), *Courier-Mail*, 15 September 1993, p. 8.
26 Peter Corrigan, 'Brave new worlds', *Age*, 16 October 1993, p. 11.
27 Manne, 'A holy cow called history', *Age*, 1 September 1993, p. 16, republished as 'Manning Clark, Peter Ryan and Us', *Quadrant*, vol. 37, no. 10, October 1993, pp. 2–3.

on to ask, quite reasonably, whether 'one of [Australia's] most important thinkers should be placed under a semi-permanent moratorium', and whether Clark had considered the feelings of Dame Pattie and her family when repeatedly denigrating long-serving Liberal Prime Minister R.G. Menzies (1894–1978) in Volume 6 of the *History*. Manne also claimed that, far from committing a cowardly action, Ryan had shown considerable courage in publishing his article given the wrath that would come down on his head, and he assured readers that the timing of Ryan's article had not been planned to coincide with the publication of Cathcart's abridgment of the *History* in the hope of damaging sales. He was unaware of the book's imminent publication; and a delighted MUP promptly printed 4,000 further copies to meet the anticipated extra demand.[28]

Manne also disputed the claim that *Quadrant* had run recurrent attacks on Clark down the years, stating that the magazine had published only four significant critiques. He was mistaken. Although there had been two pieces favourable to Clark,[29] there were at least 17 articles in which he received unfavourable mention, seven of which could be described as 'significant' (Appendix 1). But the burden of Manne's argument was to rebut the accusations of vilification, claiming that Ryan had instead revealed the interconnectedness between the faults in Clark's work and the faults in his character—a point that I will go on to dispute. The other justification for *Quadrant* publishing Ryan's article was that discussion on Clark's work was long overdue, but this can hardly be countenanced given how much assessment had already taken place (Appendix 2). A notable example, among many, was R.W. Connell's 1978 critique of Clark's methods, including the charge that Clark lacked a 'formulated concept of structure and structural change'.[30] At that point Clark would probably have been the most discussed Australian historian after W.K. Hancock (1898–1988). Indeed, Clark's public profile as an historian was indicated

---

28 'Quiet delight over Clark row', *Canberra Times*, 28 August 1993, p. 4; 'History's success puts criticism into perspective', *Uni News*, University of Melbourne, 3 September 1993, p. 1; Rod Campbell, 'Fracas over historian's work helps sales', *Canberra Times*, 7 September 1993, p. 12.
29 Heinz Arndt, 'The Real Manning Clark', *Quadrant*, vol. 20, no. 11, November 1976, pp. 18–19; J.J. Eddy, 'The Clark Paradox', review of *Manning Clark and Australian History*, by Stephen Holt, *Quadrant*, vol. 26, no. 8, August 1982, pp. 62–64.
30 R.W. Connell, 'Manning Clark and the Science of History', *Meanjin Quarterly*, vol. 37, no. 2, 1978, pp. 262–68.

by the appearance of Stephen Holt's intellectual biography of Clark, published in 1982.[31] If anything, discussion on Clark's work amounted to overkill.

In addition to Manne's defence, Ryan received a considerable measure of wider public support. Both the *Australian* and the *Age* editorialised that he had acted 'responsibly', in contrast to the *Sydney Morning Herald* and *Canberra Times* editorials that Clark's *History* would live on.[32] There were letters to newspapers, thanking Ryan for exposing the fraudulence of Clark and his *History* and deploring Clark's baleful effect on Australian public life.[33] Several regular newspaper columnists also delivered hosannas, with one exclaiming that

> at the risk of being lynched by the historian's many admirers, I think Ryan's piece is one of the best examples of the art of essay writing I have ever seen. To me, it is not so much an attack as a frank and well-rounded portrait of a fascinating Australian personality.[34]

Another columnist was a former history professor, Austin Gough, who used Ryan's article (which he had not actually seen) as the vehicle for a perceptive and generally temperate critique of the *History*, especially the religious aspects.[35]

---

31 Stephen Holt, *Manning Clark and Australian History, 1915–1963*, Brisbane: University of Queensland Press, 1982.
32 'Historic battles', *Age*, 27 August 1993, p. 12; 'The fatal flaws of history', *Weekend Australian*, 28–29 August 1993, p. 20; 'Manning Clark's history lives', *Sydney Morning Herald*, 28 August 1993, p. 28; 'Manning Clark will outlast most critics', *Canberra Times*, 28 August 1993, p. 12.
33 For example, 'Debunking a national icon', *News Weekly*, 11 September 1993, p. 7; Paul Lynch, 'Ryan's decision to publish proved responsible' (letter) *Australian*, 11–12 September 1993, p. 18; Colin Kennedy, 'Manning Clark unreliable' (letter), *Canberra Times*, 23 October 1993, p. 3.
34 Paul Gray, 'When praise turns abruptly into farce' (by-line column), *Herald Sun*, 2 October 1993, for quotation see p. 18; David Clark, 'Critics miss fatal flaws' (by-line column), *Australian Financial Review*, 30 August 1993, p. 17; Frank Devine, 'Clark a captive of Gaullist delusions' (by-line column), *Australian*, 2 September 1993, p. 15; Les Carlyon (by-line column), *Business Review Weekly*, 3 September 1993, p. 16; Ronald Conway, 'A cry of support for Clark's critic', *Australian*, 15 September 1993, p. 19.
35 Austin Gough, 'Singular view of our past exposed' (by-line column), *Mercury* (Hobart), 4 September 1993, p. 28. A.G. Gough (1926–1997), emeritus professor of history at the University of Adelaide, was living in retirement in Tasmania. As well as his fortnightly column in the *Mercury*, he was an regular contributor to the conservative *Adelaide Review*. See Don Longo, 'The Fin-de-siècle Academy and its Discontents: Austin Gough and the Betrayal of the Intellectuals', *Journal of Labor and Society*, vol. 20, no. 3, 2017, pp. 285–305, doi.org/10.1111/wusa.12293.

However, the conservative side of politics was not unvarying in its defence. Ryan was tellingly reproached from an unexpected quarter when Gerard Henderson, the director of the Sydney Institute, stated that he had said nothing new and went on to rebuke him for not speaking out much earlier: 'Welcome aboard Peter—but where were you when we needed you?'[36]

* * *

Ryan rounded on his opponents in a follow-up article in the October 1993 issue of *Quadrant*, titled simply 'A Reply to my Critics'. He opened by expressing surprise at being on the receiving end of a 'hubbub of abuse'.

> Whew! An old publisher submits an essay to a small-circulation literary journal in Melbourne; a few home-truths about an Australian sacred cow escape into the atmosphere; a national media bushfire ignites. Truly, Australia remains a very provincial place.[37]

The surprise was hardly genuine in the light of Manne's statement that when Ryan first proposed his attack, he was

> already imagining the anger of Manning [who was still alive at the time] and the social ostracism which would be visited upon him by his vast network of friends and admirers. Never mind, it had to be done.[38]

One of Ryan's tactics was to ignore telling or inconvenient criticism, including that of Gerard Henderson. The other stratagems were to concentrate on points of weakness in his critics' arguments rather than addressing their wider concerns, and to twist the meaning of what they said. Thus, historian and writer Don Watson's description of Ryan as a 'cannibal' is used as an example of the abuse heaped upon him and at the same time making Watson look somewhat daft.[39] What Watson actually said was that Ryan's posthumous attack on Clark was 'an act of double cannibalism really. You live off him in life and when he's dead you live off

---

36   Gerard Henderson, 'Bless him, it is 30 years since he sinned', *Age*, 27 August 1993, p. 13; Henderson, 'The belated Mr Ryan owes us a penance', *Sydney Morning Herald*, 27 August 1993, p. 11.
37   Peter Ryan, 'A Reply to my Critics', in his *Lines of Fire: Manning Clark & Other Writings*, edited by A.K. Macdougall, Binalong, NSW: Clarion Editions, 1997, pp. 214–22, for quotation see p. 214.
38   Manne, 'A holy cow called history', *Age*, 1 September 1993, p. 16.
39   Ryan, 'A Reply to my Critics', p. 215.

him again'.⁴⁰ In similar fashion, Paul Bourke (1938–1999), director of the Research School of Social Sciences at The Australian National University, is derided for the inscrutable title of his critique in the *Canberra Times* ('Ryan is playing with the "pornography of power"'). Bourke was referring to the obscenity of visceral public attacks on prominent figures in the community, but the title of his piece (the work of a sub-editor) makes little sense in and of itself.⁴¹ Ryan, however, was within his rights to suggest a conflict of interest in that Bourke was in the throes of raising funds for a Manning Clark Chair of History at ANU.⁴² Ryan didn't realise that Bourke, while publicly supportive of Clark, was in fact highly critical of the latter's scholarship, or else Ryan would have had another point of attack against Bourke, who should not have entered the fray in the first place.⁴³

A third target was Peter Craven, who had referred to the

> bizarre attack by the man personally responsible for the state in which Manning Clark's *A History of Australia* was presented to the public ... Clearly in Ryan's own terms he was a failure as a publisher.⁴⁴

(As will be seen in Chapter 8 of this book, it was not so straightforward because Clark was hardly a compliant author.)

Ryan's stock answer to such criticisms was not to answer them at all, but to describe Craven's intervention as a 'tizzy' that 'splutters rather than speaks', and to

> offer a small prize—say a genuinely unread copy of the Manning Clark abridgement—to the first person who can elucidate the meaning of Craven's concluding paragraph when he wanders off inexplicably to Edmund Wilson.⁴⁵

---

40 'Quiet delight over Clark row', *Canberra Times,* 28 August 1993, for quotation see p. 4; Gerard Henderson, 'Backroom maestro finds the limelight', *Age,* 19 October 1993, p. 13.
41 Paul Bourke, 'Ryan is playing with the "pornography of power"', *Canberra Times,* 28 August 1993, p. 4; Peter Ryan, *Final Proof: Memoirs of a Publisher,* Sydney: Quadrant Books, 2010, p. 49.
42 Ryan, 'A Reply to my Critics', p. 218.
43 Austin Gough to Ryan, 6 September 1993, Ryan Papers, NLA, MS 9897, Series 6, Box 10, Folder 2; Ryan to Bourke, 26 August 1994 (faxed message), Ryan Papers, NLA, MS 9897, Series 6, Box 10, Folder 5; Ryan to Heinz Arndt, 17 May 1992 [should be 1994] (faxed message), Ryan Papers, NLA, MS 9897, Series 6, Box 9, Folder 1.
44 Craven, 'Publisher damned by attack on Clark', *Australian,* 1 September 1993, p. 15.
45 Ryan, 'A Reply to my Critics', p. 219.

University of Melbourne historian Stuart Macintyre is also taken to task for his comment on the 'PM' radio station that Ryan was unqualified, as a non-historian, to criticise Clark.[46] Aged 46, Macintyre was already a leading figure in the Australian historical profession. His statement gives the impression of academic arrogance, yet elsewhere Ryan admits to achieving only 'an undistinguished second-class Honours BA'.[47] Certainly, Ryan had nothing original to say about the *History*, either then or later. But it was Macintyre's accusation of cowardice in launching the posthumous betrayal of Clark that stuck in Ryan's craw. As we have seen with Andrew Clark's comments, Macintyre was by no means alone in making such an observation, but Ryan's pugnacious reaction was as though it were:

> It is not an accusation I often face and I cannot, offhand, recall the name of any survivor. If Macintyre means that it does not take much courage to face a yapping pack of briefly woken-up Australian historians, he may be right. If he means something else, he is invited to stand within arm's reach the next time he says it.[48]

To which, one of Ryan's friends responded that he hoped to be present, camera in hand, in the event of 'fisticuffs'.[49] A commentator later asserted:

> [Macintyre's] accusation of cowardice was particularly bizarre, since Macintyre, like Clark, had probably never touched a toy gun, whereas Ryan served with conspicuous gallantry in New Guinea in the jungle and mountains.[50]

It is not a helpful statement, except perhaps to demonstrate that the often-personalised mode of debate continued well after 1993. (In fact, Macintyre had practised with a .303 rifle containing live ammunition during compulsory Cadets at Scotch College, Melbourne.) Seventeen years later, Ryan announced that 'the offer [to fisticuffs] remains open', implying that Macintyre had been too gutless to tangle with him.[51]

---

46   Ryan, 'A Reply to my Critics', p. 215. Various radio stations ran interviews with interested parties in the two days following the disclosure of Ryan's first *Quadrant* article. There are three listings of these interviews in undated notes by Ryan to himself, in the Ryan Papers, NLA, MS 9897, Series 6, Box 10, Folders 2, 3 & 4.
47   Ryan, *Final Proof*, pp. 20, 106.
48   Ryan, 'A Reply to my Critics', p. 216.
49   Michael [Cannon] to Ryan, 5 September 1993, Ryan Papers, NLA, MS 9897, Series 6, Box 10, Folder 3.
50   Geoffrey Partington, *Making Sense of History*, Bloomington, IN: Xlibris, 2013, p. 189.
51   Peter Ryan, 'My Life as a Leper', *Quadrant*, vol. 55, nos 1–2, January–February 2011, pp. 127–28, specifically p. 128.

Figure 6. Michael Cathcart (foreground) and Stuart Macintyre were both critics of Peter Ryan.

They are pictured at the launch of a careers in arts brochure at the University of Melbourne Union, 24 July 2000.

Source. © Michael Silver 2000 (Magnet Galleries Melbourne Inc., magnet.org.au). Reproduced with the permission of photographer and subjects.

It was actually Ryan who lacked the courage of his convictions by avoiding Macintyre's offers at the time to debate the issue on radio or television, or even to appear on such media (for example, Mary Delahunty's ABC-TV cultural program), preferring instead to confine himself to print where he could not be immediately challenged.[52] Macintyre came to see the futility of it all, given that Ryan's 'mixture of personal abuse and misunderstanding of history provided little of substance to discuss'.[53] Less than a year later, Ryan misrepresented the situation by telling a correspondent that 'hardly anyone was prepared to sit down [at the time] and have a face-to-face argument—even a shouting match, if they had wanted'.[54]

---

52   Stuart Macintyre, 'Why do the Tories hate Manning Clark?' in ('Symposium Defending Manning Clark'), *Evatt Papers,* vol. 1, no. 2, 1993, pp. 17–21, specifically p. 17; Stuart Macintyre and Anna Clark, *The History Wars,* 2nd edn, Melbourne: MUP, 2004, p. 226.
53   Macintyre, 'Why do the Tories hate Manning Clark?', pp. 17–20, for quotation see p. 17; Peter Ryan, notes of phone conversation with Brian Millership, 6 March 1995, Ryan Papers, NLA, MS 9897, Series 6, Box 10, Folder 8.
54   Ryan to John Parsons, 21 August 1994, Ryan Papers, NLA, MS 9897, Series 6, Box 10, Folder 5.

Neither does Ryan mention the level of private support he received; it suited his purposes to represent himself as a victim of serial abuse. In fact, he was favoured with numerous letters of affirmation from friends and strangers alike. Some of the latter were 'Concerned Australian[s]', as one described himself, whose alarmist sentiments indicate that the mere mention of Manning Clark was a political statement in itself:

> I have genuine sympathy for the wife and other family members of Manning Clark. However, I would ask them to understand that [Peter Ryan's article] is akin to the lancing of a huge, painful carbuncle for those of us who have suffered for so long … I believe Manning Clark and his supporters (the Whitlams, the Hawkes, the Keatings, et al) have been in no small part responsible for what I see as the destruction of Australian values, culture and independence during the 70's and 80's. I live in the hope that those of us of the opposite persuasion may prevail over the next several decades, in order to rescue Australia from the edge of the terrible abyss upon which it currently teeters.[55]

Another such product of the History Wars came from 'a plain man of advancing years':

> Oh, my! what a to-do, what a fox to loose among the academic chickens; oh! the feathers that will fly; the dust that will be raised … I am sure that I speak for the majority of Australians—that mysterious 'silent majority' who, like me, seldom put pen to paper, but who, thank God, still have the power—when I congratulate you on having the courage to say what you thought about a work which, if not questioned, could be accepted as gospel by future generations of young Australians.[56]

A friend also wrote to Ryan saying that 'I agree with everything you've said and I haven't read the fucking history', and a stranger reassured him that

> I think it was right and good *what* you did, *when* you did, and I hope that others who think the same will, like me, overcome their diffidence to write and let you know of their support.[57]

---

55 Brian J. Hurlock, letter to the *Australian* (unpublished), 30 August 1993, attached to Hurlock to Ryan, 6 September 1993, Ryan Papers, NLA, MS 9897, Series 6, Box 10, Folder 2. Actually, Clark and Hawke were not enamoured with each other. See McKenna, *An Eye for Eternity*, pp. 10, 302, 609.
56 L. George Martin to Ryan, 31 August 1993, Ryan Papers, NLA, MS 9897, Series 6, Box 10, Folder 4.
57 (Signature indecipherable) to Ryan, 29 August 1993; Zoe Osman to Ryan, 4 September 1993, respectively, both in Ryan Papers, NLA, MS 9897, Series 6, Box 10, Folder 3.

Yet another correspondent noted, after itemising numerous errors of Clark's concerning a forebear, that Volume 2 of the *History* made 'a good door stop against the wind'.[58]

Ryan also had academic endorsers. An academic lawyer congratulated him for having 'cracked the whole "PC" closed shop'.[59] Archivist Barbara Ross told Ryan, 'I have greatly admired your honesty and forthrightness in writing as you did. And it has become so very necessary that someone should say all that you said'.[60] Support from another unexpected quarter came from ANU anthropologist Derek Freeman (1916–2001), the nemesis of fellow anthropologist Margaret Mead (1901–1978), who wrote to Ryan as a fellow sufferer, having borne the slings and arrows of Mead's devotees. Freeman's repudiation of Mead was also posthumous, the difference being that he confronted Mead about his concerns over her work 14 years before she died.[61]

In short, Ryan cast himself in the role of a victim without indicating that many supported his stance and applauded his heroic exposé of the emperor's lack of clothes. Ryan never publicly acknowledged the level of endorsement he received, instead depicting himself as an innocent set upon by a bunch of thugs. As we shall see, these are just two of the distortions that leave his version of events having little credibility.

---

58   Edna Bateman Rich[ards?] to Ryan, undated, Ryan Papers, NLA, MS 9897, Series 6, Box 10, Folder 2.
59   Geoffrey deQ. Walker (University of Queensland) to Ryan, 4 March 1994, Ryan Papers, NLA, MS 9897, Series 6, Box 10, Folder 6. Similar sentiments were expressed in Simon H. Haskell (Deakin University) to Ryan, 10 September 1993, Ryan Papers, NLA, MS 9897, Series 6, Box 10, Folder 2.
60   Barbara Ross to Ryan, 14 November 1994, Ryan Papers, NLA, MS 9897, Series 6, Box 10, Folder 5. At one point, Ross (1929–2005) had been attached to the history department at ANU in the Research School of Social Sciences—an institution that Clark viewed askance.
61   Derek Freeman to Ryan, 4 October 1992 [should be 1993], Ryan Papers, NLA, MS 9897, Series 6, Box 10, Folder 2; Peter Hempenstall, *Truth's Fool: Derek Freeman and the War over Cultural Anthropology*, Madison: University of Wisconsin Press, 2017, pp. 98–100, doi.org/10.1111/aman.13063.

4

Errors, Great and Small

> History is in deep trouble once it leaves its empiricist base.
> Robin W. Winks (2001)[1]

Peter Ryan observed that 'of all the people I have met, Manning's character was the most elusive, the most baffling to pin down and describe'.[2] But he reckoned that he had cracked the code by virtue of 'the Doctor Johnson factor':

> If Doctor Johnson is correct, that no man may write about the life of another 'but those that have eat and drunk and lived in social intercourse with him',[3] [then] I have that qualification, in regard to the man and also in regard to his book.[4]

It is not as it seems. Despite their long association, Ryan states that Manning Clark had 'beaten the grog'[5] and in fact many of Clark's friends and associates were also under the impression that Clark had renounced the demon drink.[6] Clark's problem was that he suffered from

---

1   Bruce Harding, 'The Historian as Detective: Interview with Professor Robin Winks', *History Now*, vol. 7, no. 4, 2001, pp. 2–4, specifically p. 4.
2   Ryan, Peter, 'Manning Clark', in his *Lines of Fire: Manning Clark & Other Writings*, ed. A.K. Macdougall, Binalong, NSW: Clarion Editions, 1997, pp. 179–214, specifically p. 201.
3   John Wilson Croker (ed.), *Boswell's Life of Johnson: Including their Tour to the Hebrides*, London: John Murray, 1848, p. 235.
4   Ryan, 'Manning Clark', p. 181.
5   Ryan, 'Manning Clark', p. 201.
6   Geoffrey Dutton, *Out in the Open: An Autobiography*, Brisbane: University of Queensland Press, 1994, p. 492; Humphrey McQueen, *Suspect History: Manning Clark and the Future of Australia's Past*, Adelaide: Wakefield Press, 1997, p. 121; Bruce Grant, *Subtle Moments: Scenes on a Life's Journey*, Melbourne: Monash University Publishing, 2017, p. 54. Ryan repeats the assertion that Clark had beaten the grog in 'Folk Memory v History', *Quadrant*, vol. 43, no. 10, October 1999, pp. 70–72, specifically p. 72.

grand mal epilepsy and, in consequence, was a two-pot screamer.[7] It was during a study leave in Oxford in 1956 that Clark resolved to give up drinking and to start writing the *History*.[8] He largely avoided alcohol thereafter, although there were spectacular lapses, including the occasion in 1969 when he disgraced himself in Government House at a gathering of writers and artists.[9] But Ryan categorically states that Clark had become 'a strict and faintly tedious teetotaller'[10] and he claims to be speaking from a position of Johnsonian authority.

Ryan makes mistake after mistake about the person he berates for inaccuracies. He criticises Clark for misspelling a friend's surname,[11] to which Stuart Macintyre remarked that neither Ryan nor Manne was able to spell his own surname correctly.[12] More seriously, Ryan states that Clark found satisfaction and enjoyed academic freedom during his early years at Canberra University College.[13] Rather, this was a frustrating time for Clark. Thanks to ASIO intervention, the course he taught to diplomatic cadets was taken from him.[14] Neither did Clark care for Canberra's lack of 'refinement', and he liked even less his department's courses and exam results having to be approved by the parent department at the University of Melbourne. A further source of discontent was the contiguous Australian National University, whose academics had no undergraduates and were able to concentrate on their research. In fact, Clark was desperate to get back to the University of Melbourne and was acutely disappointed when his attempt to occupy the newly created second chair of history came to nothing.[15]

---

7   Katerina and Axel Clark, interviewed by Susan Marsden, 19 June 2001, NLA, ORAL TRC 4770 (p. 11 of transcript). At the time of the interview, Katerina Clark was under the impression that her father had petit mal epilepsy. She later discovered that it was more likely he had grand mal epilepsy. Katerina Clark, email to author, 3 August 2019.
8   Katerina Clark, email to author, 2 August 2019.
9   Geoffrey Bolton, *Paul Hasluck: A Life*, Perth: UWA Publishing, 2014, p. 431; Brian Matthews, *Manning Clark: A Life*, Sydney: Allen & Unwin, 2008, p. 302.
10 Ryan, 'Manning Clark', p. 181.
11 Ryan, 'Manning Clark', p. 207.
12 Stuart Macintyre, 'Why do the Tories hate Manning Clark?', in ('Symposium Defending Manning Clark'), *Evatt Papers,* vol. 1, no. 2, 1993, pp. 17–20, specifically p. 17.
13 Ryan, 'Manning Clark', pp. 190–91.
14 Manning Clark, *The Quest for Grace*, Ringwood: Penguin, 1991, p. 204; Mark McKenna, *An Eye for Eternity: The Life of Manning Clark*, Melbourne: Miegunyah Press, 2011, p. 395.
15 Fay Anderson, *An Historian's Life: Max Crawford and the Politics of Academic Freedom*, Melbourne: Melbourne University Press (hereafter MUP), 2005, pp. 230, 246–50, 280–89; Stephen Holt, 'War of words', *Courier Mail Weekend* (Brisbane), 2 August 1997, p. 7.

4. ERRORS, GREAT AND SMALL

To complain about low-grade inaccuracies risks the charge of being 'obsessed with little things of the mind and spirit', the phrase used in an excoriating review of Volume 1 of the *History*.[16] Rather, Ryan's minor inaccuracies are forewarning that larger errors of fact and representation are afoot, one of them being Ryan's depiction of the publishing trajectory of Clark's *History*. He asserts that the Sydney publisher Angus & Robertson's experience of publishing Clark's two-volume *Documents in Australian History* was so off-putting that they turned down his *History* and shuffled it on to Gwyn James, Ryan's predecessor at MUP.[17] Actually, Clark chose MUP over Angus & Robertson because he felt his *History* was 'appropriate for a University press' and because 'Melbourne was the place where the passion for these things was first conceived'.[18] Clark was formally invited to commit his *History* to MUP by James, who added his remorse at having turned down Clark's two-volume *Documents* a decade earlier.[19] For their part, Angus & Robertson regretted not being chosen to publish the *History* and were 'delighted' with the consolation prize of Clark's *Meeting Soviet Man* (1960)—a book that caused him much grief in the years to come.[20]

More seriously, Ryan misrepresents the nature of Clark's contractual arrangements with MUP. This was not a matter of debate in late 1993 because no one had reason to doubt Ryan's explanation that he was locked into the contract he had inherited from Gwyn James. Ryan is adamant on this point,[21] which he repeats on subsequent occasions, culminating with assertions in his autobiography that

---

16 Malcolm Ellis, 'History without Facts', *Bulletin,* 22 September 1962, pp. 36–37, specifically p. 36.
17 Peter Ryan, *Final Proof: Memoirs of a Publisher,* Sydney: Quadrant Books, 2010, pp. 32, 96; Ryan, 'Hollow Man of Yesterday', review of *Manning Clark: A Life,* by Brian Matthews, *Quadrant,* vol. 53, nos 1–2, January–February 2009, pp. 127–28, specifically p. 127.
18 Roslyn Russell (ed.), *Ever, Manning: Selected Letters of Manning Clark, 1938–1991,* Sydney: Allen & Unwin, 2008, p. 178 (Clark to George Ferguson, 13 January 1961). Instead, Angus & Robertson published Marjorie Barnard's 710-page *A History of Australia.* It appeared in the same year as Volume 1 of Clark's *A History of Australia,* and was eclipsed by it.
19 G.F. James to Clark, 10 March 1959, Manning Clark Papers, National Library of Australia (hereafter NLA), MS 7550, Series 1, Box 3, Folder 23; C.M.H. Clark (ed.), *Documents in Australian History,* 2 vols, Sydney: Angus & Robertson, 1950 and 1956.
20 Beatrice Davis to Clark, 26 June 1959, Manning Clark Papers, MS 7550, Series 1, Box 3, Folder 22; Ferguson to Clark, 23 January 1961, Manning Clark Papers, MS 7550, Series 1, Box 5, Folder 34.
21 Ryan, 'Manning Clark', p. 180.

the Press had made an open-ended commitment to Manning to publish succeeding numbers in the series without the slightest idea of how many volumes that might eventually be, nor over how many years [and, further, that] ... under our contract, MUP was committed to completing the *History*.[22]

Such claims are a travesty. When James enquired, in March 1959, whether Clark would be interested in having MUP publish his forthcoming *magnum opus,* he did have in mind an open-ended arrangement whereby Clark would be allowed 'whatever number of volumes' it took to complete his *History of Australia*.[23] But James's offer required confirmation by MUP's Board of Management. The board was cautious and, in September 1960, deferred its decision until the complete manuscript of Volume 1 was to hand.[24] In January 1961, upon receipt of the first five chapters of Volume 1, Clark was informed that Macmahon Ball, in his capacity of chairman of the MUP Board, had 'confirmed the acceptance of the entire project'.[25] At this point it starts to get murky. Ryan states that Ball had opposed taking on the *History*,[26] and he repeats himself in his autobiography.[27] But the MUP Board minutes corroborate that the commitment to publish the work rested with the chairman's action. Clearly, James had managed to prevail upon a reluctant Ball, probably on the back of Cambridge University Press agreeing to take significant numbers of unbound copies (or 'sheets', in publishing parlance). A disgruntled Ball then got a measure of revenge by 'browbeat[ing]' the board into reducing the proposed print run of Volume 1 and accusing James of 'culpably under-pricing' the cost of sheets to Cambridge University Press. Whatever the justice of the allegation, James's economic management had been deficient in other respects, resulting in a horrendous overdraft and ultimately in his

---

22   Peter Ryan, 'Folk Memory v History', review of *A Short History of Manning Clark*, by Stephen Holt, *Quadrant*, vol. 43, no. 10, October 1999, pp. 70–71, specifically p. 71; Ryan, 'My Life as a Leper', *Quadrant*, vol. 55, nos 1–2, January–February 2011, pp. 127–28, specifically p. 128; Ryan, *Final Proof*, p. 31 for quotation, also p. 138. Clark initially intended the *History* to comprise two volumes but it blew out to six. Stuart Macintyre and Anna Clark, *The History Wars*, 2nd edn, Melbourne: MUP, 2004, p. 55; McKenna, *An Eye for Eternity*, p. 343.
23   James to Clark, 10 March 1959, Manning Clark Papers, MS 7550, Series 1, Box 3, Folder 23.
24   Minutes of the Board of Management, 26 September 1960, Records of Melbourne University Press (hereafter MUP Records), 2003.0118.
25   James to Clark, 5 January 1961, Manning Clark Papers, MS 7550, Series 18, Box 156, Folder 1.
26   Ryan, 'Manning Clark', p. 182.
27   Ryan, *Final Proof*, pp. 16–17.

constructive dismissal; in a restructuring of the press, he was to remain as director but without a place on the board. Rather than submit to such indignity, he resigned.[28]

There is a second point of contention. Contrary to Ryan's assertions, no actual contract had been drawn up by the time that Volume 1 of the *History* was published in September 1962, some months after James's departure. Ryan did not inherit a contract as he claimed but presented Clark with one (technically an 'agreement') the following year. It was the standard MUP contract and it specified, in Ryan's handwriting, that the *History* would comprise four volumes and that each volume be delivered at two-yearly intervals, unless extensions of time had been granted.[29] The formal contract for four volumes, of course, overrode the open-ended but informal offer from James to write as many volumes as Clark chose.

Then we come to another contractual matter. Historian Geoffrey Bolton did wonder—and doubted—whether MUP had followed the usual procedure that the manuscripts of successive volumes had been sent to 'one or two qualified readers' for comment on their suitability.[30] This was not the case, because Ryan had neglected to make any such provision. Although the first volume of the *History* had already been published, provision for subsequent refereeing ought to have been written into the belated contract. In other words, it was Ryan's doing that subsequent volumes of the *History* were not subject to peer review, something he never publicly acknowledged. As Ryan would have said, this is 'no way to run a long-term publishing venture'.[31]

---

28 Minutes of the Board of Management, 27 March 1961, MUP Records, 2003.0118; James to Clark, 5 January 1961, and James to Clark, 5 April 1961, both in Manning Clark Papers, MS 7550, Series 18, Box 156, Folder 1; James to Clark, 6 August 1987, Manning Clark Papers, MS 7550, Series 18, Box 160, Folder 29; Stephen Holt, *A Short History of Manning Clark*, Sydney: Allen & Unwin, 1999, pp. 129–31.
29 Ryan to Clark, 17 July 1963 and 19 August 1963, MUP Records, 2003.0129, Unit 20 (Folder: History of Australia, vol. 1). An unsigned copy of the contract, but containing Ryan's handwritten insertions, is in the MUP Records, 2003.0129, Unit 20 (Folder: History of Australia, vol. 2). Ryan's intention that there be four volumes seems to have been known around town. In his review of Volume 1 of the *History*, Stuart Sayers (literary editor of the *Age*) refers to 'what promises to be a four-volume work'. See Sayers, 'A new history of Australia: "restless human forces and passions"', *Age*, 8 September 1962, p. 17.
30 Geoffrey Bolton, 'Don't smash the icon', *Bulletin*, 12 October 1993, pp. 42–43, specifically p. 43. Bolton (1931–2015) was prominent within the Australian historical profession. He was an exponent of 'the middle way' and in public debate he instinctively assumed the role of 'an observer rather than a controversialist'. Stuart Macintyre, 'Geoffrey Bolton, A Lifetime in History', in Stuart Macintyre, Lenore Layman and Jenny Gregory (eds), *A Historian for all Seasons: Essays for Geoffrey Bolton*, Melbourne: Monash University Publishing, 2017, pp. 1–39, for quotation see p. 31.
31 Ryan, *Final Proof*, p. 31.

Ryan's autobiography contains a confusion of ideas and statements that Volume 1 had been foisted upon him. On the one hand, he asserts that its publication came at a most opportune moment for the financially beleaguered MUP. A few pages earlier, however, he expresses dissatisfaction that he had to 'get in the nation's bookshops a work of which I had not previously read the manuscript before recommending it to the [MUP Board of Management] for acceptance', as though something untoward was afoot.[32] But every incoming managing editor of a publishing house inherits a list. Ryan wants it both ways, because he also complains that the existing list, when he commenced duties, 'would [only] hold the MUP fort briefly; after that, a void, unless urgent steps were taken to fill it'.[33] Such inconsistencies, as we will see, are typical of the manner in which Ryan's arguments can shift around.

* * *

As mentioned, Ryan asserts that he was locked into an association with Clark from which there was no exit door, unless Clark decided to cease producing volumes. On the contrary, Ryan had ample opportunity to terminate the project. In his original *Quadrant* article, Ryan mentioned that 'Manning more than once, in disgust and discouragement, declared to me his intention to abandon all thought of future volumes'.[34] Surprisingly, no one noticed in late August/early September 1993 that Clark had provided escape routes, or else questions would have been asked as to why Ryan had persisted with a work he described as 'unworthy of the imprint of a scholarly publishing house'.[35] In fact, Ryan had the chance to sign off as early as July 1964 when Clark 'wondered whether it is worthwhile going on'. In despair at some of the reviews, Clark thought 'it may be wise to write no more'. To which Ryan promptly responded:

> Of course we think it worth going on with. It is certainly one of the most distinguished and exciting titles in our List ... your great history will certainly be one of the best known pieces of Australian scholarship and literature for many, many years to come.[36]

---

32 Ryan, *Final Proof*, p. 30.
33 Ryan, *Final Proof*, p. 28, for quotation see p. 36, also pp. 63–65.
34 Ryan, 'Manning Clark', p. 194.
35 Ryan, 'Manning Clark', p. 181.
36 Russell, *Ever, Manning*, p. 230 (Clark to Ryan, 28 July 1964); Ryan to Clark, 1 July [should be August] 1964, Manning Clark Papers, MS 7550, Series 1, Box 5, Folder 40.

4. ERRORS, GREAT AND SMALL

A further opportunity presented itself three years later, in September 1967, when Clark asked Ryan 'to tell me honestly if you and the M.U.P. want me to write a third volume'.[37] Ryan's blandishments then switched from praise of quality to public interest in the project, which are two different things.

> This is in reply to your letter of 5 September, asking whether we *really* want a third (and indeed a fourth) volume from your pen. The answer is clearly and emphatically 'Yes', and upon several counts. Firstly … we feel that there is an obligation, following the announced plan of the work years ago, to carry it through. Secondly, volume I established for itself a place quite unique in Australian history, and the continuing level of interest is proved by the fact that, (yet again!) it has to be reprinted to meet the demand. Thirdly, the advance interest in volume II is keen, and we have not the slightest doubt that it will be a great success. So how can you doubt that volume 3 could be anything but one of the most eagerly awaited MSS. we have upon our list?[38]

Clark was having a difficult time with Volume 3 and the following year he burdened Ryan with further self-doubts:

> Chance and circumstance may well cause me to stop at 1851 or December 1852, call it a day, and call the whole work, *A History of Australia down to the discovery of Gold.* Then I could get on with other things, and bow out from the world of the men who presume to establish a standards' laboratory for the great questions of the human heart.[39]

And again his publisher mounted a rescue mission:

> I hope you will not, upon reflection, conclude your history with volume 3 in 1852. This would be a disappointment to your immense and avid public, *and a great loss to Australians' awareness of themselves* [my emphasis].[40]

Ryan followed up a few months later, and his argument switched back to quality. Fondly recalling his days as Clark's student at the University of Melbourne, he expressed the hope that Clark would continue 'at least up to 1901 … It is unthinkable that all this should not eventually be gathered

---

37 Russell, *Ever, Manning,* p. 262 (Clark to Ryan, 5 September 1967).
38 Ryan to Clark, 7 September 1967, MUP Records, 2003.0129, Unit 20 (vol. 2).
39 Russell, *Ever, Manning,* p. 270 (Clark to Ryan, 28 March 1968).
40 Ryan to Clark, 9 April 1968, MUP Records, 2003.0129, Unit 20 (vol. 2).

into the great work'.⁴¹ Even then, Clark continued to voice his doubts and again Ryan urged him to forget the 'nitpickers' and to forge ahead.⁴² All this cajoling amounted, in a phrase of Ryan's in another context, to 'moral evasiveness'.⁴³

Clark's crises of confidence provide insight as to what Ryan was up against; and Clark may just have been angling for reassurance. But, why was Ryan so anxious for subsequent volumes of a work about which he was becoming increasingly disenchanted? He could have taken the ostensibly humanitarian approach by letting Clark go in peace, citing concerns for his health and welfare in the face of a task that was grinding him down. The impediment to ditching the *History*, according to Ryan, was that it was 'highly doubtful' he could prevail upon MUP's Board of Management to discontinue Clark's *History*.⁴⁴ 'The book was a success, wasn't it. Sales were stupendous, weren't they? The professional historians seemed to approve, didn't they? So who was I to judge such matters?'⁴⁵ Geoffrey Bolton wondered—and, again, doubted—whether this was a valid argument, stating that Ryan was casting aspersions on his Board of Management and noting that he could have sought outside opinions on Clark's work.⁴⁶ Armed with negative outside advice there is reason to believe that Ryan's misgivings would have prevailed. In his autobiography he represents the board as comprising sensible chaps who would listen to reason, whose interactions with the director were based on mutual trust and who were motivated by an overriding concern for the good standing of the press.⁴⁷ Yet Ryan never raised with the board, much less with Clark, his qualms about the quality of the *History* and his perception that it was putting MUP's reputation at risk. A former chairman of the board attests that Ryan 'meticulously ... briefed the Board and its various committees',

---

41   Ryan to Clark, 21 May 1968, MUP Records, 2003.0129, Unit 20 (vol. 2). Shortly after taking up the reins at MUP, Ryan told Clark that Volume 1 of the *History* was 'a great work'. See Matthews, *Manning Clark*, p. 229.
42   Russell, *Ever, Manning*, pp. 277–78 (Clark to Ryan, 14 August 1968 and 3 September 1968) and p. 384 (Clark to Ryan, 8 November 1978); Ryan to Clark, 16 September 1968, MUP Records, 2003.0129, Unit 21 (vol. 3).
43   Peter Ryan, 'Journey into Greenland' (1989), in his *Lines of Fire*, pp. 75–79, specifically p. 76.
44   Ryan, 'Manning Clark', p. 196.
45   Ryan, 'Manning Clark', p. 182.
46   Geoffrey Bolton, 'Don't smash the icon', *Bulletin*, 12 October 1993, pp. 42–43; Christopher Bantick, 'Clark's place in historical discourse', *Australian*, 8 September 1993, p. 22.
47   Ryan, *Final Proof*, pp. 28–29, 42, 65, 67, 74, 144.

and another board member avers that 'he ran a lean and orderly ship'.[48] But instead of sharing his concerns with the MUP Board of Management he lays the blame on others, arguing that academic approval of the *History* precluded him from approaching the board with a view to terminating the project.

Ryan's other explanation for not ditching the *History* was the press's precarious financial position. When he took up duties in mid-1962, MUP was still paying off a sizeable overdraft and 'the *History* was a valuable revenue earner … income not lightly to be thrown away'.[49] Moreover, 'The reception given to Volume 1 was everything a publisher prays for— keen and occasionally acrimonious criticism, extending over months. Sales soared'.[50] Volume 1, in fact, came at a heaven-sent moment for both the beleaguered MUP and the newly arrived Ryan: 'Apart from providing urgently needed sales revenue … it gave reassurance to both booksellers and the public that "MUP is still *definitely* in business"'.[51] The notion among MUP staff that 'Manning pays all our wages'[52] is an exaggeration but revenue from the earlier volumes of the *History* was clearly of great help to the firm's straightened finances. The *History* was indeed a high-selling title—'at almost any time one volume or another was in the printer's hands for a reprint'[53]—to the extent that it had 'chalked up aggregate prints of over 40,000 copies' by 1988.[54] Such was the success

---

48 John Poynter, 'Peter Ryan the Publisher', *Quadrant*, vol. 60, no. 3, March 2016, pp. 58–59, specifically p. 59; Geoffrey Blainey, 'Peter Ryan's Life (2)', *Quadrant*, vol. 60, no. 3, March 2016, pp. 57–58, specifically p. 58. The minutes of the MUP Board of Management are a record of decisions; only occasionally do they relate the discussions leading to a decision. Still, it is inconceivable that a matter of such importance as abandoning Clark's *History* would have escaped being recorded in the minutes, had the subject been raised. Once the *History* had been formally accepted, the board minutes simply record such routine matters as the receipt of Clark's manuscripts, the stage of editing, printing processes and the size of the print runs.
49 Ryan, *Final Proof*, p. 31, for quotation see p. 138. Both Ryan and Ball were assiduous in finding ways to reduce the overdraft: e.g. Ball to F.R. Mansridge (Cambridge University Press, New York), 21 March 1963, Ball Papers, NLA, MS 7851, Series 1, Box 3, Folder 22; Ryan to Jim Main, 12 September 1966, J.M. Main Archive, Special Collections, Flinders University Library, PGp 2/183/10; Ryan to Douglas Pike, 1 December 1966, Pike Papers, NLA, MS 6869, Box 8, Folder 4.
50 Ryan, 'Manning Clark', p. 192.
51 Ryan, *Final Proof*, p. 38.
52 Dymphna Clark, interviewed by Heather Rusden, 13 February 1997 (starting at 71.53 minutes), NLA, ORAL TRC 3548, available at: nla.gov.au/nla.obj-217338911/listen.
53 Ryan, 'Manning Clark', p. 205.
54 Ryan to Sayers, 16 October 1973, MUP Records, 2003.0129, Unit 21 (vol. 3). Sales figures for various volumes of the *History* are provided by Matthews, *Manning Clark*, pp. 229–30, 267, 363; McKenna, *An Eye for Eternity*, pp. 438, 592, 615, 772 n.80.

that eventually hardback and paperback sets of the entire six volumes of the *History* were 'selling strongly at recommended retail prices of \$210 and \$155.70, respectively'.[55]

A key phrase in Ryan's critique went unnoticed at the time, namely the assertion that 'Manning's sales revenues were large and they were welcome, but the Press would not have sunk without them'.[56] Indeed, the overdraft, which stood at £161,000 (or \$322,000) at the end of 1962, was extinguished in 1971.[57] An important factor in MUP's return to financial health was the sale of the printery and the building it occupied, which 'yielded a handsome sum in ready cash'.[58] Although MUP was out of financial danger and had other high-selling titles,[59] Ryan, by his own account, sold his soul and continued to publish the *History*—whose limitations, he said, were 'conspicuous and disappointing'.[60] In other words, after Volume 3 the *History* was by no means the economic be-all-and-end-all that justified Ryan persisting against his 'better judgement'.

He was then reduced to flattery to deceive, as people attest. David Carment, a former postgraduate student of Clark's, recalls an occasion in the late 1970s at the Clarks' home when Ryan was loud in his praise for the forthcoming volume of the *History*; and Clark's son Axel told Roslyn Russell that Ryan always flattered his father outrageously.[61] It is not that the family resented criticism *per se*; responding to historian James Griffin's review of Cathcart's abridgement of the *History*, Axel reassured Griffin that his 'severe judgments' constituted 'serious criticism' and that no offence had been taken.[62]

---

55 Nick Walker (MUP Manager – Sales & Marketing) to Ryan and others, 8 March 1988, and Walker to 'Dear Bookseller', 1 December 1987, both in MUP Records, 2003.0129, Unit 21 (vol. 6).
56 Peter Ryan, 'A Reply to my Critics', in his *Lines of Fire*, pp. 214–22, specifically p. 218.
57 Ryan to Macmahon Ball, 19 July 1963, Ryan Papers, NLA, MS 9897, Series 1, Box 1, Folder 1; John Poynter and Carol Rasmussen, *A Place Apart: The University of Melbourne: Decades of Challenge*, Melbourne: MUP, 1996, pp. 438, 513 n.16.
58 Ryan, *Final Proof*, p. 61.
59 Ryan, *Final Proof*, pp. 73, 86–88, 95, 102–3, 109, 119–21, 163.
60 Ryan, 'Manning Clark', p. 206.
61 Carment, 'Exemplary scholar' (letter), *Australian*, 31 August 1993, p. 10; Carment to Dymphna Clark, 27 August 1993, Dymphna Clark Papers, NLA, MS 9873, Series 10, Box 35, Folder 1; Roslyn Russell, email to author, 31 August 2017.
62 James Griffin, 'Selected histrionics', *Weekend Australian Review*, 26–27 September 1993, p. 9; Axel Clark to Griffin, 6 September [should be October] 1993, Dymphna Clark Papers, NLA, MS 9873, Series 10, Box 35, Folder 2.

4. ERRORS, GREAT AND SMALL

For all his cajoling and flattery, Ryan had never been enamoured of the *History* as history. At an early stage he told an associate at Cambridge University Press (the *History*'s copublisher) that Clark was an oddball character writing oddball history:

> We think [the *History*] will cause a good deal of controversy and interest. It is highly opinionated, and I am sure it will drive a lot of historians mad. I must say it is not my own cup of tea, as a once-professional historian. *Nevertheless, as a publisher I am sure that we have a most valuable work* [my emphasis]. And if I may close on a very private note, thank God volume 2 is almost out of the way. He is a charming fellow … but for temperamental difficulties, give me Kitson Clark any day![63]

When corresponding with Clark, however, Ryan was repeatedly complimentary (apart from complaints about the technical faults in the manuscripts that Clark submitted). In a letter of encouragement in 1968, he beseeched Clark not to

> underestimate the importance of the work, nor the impact it has made upon historians and plain readers alike, nor the very high level of excited anticipation with which the public awaits the next volume. When our sales representatives call upon bookshops or meet history teachers, the question they are most likely to be asked is: 'When will there be another volume of Manning Clark?' It continues to sell steadily. Not one day passes without orders for 4s and 6s and 12s. This may sound sensational, but to continue like that (both volumes) is much better than a brief burst of interest, and then eclipse. It is my very firm belief that your History of Australia will go on attracting readers in large numbers long after you or I are here to know anything about it.[64]

He later told Clark that 'it is splendid news that we are to have a fourth volume',[65] and the year after that he was importuning:

> The booksellers and many individuals ask me … 'when can we expect volume 4?' Of course I say that Rome wasn't built in a day, that even God laboured seven days over the Creation, etc. etc.,

---

63 Ryan to P.J. Tickell, 9 March 1967, MUP Records, 2003.0129, Unit 20 (vol. 2). George Kitson Clark (1900–1975) of Cambridge University was a 'character' and was accustomed to getting his own way. He came to Melbourne in 1964 to deliver the George Ascott Lectures at Ormond College, which were published as *An Expanding Society: Britain 1830–1900,* Melbourne: MUP, 1967.
64 Ryan to Clark, 22 August 1968, MUP Records, 2003.0129, Unit 21 (vol. 3).
65 Ryan to Clark, 7 May 1973, MUP Records, 2003.0129, Unit 21 (vol. 3).

which they take in good part but with impatience. It is good to have such an eager audience in keen anticipation, and I wondered whether you might like to give me a tentative date. Like the old song, it's never too late but it's never too soon![66]

Upon receipt of the manuscript of Volume 4, Ryan switched back to praising the quality of Clark's work:

> Vintage Clark! Your innumerable fans will go wild. The thematic treatment is wholly successful, and the episodes you have selected for close scrutiny are very discriminatingly chosen. The individual persons used to typify trends and arguments and social attitudes (Stawell, Clarke etc.) are a really rich and representative gallery.[67]

And his exuberant reaction to the first instalment of Volume 6 was to tell Clark that he had

> read the first seven chapters in two long sittings—yesterday and this morning—and write hot from pleasure. (*You* know which pleasure!) Verdict: Vintage Clark; a fine keystone to complete the arch.[68]

Yet in his first attack in *Quadrant,* Ryan refers to Clark's 'high-flown style, the vague, pretentious sentences, the ill-carpentered paragraphs, [and] the cavalcades of clichés',[69] as well as Clark's characters being a 'dismal gallery of distorted portraits'.[70] In 1997 he described Clark's books as being 'sloppy, slanted and boring'.[71] Ryan's posthumous attacks on Clark's *History* are in stark contrast to his public effusions and private flattery, yet he told Mark McKenna in 2007 that 'Manning was a hypocrite'.[72]

* * *

Ryan's determination to hang on to the *History* stemmed from a quirk of personality as much as it did an early preoccupation with dollars. He was a turf warrior with a strong desire to have and to hold. The *History* was 'his', in a sense, and he was not prepared to let it go despite his qualms *and*

---

66   Ryan to Clark, 12 February 1976, MUP Records, 2003.0129, Unit 21 (vol. 4).
67   Ryan to Clark, 15 June 1976, MUP Records, 2003.0129, Unit 21 (vol. 4).
68   Ryan to Clark, 13 January 1987, Manning Clark Papers, NLA, MS 7550, Series 18, Box 158, Folder 28.
69   Ryan, 'Manning Clark', p. 199.
70   Ryan, 'Manning Clark', p. 210.
71   Peter Ryan, 'Sunk from the start', *Courier-Mail,* 14 June 1997, p. 8.
72   Quoted in McKenna, *An Eye for Eternity,* p. 690.

the opportunities to be rid of it. His handwritten codicil to the contract provided that successive volumes be submitted at two-yearly intervals, which was a palpably untenable timetable. Clark was invariably late and Ryan would have been within his legal rights to abandon the project rather than giving extensions of time; he was tempted to do so at least as early as 1968 simply to see the back of an author whom he feared lacked

> the staying power to carry it through—& he's getting odder and odder … [sic]. One always suspects, of course, that he'll then switch instantly to (say) Cassells for an advance of $10,000. Do we care?[73]

Various other publishers—Cassells, Angus & Robertson, Penguin, Macmillan, Ure Smith and, in particular, Sun Books—were all clamouring for the paperback rights, but Ryan kept them at bay by one means or another.[74]

In the event Ryan's instinct proved correct: the *History* was 'a tidy little earner' that sold in ever-increasing numbers, with the appearance of each new volume stimulating the sales of its predecessors. There was also the bonanza, in 1988, when the Australia New Zealand Foundation funded the purchase of 450 boxed sets of all six volumes for distribution to every secondary school in New Zealand.[75] That boosted total sales to 170,000 copies and 22,000 for Volume 6 in the eight months following its release.[76] In a sense, the high profile and the profitability of the *History* worked to Ryan's disadvantage, in that it became increasingly difficult to terminate Clark's profitable association with MUP as time moved on, even had he wanted to. To add to Ryan's quandary, the *History* was routinely winning book awards—some of which Ryan nominated himself.

Yet, had Ryan played his cards carefully—and he was a shrewd negotiator—he could have off-loaded the *History* to another eager publisher at least as early as 1968, and in all likelihood, there would have been a bidding war. It was a risk that he was obliged to take given his feelings about the *History*'s quality and his view that MUP's 'duty was to scholarship, and

---

73 Ryan, handwritten note to MUP deputy director [1968], MUP Records, 2003.0129, Unit 21 (vol. 3).
74 McKenna, *An Eye for Eternity*, pp. 588, 596, 770 n.46; Matthews, *Manning Clark*, pp. 311–12.
75 New Zealand High Commissioner (Canberra) to Clark, 24 February 1988, Manning Clark Papers, NLA, MS 7550, Series 18, Box 159, Folder 35; 'Manning Clark's History—wall to wall!' *University [of Melbourne] News*, May 1988 (clipping in Manning Clark Papers, NLA, MS 7550, Series 18, Box 159, Folder 36); 'Gift of Australian history', *Dominion* (Wellington), 2 July 1988, p. 2.
76 Patricia Rolfe, 'Maggie Thatcher, Sales Catcher', *Bulletin,* 3 May 1988, p. 25.

the high standing of its parent university'.[77] Ryan also had the option of insisting that the project be wrapped up with Volume 4, as per the contract, or of bowing to Clark's suggestion to terminate the project at 1851, or even with the publication of Volume 2. As mentioned, he could also have enforced the two-year period between volumes, as per the contract. Another alternative was to vary the terms of the contract by inserting a clause that future volumes be refereed in accordance with MUP policy and indeed with scholarly practice.[78]

But it was not within Ryan to either enforce or vary the contract; although he was capable of lording it over authors of junior status, he seemed unwilling or unable to bring big-name authors such as Manning Clark and architect Robin Boyd (1919–1971) to heel.[79] Perhaps he wanted to avoid the rancour he had experienced in his early years at MUP with Sir John Barry (1903–1969), the criminologist and judge, over the latter's biography of the penal administrator John Price.[80] In the event, Ryan hung on to the *History* to the bitter end and in doing so subjected himself to much aggravation.

Another aspect of Ryan's turf warrior mentality was his resentment when potential books went to other publishers. When offered the manuscript of *Studies in the Australian Capital Market* (1964), the dismayed editors learned that it would take 12 months to publish. They took it to Cheshire, who got it out in three months. Ryan's reaction to this rebuff, when he next saw one of the editors, was to tell him that 'you're no gentleman!'[81] On a later occasion, invoking MUP's on-campus monopoly of book sales, he unsuccessfully tried to prevent the launch on university premises of a book he had declined to publish.[82] He also lobbied vigorously for MUP to become the principal beneficiary of the Grimwade bequests. Failing to appreciate the complexities of the wills, he was volubly aggrieved when this did not come to pass.[83]

---

77 Ryan, *Final Proof*, p. 29.
78 Ryan, *Final Proof*, pp. 36, 66–67, 93, 159.
79 For Boyd, see Ryan, *Final Proof*, p. 181.
80 Mark Finnane with the assistance of John Myrtle, *J.V. Barry: A Life*, Sydney: UNSW Press, 2007, pp. 249–50.
81 Robert Wallace, discussion with author (Adelaide, 31 July 2015) and follow-up email (4 May 2016); R.R. Hirst and R.H. Wallace (eds), *Studies in the Australian Capital Market*, Melbourne: Cheshire, 1964.
82 Patricia Grimshaw and Lynne Strahan (eds), *The Half-Open Door: Sixteen Modern Australian Women Look at Professional Life and Achievement*, Sydney: Hale & Iremonger, 1982.
83 John Poynter and Benjamin Thomas, *Miegunyah: The Bequests of Russell and Mab Grimshaw*, Melbourne: Miegunyah Press, 2015, pp. 85–91, 131–33, 252; John Poynter, 'Peter Ryan the Publisher', *Quadrant*, vol. 60, no. 3, March 2016, p. 59; Ryan, *Final Proof*, pp. 171–77.

Ryan demonstrated his possessiveness even more resolutely in 1988, bringing in the lawyers against the producers of *Manning Clark's History of Australia: The Musical* and threatening that the show would not open if Penguin Books attempted to sell copies of its reprint of Clark's *Short History of Australia* in the foyer in competition with the six volumes of the *History*. Dymphna recalls that 'he was very, very nasty about it and totally unrelenting'.[84] In schoolboy parlance, he was playing for keeps, despite thinking that MUP should in no way be associated with what he regarded as a farcical show, and all on behalf of a book for which he only had contempt.[85] After his departure from MUP, Ryan took his proprietorial attitude to new heights. Upon hearing that his chosen successor had not been appointed, he returned his retirement gifts. The futility of the gesture is only matched by an astonishing lack of self-awareness that he was being downright churlish, not to mention that he had no right to be so presumptuous in the first place.[86]

* * *

Clark's defenders took the wrong tack in that the thrust of their criticisms of Ryan went into defending Clark's character and in asserting, rather than demonstrating, the merits of his work. In doing so they were debating issues on Ryan's terms, which got them nowhere. Historian Alan Powell, for one, felt that Clark's supporters did little more than 'pussyfoot around the vital core of Ryan's charges'.[87] Much of the reaction was based on indignation at Ryan's ad hominem approach, his betrayal of a friendship and the breach of publishing ethics—deploring his tactics and condemning his bad taste. In the view of Pulitzer Prize winner and La Trobe University historian Rhys Isaac (1937–2010), Ryan was 'as much an ignorant fool as a treacherous bastard!'[88] There were certainly some angry retorts, but

---

84 Dymphna Clark, interviewed by Heather Rusden, 13 February 1997 (starting at 74.20 minutes), NLA, ORAL TRC 3548, available at: nla.gov.au/nla.obj-217338911/listen; John Timlin, 'A Little Footnote to *A History of Australia*', *Australian Book Review*, no. 98, March 1988, pp. 46–48; John Rickard, '"A fine song and dance": Manning Clark's History—The Musical', *Victorian Historical Journal*, vol. 59, nos 3–4, 1988, pp. 3–20; Ryan, *Final Proof*, pp. 135–36.
85 Ryan, 'Manning Clark', pp. 203–4.
86 Ryan, *Final Proof*, pp. 203–5. Even Ryan's gentle biographer says that 'the decision on his replacement was actually none of his business. Nor should it have been'. John Tidey, *Ryan's Luck: A Life of Peter Ryan MM*, Melbourne, Arcadia, 2020, p. 95.
87 Alan Powell, 'Manning Clark's Imagination of Australia', review of *Manning Clark*, ed. Carl Bridge, *Northern Perspective*, vol. 18, no. 2, 1995, pp. 226–28, specifically p. 227. Powell (1936–2020) was Emeritus Professor of History at Charles Darwin University.
88 Rhys [Isaac] to Stuart Macintyre, 1 September 1993, Macintyre Papers, NLA, MS 9389, Series 1, Box 5, Folder 32.

generally less immoderate in tone than Ryan makes out; he didn't touch off a powder keg. All the same, the critics' responses were anything but a convincing endorsement of Clark's *History*. They were caught in a bind of their own making. They tried to mount defences of a work that was not held in high esteem as historical scholarship but, in doing so, they fellback on assertions that Clark had a vision and was no fraud. Such an approach played into Ryan's hands and let him off the hook, at least in those respects. A better strategy would have been to concentrate on the sheer unoriginality of Ryan's assessment of the *History*, which would have exposed his intellectual deficiencies. McKenna has pointed out that 'the substance of Ryan's criticisms of Clark's work was hardly startling', but no one, apart from Gerard Henderson, said this at the time.[89]

Apart from deploying the wrong tactics, the critics were poorly placed to mount an effective counterattack, despite *Quadrant* and the *Australian* giving them generous enough column inches to do so. Crucially, the critics had no way of knowing that Ryan had misrepresented MUP's contractual arrangements with Clark and everyone missed Ryan's statement that Clark had wanted to terminate the project at an early juncture.[90] Posing these issues would have left Ryan vulnerable to counterattack; and it was unfortunate that MUP did not check its own records at the time and enlighten the public accordingly. All the same, the critics might have been more effective had they hammered away at Ryan's obvious point of weakness—that he was the *History*'s publisher and therefore culpable and complicit. As the writer and social critic Donald Horne (1921–2005) put it:

> I think it is absolutely disgusting that Peter Ryan was at MUP for that whole period and did not express those views to Manning Clark directly at the time. Here is a man who was publishing Manning Clark for 30 [should be 25] years and apparently did not have any honest conversations with him.[91]

---

89 McKenna, *An Eye for Eternity*, p. 687; Gerard Henderson, 'Bless him, it is 30 years since he sinned', *Age,* 27 August 1993, p. 13; Henderson, 'The belated Mr Ryan owes us a penance', *Sydney Morning Herald,* 27 August 1993, p. 11.
90 Ryan, 'Manning Clark', p. 194.
91 Quoted in Lisa Clauden, 'Publisher ridicules Manning Clark work', *Advertiser* (Adelaide), 27 August 1993, p. 5. Ryan returned the favour when reviewing Horne's omnibus autobiography. See Peter Ryan, 'Donald Horne: A Self-Made Man', review of *An Interrupted Life* by Donald Horne, *Quadrant*, vol. 42, no. 9, September 1999, pp. 28–33, the final sentence of which reads, 'This one is "For Your Dustbin", but fit a non-corrosive bottom first'.

The only time on record when Ryan expressed negative feelings about the content of the *History* to Clark himself was in 1968, and in decided undertones:

> I don't by any means always agree with your writings or your approaches myself, but this doesn't stop me from seeing that much of the criticism you receive comes from people whose books nobody much wants to read, but who resent the fact that people *do* want to read yours.[92]

Ryan's critics might also have paid greater attention to the fact that Ryan continued to publish successive volumes of the *History*, which he claimed were becoming a liability to MUP's scholarly reputation. The Melbourne writer, Christopher Bantick, did state that Ryan's rationalisations for persisting with the *History* were 'totally inadequate and unconvincing'.[93] But no one followed-up on this central issue, apart from Geoffrey Bolton, who raised questions about 'MUP's role in all this':

> Ryan had apparently convinced himself that Clark was a fraud. Yet his firm still invested its resources in Clark's writings, gave its extremely respectable name to his publications and took the public's money for them. Authors have a particular bond of trust with their publishers. Their endorsement is a guarantee of quality. If an author's work needs improvement, it is the publisher's job to give that advice. If the work is no good, it should be rejected. This should be done during the author's lifetime. Ryan has added a new terror to death.[94]

What should have happened, then and later, was to insistently demand that Ryan explain why he published successive volumes of the *History*, which he described as 'gooey subjective pap',[95] rather than allowing him to dodge the issue by remaining silent. The critics might also have made capital out of the fact that Ryan actually wanted the *History* to fail and be laughed out of court.[96] It is not just the spitefulness of such an attitude but the incongruity of it all—expending enormous effort on a project

---

92 Quoted in Matthews, *Manning Clark*, pp. 266–67.
93 Christopher Bantick, 'Clark's place in historical discourse', *Australian*, 8 September 1993, p. 22; also 'Questions of history', *Independent Monthly*, September 1993, p. 45.
94 Geoffrey Bolton, 'Don't smash the icon', *Bulletin*, 12 October 1993, pp. 42–43.
95 Ryan, 'A Reply to my Critics', p. 221. Rebuttals that cover most of the bases include Bolton, 'Don't smash the icon', *Bulletin*, 6 October 1993, p. 43; and 'Manning Clark's history lives', *Sydney Morning Herald* (editorial), 28 August 1993, p. 28, but these were too thinly spread to make a widespread impression.
96 Ryan, 'Manning Clark', pp. 208, 211–12.

that one part of him wanted to clap out. There was also a feeling among Ryan's critics that to dignify him with further responses would lead to a never-ending slanging match, which would only serve to give Ryan further traction and from which no good would emerge.[97] As it was, the divisive History Wars atmosphere of the time meant that positions were entrenched. Lines had been drawn in the sand, and no amount of reasoning was likely to change people's minds either way.

---

97   Stuart Macintyre to Dymphna Clark, 8 October [1993], Dymphna Clark Papers, NLA, MS 9873, Series 1, Box 10, Folder 55; Macintyre, 'Why do the Tories hate Manning Clark?' *Evatt Papers,* vol. 1, no. 2, 1993, pp. 17–20, specifically p. 17.

5

Justified or Not?

> The raking over of a life … is the proper role of the biographer, and who would fairly dispute this responsibility? Less clear is the way information which may only become available after death is used.
>
> Christopher Bantick (1994)[1]

In October 1994, some 13 months after his first onslaught, Ryan wrote a further reply to his critics. Titled 'The Charge of the Lightweight Brigade', the denigration continues unabated. Part of the equation is that Ryan is such a good writer—too good for his own good unless harnessed by a sense of restraint—with a powerful prose style, an expansive vocabulary, a fine turn of phrase and the gift of evocative imagery, all enhanced by wide reading. But he lacked a sense of self-control and was prone to distortion.[2] At one point he pours scorn on Geoffrey Bolton's statement, which he quotes out of context, 'that there may be cause to remove [Clark's] icon to a lower shelf. It would be conceding too much to the Australian habit of self-hatred if we smashed it altogether'.[3] To which Ryan responded, 'Bolton wins first prize for facing both ways at once'.[4]

---

1 Christopher Bantick, 'Death by character assassination', *Canberra Times,* 9 October 1994, p. 19.
2 The positive and negative aspects of Ryan as a writer are on full display in 'New Guinea and I', review of *Throwim Way Leg,* by Tim Flannery, *Quadrant,* vol. 42, no. 5, May 1998, pp. 71–72.
3 Geoffrey Bolton, 'Don't smash the icon', *Bulletin,* 12 October 1993, pp. 42–43, specifically p. 43.
4 Peter Ryan, 'The Charge of the Lightweight Brigade', in his *Lines of Fire: Manning Clark & Other Writings,* ed. A.K. Macdougall, Binalong, NSW: Clarion Editions, 1997, pp. 222–34, specifically pp. 225–26.

Ryan had a merry time in traducing his critics with whatever weapon came to hand, but he deludes himself by claiming that his criticism of Clark 'nowhere transgresses propriety'[5] and was 'politely phrased'.[6] One would have to be tone deaf not to realise that unusually vitriolic, vindictive and belittling elements were at play. Take, for example, Ryan's trash-talk:

> The six volumes [of the *History*] are almost unbelievably prolix— the opinion of one who has read the entire work not merely once throughout, but three times, and some parts oftener. It is a vast cauldron of very thin verbal soup, in which swim morsels of nourishing meat, widely spaced. I have been told that a single-volume abridgment is in preparation. The scholar preparing it can hardly find his commission a serious challenge. He need— metaphorically—merely stick a pin in the mass and allow the gaseous verbal excess to hiss its way out.[7]

It is hard to imagine anything more impolite. Nothing could be less calculated to generate the reasoned debate that Robert Manne wanted to encourage; and Manne himself was criticised for allowing the 'animus', which had 'no relevance to Ryan's central thesis of Clark being a bad and wayward historian', to be waved through.[8]

Writer Helen Garner lamented:

> Perhaps if Mr Ryan were prepared, even a little, to address the source of this rage in himself, he might be able to present his criticisms in a form which would invite a decent response.[9]

But Garner misses the point entirely. Ryan had no interest in a reasoned and evidentiary-based discussion of Clark. Rather than attempting to lower the temperature, he sought to raise it. He wanted to start a shouting match as distinct from engaging in a conversation about the pros and cons

---

5   Peter Ryan, 'A Reply to my Critics', in his *Lines of Fire,* pp. 214–22, specifically p. 220.
6   Ryan, 'The Charge of the Lightweight Brigade', p. 230.
7   Peter Ryan, 'Manning Clark', in his *Lines of Fire,* 179–214, for quotation see p. 213; Ryan, 'The Charge of the Lightweight Brigade', p. 223. To the contrary, Cathcart's commission proved unexpectedly difficult, taking a full two years. It was not a matter of omitting five out of every six paragraphs but of significant deliberation and rearrangement. Cathcart, 'Preface' to *Manning Clark's History of Australia,* Melbourne: Melbourne University Press (hereafter MUP), 1994, pp. ix–xi; Cathcart, telephone interview with author, 20 October 2017; Mark McKenna, *An Eye for Eternity: The Life of Manning Clark,* Melbourne: Miegunyah Press, 2011, p. 459.
8   Christopher Bantick, 'Clark's place in historical discourse', *Australian,* 8 September 1993, p. 22.
9   Helen Garner, 'Dumping One's Shadow' (letter), *Quadrant,* vol. 38, no. 11, November 1994, p. 6.

of the *History* and its author. Ryan's intention was to insult and to provoke a diarrhoea of outrage; and he knew that his status as Clark's 'friend' and former editor gave his attack a seeming authenticity that no one else could muster. In the heightened divisiveness of the History Wars, it was more important to bring Clark down, by whatever means, than to engage in disinterested debate.

At this point we return to the role of Manne. He had little regard for Clark as a scholar, describing him as 'cavalier with facts, unreliable in his mastery of documentary sources, [and] uninterested in the work of other historians', all of which are correct.[10] As mentioned, Manne states that a particular value of Ryan's essay was to show the interconnectedness and the linkages between Clark and his writings. Manne also insisted Ryan had demonstrated that Clark's 'long decline as an historian' was due to 'what Clark might have called his fatal flaw—extraordinary vanity', together with an 'extraordinary unwillingness to listen to criticism, his self-absorption, above all his determination to fabricate for himself a grand prophetic persona'.[11]

Manne wanted a serious discussion of Clark's work, but he took Ryan's authority, as Clark's publisher and long-time associate, too much on trust. If vanity is all that Ryan can come up with to explain the relationship between Clark's life and work, then his article should have been rejected on those grounds alone. At no time, for example, does Ryan so much as mention the central point that the *History* had assumed an increasingly autobiographical dimension, which had been commented on by others since at least 1987.[12] Of course, a great deal of historical writing contains an element of concealed autobiography. The very choice of subject can be rooted in the historian's own past and conclusions may unduly derive from personal experience, but Clark took the self-referential side of history to extremes. The autobiographical element was 'so noticeable in Manning Clark', his friend Edmund Campion, a Catholic priest and historian, remarked, 'that when I first read Volume Six I thought of suggesting to

---

10   Robert Manne, 'The Puzzles of Manning Clark' (editorial), *Quadrant*, vol. 38, no. 11, November 1994, pp. 2–3, specifically p. 2; see also Manne, 'Clark's fading vision of colonial struggle', *Age*, 19 October 1994, p. 17.
11   Robert Manne, 'A holy cow called history', *Age*, 1 September 1993, p. 16.
12   See Mark McKenna, '"National Awakening", Autobiography, and the Invention of Manning Clark', *Life Writing*, vol. 13, no. 2, 2016, pp. 207–20, specifically p. 211, doi.org/10.1080/14484528.2016.1162263.

Melbourne University Press that they rejacket it as his autobiography'.¹³ Historian Frank Clarke complained that attention was being diverted from an analysis of the *History* and centred 'on the personality of the author', but this was hard to avoid when Manning Clark's writings were so self-referential.¹⁴ Ryan's obvious vilification might also have given Manne pause for thought, if only to go no further than requiring Ryan to tone down his reproofs and thus make his message more effective.

This raises a further question: where, on the spectrum of authorial autonomy, does a journal editor draw the line? Put another way, are editors supposed to publish only what they agree with? Authors rightly require large areas of discretion but there are limits, and Manne did reject a submission in which Clark was accused of being anti-Semitic.¹⁵ Besides, there had already been three *Quadrant* articles in which Clark had featured since his death only two-and-a-half years before—the critiques by La Trobe University historians John Barrett and John Hirst, and in Geoffrey Blainey's Latham Lecture on black-armband history.¹⁶ In the latter, Clark is the subject of a single paragraph but it carried a double significance—namely that Clark and Blainey, who were both atypical of the academic profession, had always been publicly supportive of the other and held each other in warm regard, despite their increasingly divergent political views.¹⁷

It could be argued either way if these three articles were sufficient for the time being or whether more needed saying about Clark's view of Australian history and his merits as an historian. All the same, it is a bit much that Ryan, having set the tone, should conclude his second *Quadrant* article

---

13   Edmund Campion, 'Manning Clark', *Scripsi*, vol. 5, no. 2, 1989, pp. 183–87, specifically pp. 185–86.
14   F.G. Clarke, review of Volume 5 (1890–1915), *American Historical Review*, vol. 87, no. 5, 1982, pp. 1450–51, specifically p. 1450, doi.org/10.2307/1857052. Clarke is emeritus professor of Australian history at Macquarie University.
15   Peter F. Alexander, *Les Murray: A Life in Progress*, Melbourne: Oxford University Press, 2000, p. 283.
16   John Barrett, 'Manning Clark: The Historian', *Quadrant*, vol. 35, nos 7–8, July–August 1991, pp. 8–9, republished as 'Two Clarks', in Carl Bridge (ed.), *Manning Clark: Essays on his Place in History*, Melbourne: MUP, 1994, pp. 113–16; John Hirst, 'Australian History and European Civilisation', *Quadrant*, vol. 37, no. 5, May 1993, pp. 28–38, first section republished as 'The Whole Game Escaped Him', in Bridge, *Manning Clark*, pp. 117–21; Geoffrey Blainey, 'Drawing up a Balance Sheet of Our History', *Quadrant*, vol. 37, nos 7–8, July–August 1993, pp. 10–15. Hirst (1942–2016) was an historian and social commentator of right-wing leanings and widely admired even by those who did not share his viewpoint.
17   Geoffrey Blainey, *Before I Forget: An Early Memoir*, Melbourne: Hamish Hamilton, 2019, pp. 154–57; Blainey, 'Manning Clark: a gifted man of quiet dignity', *Age*, 24 May 1991, p. 11; Carl Bridge, 'Introduction', to Bridge, *Manning Clark*, pp. 1–9, specifically p. 7.

by stating that 'we should forget name-calling and have a fresh and critical examination of the truth and value of the *History* of Manning Clark',[18] while all the time exempting himself from his own injunction. Michael Cathcart's hope that 'the debate [would] continue with better grace than that with which it begun' was a prayer unanswered.[19]

There is a sequel that illustrates the depth of Ryan's dislike of Clark. Sometime after the publication of the abridged edition of the *History*, a mutual friend arranged a lunch at the Melbourne Club so that Cathcart and Ryan could meet, and perhaps even find common ground. Instead, Ryan launched into 'toxic gossip' that was delivered with 'venom' and obvious relish. He shared 'detailed dirt on people' including Clark, who he said, among other things, was a homosexual. Cathcart's lasting impression was that Ryan was 'a very bitter and unpleasant man'.[20]

* * *

The question is, how far did Ryan go in satisfying Robert Manne's statement that he had revealed the relationship between Clark the man and Clark the historian? In his first *Quadrant* article, Ryan stated that Clark's *History* was 'utterly a projection and a part of the author's personality',[21] which is true enough. But having made the statement, Ryan then neglects to develop his case. He does not demonstrate how particular facets of Clark's character resulted in specific faults in the *History*. How, for example, did Clark's inability to hold his liquor impinge on the *History*. And one does wonder whether Ryan was an innocent bystander in Clark's drunken escapades in the late 1940s[22] given the heavy drinking culture at the Directorate of Research and Civil Administration (DORCA) and the fact that several of Ryan's fellow students at the University of Melbourne affirm 'that the escapades he attributes to the drunken Manning were more than matched by [his own]'.[23] Edmund Campion saw a link between Clark's problems with alcohol and the *History*, remarking that Clark had 'a special place for those who battled the booze, almost as if he were writing an alcoholic history of Australia', but the connection

---

18 Ryan, 'A Reply to my Critics', p. 222.
19 Michael Cathcart, 'The sage under siege', *Age,* 27 August 1993, p. 13.
20 Michael Cathcart, email to author, 19 October 2017.
21 Ryan, 'Manning Clark', p. 184.
22 Ryan, 'Manning Clark', pp. 186–87.
23 Stuart Macintyre, email to author 3 April 2018. Ryan refers to his own earlier 'drinking days' in 'The Foreign Legion' (1997), in his *Lines of Fire,* pp. 115–18, specifically p. 117.

eluded Ryan.[24] Only once in Ryan's somewhat meandering text does he come close to identifying any linkages between Clark the man and Clark the historian—namely, that Clark's disdain for 'Yarraside' (middle-class rectitude) accounts for his 'repeated sneers at the bourgeoisie', or what one historian described as his 'pathological hostility towards "Yarraside" and the straighteners of the "Protestant Ascendancy"'.[25] Or, as Cathcart observed, '[Clark] saw himself as a firebrand radical—yet he was, in so many ways, an eccentric aristocrat'.[26]

Ryan is quite right to point out the incongruity of Clark's disparagement of the bourgeoisie.[27] Of course, such attitudes were routinely expressed among Clark's generation. 'Oh, you're so bourgeois!', or 'How bourgeois!' were commonly heard put-downs of the time—which make Clark's strictures all-the-more-silly considering he lived contentedly enough in Canberra suburbia while at the same time railing against what he saw as middle-class philistinism. But there is nothing to show that Ryan saw an *explicit* linkage between Clark's embrace of 'bourgeois culture' and his needless 'sneers' at the bourgeoisie. He is saying that Clark had no right to disparage the bourgeoisie given his own upbringing and lifestyle, which is fair comment. It never occurs to Ryan that Clark's counter-reaction to his own class origins might have resulted in how he depicted the bourgeoisie in the *History*—whereas Clark's near contemporary, writer and self-professed 'radical nationalist' Stephen Murray-Smith (1922–1988), was more perceptive in postulating that Clark's attitude to 'Yarraside' was a function of his 'parsonage upbringing' and his 'metaphysical yearnings'.[28]

* * *

The remarkable feature of Ryan's critique of the *History* is that it is all so familiar, precisely because it is so derivative.[29] Every one of Ryan's strictures, which he overwhelmingly presents as new information, had already been expressed in academic (and often in newspaper) reviews of the *History* and in more general discussions of Clark's work. It started with the widespread recognition that the clash of cultures—Protestantism, Catholicism and the Enlightenment—that informed the earlier volumes

---

24 Edmund Campion, 'Manning chose Ned', *Bulletin*, 5 October 1993, p. 107.
25 Carolyn Holbrook, 'Marxism for Beginner Nations: Radical Nationalist Historians and the Great War', *Labour History*, vol. 103, 2012, pp. 123–44, specifically p. 133, doi.org/10.5263/labourhistory.103.0123.
26 Michael Cathcart, email to author, 20 October 2017.
27 Ryan, 'Manning Clark', p. 202.
28 John McLaren, *Free Radicals of the Left in Postwar Melbourne*, Melbourne: Australian Scholarly Publishing, 2003, p. 203.
29 Ryan, 'Manning Clark', pp. 202, 206–13.

of the *History* was an increasingly unsuitable explanatory framework for the later volumes. In saying that Clark had 'lost his compass', Ryan was parroting what Hirst had said a few months earlier in a thoughtful critique of Clark's work—published in *Quadrant*, no less—when pointing out that that Clark's original vision of the fate of European civilisation in Australian 'had become attenuated and debased'.[30]

Contra Ryan, Clark had critics within the academy who were not backward in drawing attention to other perceived faults. There was his 'carelessness in matters of detail' and his 'sloppy' historical practice, as well as his narrow range of sources, limited range of themes, a neglect of vast impersonal forces and a corresponding preoccupation with individuals. The criticisms also included the 'tendentious or trivialised' depictions of those individuals; not to mention that Clark omnisciently divined what was going on in his historical characters' minds, whether or not the evidence justified such speculations.[31] Ryan's other criticisms of the *History* were equally in the public domain. Clark's 'mostly trivial, irrelevant and embarrassingly juvenile' sniping at the bourgeoisie;[32] his eccentric and melodramatic narrative; the overblown stylistic gestures; the resort to clichés and stock phrases as a substitute for thinking through issues;[33] the extent of his factual inaccuracies;[34] his 'lofty view of the rest of mankind, *de haut en bas*';[35] that he was writing history from the top down rather than 'history from below'; and his unduly gloomy view of the past had all been pointed out before.[36]

---

30 Hirst, 'Australian History and European Civilisation', p. 29. The quotes in the following paragraph are Ryan's.
31 Stuart Macintyre has assessed the reception of the first five volumes of the *History*, to which readers can refer for specific details. Macintyre, 'Manning Clark's Critics', *Meanjin Quarterly*, vol. 41, no. 4, 1982, pp. 442–52.
32 Ryan, 'Manning Clark', p. 202. See especially the criticisms by Brian Dickey, 'History with a personal touch', review of Volume 4 (1851–88), *Advertiser* (Adelaide), 8 April 1978, p. 21.
33 For example, Malcolm Thomis, 'Author's ideal is too elusive', review of Volume 5 (1888–1915), *Courier-Mail*, 9 January 1982, p. 24, who refers to 'the slang and the slapstick that take over when the author is in his hearty moods and applying the common touch, with homespun language and homespun philosophy'.
34 For example, K.J. Cable, review of Volume 2 (1822–38), *Australian Economic History Review*, vol. 8, no. 2, 1968, pp. 164–66, specifically p. 166, doi.org/10.1111/aehr.82br1.
35 Ryan, 'Manning Clark', p. 208.
36 See especially John Rickard, review of Volume 5 (1890–1915), *New Zealand Journal of History*, vol. 17, no. 1, 1983, pp. 90–92, available at: www.nzjh.auckland.ac.nz/document.php?wid=1132&action=null. Regarding Clark's use of the language of the times he was writing about, his former postgraduate student Michael Roe was the first to point out Clark's habit of interweaving his own words with those from the contemporary sources, leaving the reader wondering where the one begins and the other leaves off. Roe, review of Volume 1, *Quadrant*, vol. 7, no. 1, Summer 1962–63, pp. 73–76, specifically p. 75.

To give two apposite examples, the matter of the *History* being 'pervaded by a sense of failure' was troubling to Clark's former departmental colleague W.F. (Bill) Mandle. In a statement that reflected a widespread view, and which anticipated one of Ryan's major criticisms, Mandle regretted

> that a man should know so much about his own country and see so little good in its past is saddening, as saddening as to realise that this great lover of humanity finds so little in the human condition to warm the heart. The forebodings raised in volume three about the direction this great man in his great book was taking us, have in this one been confirmed. We are heading, bad or broken people, into a horrid desert.[37]

The second example involves a demolition of Volume 5 by La Trobe University sociologist Claudio Véliz whose major complaint was that Clark 'trivialis[ed] important themes', one of which was that 'Professor Clark would have his readers believe that during the quarter of a century that preceded the First World War Australia was constantly on the verge of mass violence'.[38] Other reviewers barely noticed what so exercised Véliz, but Ryan certainly did and again there is a lack of originality; he echoes the thrust of Véliz's argument, saying that 'one of [Clark's] apocalyptic signature tunes [was] dark hints of civil war and blood staining the wattle'[39] as opposed to his own (and Véliz's) view that Australia had experienced an uncommonly peaceful and prosperous history.[40] It is quite possible Ryan's decision to attack Clark in print can be traced back to a series of negative reviews and commentaries on Volume 5 by non-historians, which reinforced his misgivings about the *History* as a whole. In addition to Véliz's critique were those of another La Trobe sociologist, John Carroll, who deplored 'the mumbo-jumbo of Professor Manning Clark'; described the *History* as being 'mean and rancorous, giving a demoralising picture of the building of Australian society' and

---

37 W.F. Mandle, 'Through a Glass Compassionately', review of Volume 4 (1851–88), *Australian Book Review*, no. 1, June 1978, pp. 1 and 4, specifically p. 4. An earlier and more extended statement along these lines is by Bruce Mansfield, 'A History the Lotus has Eaten: Manning Clark's Australia', *Teaching History*, vol. 13, no. 1, 1979, pp. 3–12.
38 Claudio Veliz, 'Bad History', review of Volume 5 (1890–1915), *Quadrant*, vol. 26, no. 5, May 1982, pp. 21–26, for quotation see p. 22; see also Philip Ayres, 'The Worlds of Claudio Véliz, Part II', *Quadrant*, vol. 59, nos 1–2, January–February 2015, p. 58–64, specifically pp. 59–60.
39 Ryan, 'Manning Clark', p. 198.
40 Peter Ryan, *Final Proof: Memoirs of a Publisher*, Sydney: Quadrant Books, 2010, pp. 150–51.

'a travesty of the truth about Australia'.[41] There were also the contributions by journalists Edward Kynaston (1924–2002), who attacked Volume 5 on matters of style and substance, and Tim Hewat (1928–2004), who faulted Clark's 'monumental labour of loathing'.[42] Ryan would resurrect these same sentiments some 10 years later.

Neither was Ryan novel in contrasting the two Manning Clarks, pre- and post-1955. This notion had been emphatically stated in *Quadrant* articles by Barrett and Hirst. Whereas the first Clark was inspirational, as per his two-volume *Documents in Australian History*, according to Barrett:[43]

> The second Clark [was] a tragedy of a man because he was becoming a travesty of a historian. He might have become a historical novelist and retained his greatness. As a historian, he lost respect.[44]

Historian Beverley Kingston went one step further in stating that Clark's essentially biographical approach did not work beyond the early nineteenth century. She explained that 'while it was possible that personalities altered the dynamics of a claustrophobic society in the early nineteenth century', the technique did 'not adapt well to the larger scale of twentieth century Australia'.[45]

Had Ryan wanted to make a contribution he might have gone beyond Hirst and anticipated the analysis of historian Neville Meaney, who remarked that Clark originally intended to transcend the nationalist stereotype of the nation's past and yet Volumes 5 and 6 had reverted to just that.[46] Neither did Ryan pause to consider the extent to which

---

41 John Carroll, 'National Identity', in John Carroll (ed.), *Intruders in the Bush: The Australian Quest for Identity,* Melbourne: Oxford University Press, 1982, pp. 209–25, specifically p. 220; Carroll, 'Manning Clark's Vision Splendid', *Quadrant,* vol. 26, no. 10, October 1982, pp. 61–64, specificially p. 64.
42 Edward Kynaston, 'Turning history's pages—cliche by cliche', *Weekend Australian Magazine,* 24–25 October 1981, p. 10; Tim Hewat, 'Manning Clark's monumental labour of loathing', *Weekend Australian Magazine,* 13–14 February 1982, p. 10. On Hewat, see Michael Bromley, 'From Noted "Phenomenon" to "Missing Person": A Case of the Historical Construction of the Unter-Journalist', *Journalism,* vol. 11, no. 3, 2010, pp. 259–75, doi.org/10.1177/1464884909360919.
43 Barrett, 'Manning Clark', pp. 8–9; Hirst, 'Australian History and European Civilisation', pp. 28–38.
44 Barrett, 'Two Clarks', in Bridge, *Manning Clark,* p. 114.
45 Beverley Kingston, review of Volume 6 (1916–35), *Australian Historical Studies,* vol. 23, no. 91, 1988, pp. 204–5, specifically p. 205, doi.org/10.1080/10314618808595805.
46 Neville Meaney, 'Britishness and Australian Identity: The Problem of Nationalism in Australian History and Historiography', *Australian Historical Studies,* vol. 32, no. 116, 2001, pp. 76–90, specifically p. 77 n.2, doi.org/10.1080/10314610108596148.

The Dismissal of the Whitlam Government might have affected Clark's depiction of his country's past in later volumes of the *History*. Even less does Ryan consider the inseparability of Clark's 'spiritual searching' and the history he wrote.[47] Ryan implies the over-personalised nature of the *History* but does not discuss it.

Two vignettes sum up Ryan's lack of originality. For all his stress on Clark's 'unreliability with mere facts',[48] Ryan actually identifies very few such errors in his first *Quadrant* article.[49] He notes that Phar Lap won the Melbourne Cup only once, not twice as Clark had it, but this was pointed out to him by an MUP storeman.[50] The second instance of Ryan pinching someone else's observation concerns H.V. Evatt. Ryan rightly derides Clark's hyperbole that Evatt had 'the image of Christ in his heart'.[51] The fact remains that Ryan did not pluck this gem from the *History* but from a newspaper article by Gerard Henderson, a clipping of which is in the Ryan Papers with the operative paragraph marked up.[52]

* * *

Clearly, Ryan's intervention did not result in the informed discussion of Manning Clark and his *History* that Robert Manne expected; and it never could, given its unoriginal content and ad hominem nature. A model of how Ryan might have proceeded was provided eight years later in a curiously neglected article by historian and journalist Robert Murray. Writing in *Quadrant* and spurred by the imminent fortieth anniversary of the *History*, Murray comments:

---

47   McKenna, *An Eye for Eternity*, p. 376.
48   Ryan, 'Manning Clark', p. 190, for quotation see p. 195; Ryan, 'The Charge of the Lightweight Brigade', p. 227.
49   See Leo Scheps, 'Historical Misinformation' (letter), *Quadrant*, vol. 38, no. 12, December 1994, p. 8. In 'The Charge of the Lightweight Brigade', pp. 227–28, Ryan reveals eight factual errors of Clark's concerning Australia's first prime minister, Edmund Barton (1849–1920). He acknowledged that the information came from Rev. John Parsons, who was researching Barton, but the errors still had to be pointed out to him. The correspondence between Ryan and Parsons, which the latter initiated on 1 October 1993, is in the Ryan Papers, National Library of Australia (hereafter NLA) MS 9897, Series 6, Box 10, Folder 5.
50   Ryan, 'Manning Clark', pp. 206–7.
51   Ryan, 'Manning Clark', p. 210.
52   Gerard Henderson, 'Evatt: canonisation or cannonade?' (by-line column), *Sydney Morning Herald*, 29 December 1992, p. 9 (clipping in the Ryan Papers, NLA, MS 9897, Series 6, Box 9, Folder 1).

since the name Manning Clark still excites so much publicity, so much derision and admiration, it seems permissible to throw in a few more opinions. The first confession is that I actually enjoyed reading most of the books, partly because at their best they were good and partly because at their most, well, Manning Clark, they were so infuriating.[53]

Murray goes on to say, inter alia, that the six volumes should have been compressed into four; that they are 'over-indulgent of … reader patience with hobbyhorses, generalised insults against both people in authority … and the fickle, philistine masses'; that 'Clark's alleged Marxism and softness on communism is one of the least important things about his work'; that the 'frequent preoccupation with social class … is mostly decorative, bereft of serious analysis and seldom more than raspberries for the ruling class, bourgeoisie and squatters'; and neither can Murray 'accept that there is anywhere a great "vision", grand theme, striking "insights", nor much virtue in his "history from the heart" approach'.[54] The merits and demerits of successive volumes are discussed sequentially, in a considered manner. Murray bucks the received wisdom in some quarters, that each volume was inferior to its predecessor, arguing that Volume 3 'is a huge improvement' on Volume 2, which he considered 'a tedious disaster'. He argues that Volume 4:

> is some of the best Australian history—indeed history of any kind—I have read. The best of it approaches greatness, in that it takes a reader back, much more than a film or novel can, into the nineteenth century.[55]

Murray claims that Volume 6 'is actually a good, vivid account of Australia in this period—provided you can forgive the increasing crankiness and it being about 100 pages too long'. As will be seen, I disagree with Murray's assessment of the last three volumes and especially of Volume 6, but he does provide a platform for reasoned discussion whereas Ryan's tone and tactics were calculated to preclude fruitful debate.

---

53 Robert Murray, 'Forty Years of Manning Clark', *Quadrant*, vol. 45, no. 11, November 2001, pp. 46–53, specifically p. 46.
54 Murray, 'Forty Years of Manning Clark', p. 46.
55 Murray, 'Forty Years of Manning Clark', p. 50.

6

A Complicit Academy?

Clark's self-imposed task is awe-inspiring: to write a history of Australia is to expose oneself to slings and arrows which hurt the more if their target has offered the throwers some free ammunition. Like every historian who commits himself on paper, Clark is a standing target, especially for those who judge history only on a factual basis. Less beyond criticism are those who offer over-adulatory praise, a sort of backlash against the way volume one was greeted when it burst upon an unsuspecting public ... A history written on this scale deserves to be judged at many levels. Anything less would be unjust and patronizing.

Lloyd Robson (1968)[1]

Among those who admire him, Manning Clark has become so esteemed a prophet (by which I mean he is seen as speaking for his generation) that even if you seek to praise him you have to watch what you say; otherwise you might offend his cult followers.

Donald Horne (1981)[2]

M[anning] C[lark] was not always my cup of tea, nor anyone's I guess, but his *imagination* of Australia was a gift to us all [emphasis in original].

Donna Merwick (1993)[3]

---

1   L.L. Robson, 'Once More with Feeling: Manning Clark's History of Australia', review of Volume 2 (1822–38), *Meanjin Quarterly*, vol. 27, no. 4, 1968, pp. 497–502, specifically p. 498. Robson (1931–1990), whose PhD thesis had been co-supervised by Clark, ended his career as reader in history at the University of Melbourne.
2   Donald Horne, 'Australia fails its test', review of Volume 5 (1890–1915), *Sydney Morning Herald*, 10 October 1981, p. 45.
3   Donna Merwick to Stuart Macintyre, 16 September 1993, Macintyre Papers, National Library of Australia (hereafter NLA), MS 9389, Series 1, Box 5, Folder 32. Merwick at the time was a senior lecturer in history at the University of Melbourne.

A central plank in Ryan's argument rests on the supposed failure of an allegedly closed-shop historical profession to expose Clark as the charlatan and fraud that Ryan thought he was. It is therefore worth going into in some detail as to whether or not the Australian historical profession was soft on Clark when assessing the *History* and to dissect the bases for Ryan's allegations.

Ryan notes that *Quadrant* received 'five sheepish refusals' from historians who had been asked to review Volume 5.[4] The culpable silence of historians, according to Ryan, amounted to the '*trahison des professeurs* [betrayal of teachers] which, by degrees, allowed the *History* a free run, exempt from criticism by many of the most rigorous scholarly minds'[5]— what he also described as 'cowardice, professional complacency and critical complicity'.[6]

* * *

A trio of episodes can be used to illustrate that the historical profession was neither uncritical nor, as time went on, sufficiently critical of the *History*. Taken together, these sets of responses show that the reaction to successive volumes of the *History* was convoluted and, moreover, overlaid by personal loyalties and antagonisms that often had little to do with the *History* itself. The first two episodes also demonstrate the extent to which Manning Clark and his *History* were gaining a public profile.

The first episode—actually a series of instalments in 1962–63— concerned the fall-out from a review of exceptional harshness and vitriol titled 'History without Facts' by the journalist and historian Malcolm Ellis (1890–1969) in the Sydney *Bulletin*: 'Was ever such nonsense written?' was one of the kindlier of Ellis's remarks.[7] As the biographer of several important figures spanning the period covered in Volume 1 of the *History*, Ellis was a more than qualified reviewer. But he did so from

---

[4] Peter Ryan, 'Manning Clark', in his *Lines of Fire: Manning Clark & Other Writings*, ed. A.K. Macdougall, Binalong, NSW: Clarion Editions, 1997, pp. 179–214, specifically pp. 192–93, 198. Ryan obtained this information from A.G.L. Shaw. See Ryan, notes of telephone conversation with Shaw, 4 October 1993, Ryan Papers, NLA, MS 9897, Series 6, Box 10, Folder 4.
[5] Ryan, 'Manning Clark', p. 192.
[6] Ryan, 'Manning Clark', for quotation see p. 199; Ryan, 'A Reply to my Critics', his *Lines of Fire*, pp. 214–22, specifically pp. 220–21.
[7] Malcolm Ellis, 'History without Facts', *Bulletin*, 22 September 1962, pp. 36–37, reprinted in Carl Bridge (ed.), *Manning Clark: Essays on his Place in History*, Melbourne: Melbourne University Press (hereafter MUP), 1994, pp. 70–77.

an animus towards Clark over matters concerning their respective roles in relation to the nascent *Australian Dictionary of Biography*, which Ellis almost shipwrecked. Ellis's comments were also sharpened by his highly conservative political outlook.[8] Although Ellis took issue with some of Clark's interpretations and criticised his limited used of primary sources, the review was essentially a catalogue of factual errors.

Clark received considerable sympathy within the historical profession at being the target of Ellis's scalding and so obviously malicious review, as Ryan himself recognised.[9] In the hope of promoting more reasoned debate, the Australian Association for Cultural Freedom (in August the following year) organised a seminar to give Clark the opportunity to respond to his critics, one of whom was J.W. Forsyth, a lawyer by profession and an ardent amateur historian of the European exploration of coastal Australia. What ought to have cleared the air turned into farce when Forsyth pointed out inaccuracies in translations of Dutch sources on which Clark had relied. Whereupon Clark accused him of insulting Dymphna, who had translated those passages. Clark proceeded to hijack the meeting and then found himself cast in the role of villain for his emotional and unprofessional response to constructive criticism. In a matter of minutes, he had diminished his standing in the profession. One of those in the embarrassed audience was Allan Martin, who told me in the late 1990s that Clark had behaved badly by rounding on Forsyth in the way he did.[10] As it happened, Forsyth's strictures and a laudatory review article by a Clark admirer were published as a review forum, which epitomised the range of reactions that Volume 1 provoked.[11]

---

8   Andrew Moore, '"History without Facts": M.H. Ellis, Manning Clark and the origins of the *Australian Dictionary of Biography*', *Journal of the Royal Australian Historical Society*, vol. 85, no. 2, 1999, pp. 71–84; Kenneth R. Dutton, *Auchmuty: The Life of James Johnston Auchmuty (1909–1981)*, Mount Nebo, Qld: Boombana Publications, 2000, p.319.
9   Ryan, 'Manning Clark', p. 194; and e.g. L.R. Gardiner and A.W. Martin, 'History without Facts' (letter), *Bulletin*, 15 December 1962, p. 35; O.H.K. Spate, review of Volume 1, *Australian Journal of Politics and History*, vol. 9, no. 2, 1963, pp. 267–69, specifically p. 267, doi.org/10.1111/j.1467-8497.1963.tb01066.x; Robson, 'Once More with Feeling: Manning Clark's History of Australia', p. 498.
10 A.W. Martin (1926–2002) at the time was a history lecturer at the University of Melbourne. A political biographer, he went on to occupy the foundation chair of history at La Trobe University and ended his career at The Australian National University.
11 J.W. Forsyth, 'Clio Etwas Gebuckt: Professor Clark's "The Forerunners"', *Journal of the Royal Australian Historical Society*, vol. 49, no. 6, 1964, pp. 423–52; Jill Conway, 'A Vision of Australian History', *Journal of the Royal Australian Historical Society*, vol. 49, no. 6, 1964, pp. 453–59; see also J.W. Forsyth, 'History without Facts' (letter), *Bulletin*, 3 November 1962, pp. 31–32.

To queer the pitch was Clark's extreme sensitivity to criticism. He took the view that 'whoso attacks my [work] is undermining my deepest self'[12]—and this from someone who could be pointedly critical of the work of others. He was preposterously hurt by negative comment and his malice in the face of criticism was well known within the profession and to Ryan alike.[13] He gave early warning that he would treat critics harshly when he abruptly terminated his friendship with John McManners (professor of history at the University of Sydney) for his review of Volume 1. McManners was a cleric as well as an academic and he had taken exception to Clark's depiction of Protestantism.[14] McManners's departmental colleague A.G.L. Shaw was also consigned to outer oblivion for the same indiscretion, which was doubly sad. As well as being best man at Clark's wedding and godfather of his eldest son, Shaw was a thoroughly decent person: 'a paragon of the scholar-gentleman—cultured, disinterested, unmoved by political or intellectual fashion' and a patron of the arts.[15] Such was Clark's vindictiveness in the face of criticism that Noel McLachlan (who reappears in Chapter 7) of the University of Melbourne wrote his review of Volume 5 in the form of an ingratiating letter, taking care to preface mildly expressed criticisms with such words as 'I wonder …', and even using the phrase 'I hope, Manning, you won't mind my having been completely candid in this way'.[16]

Clearly, Clark was not held in universal esteem by the Australian historical profession, although the *History* did receive gratifying reviews from some North Americans who found his approach refreshing.[17] English reviewers

---

12   Quoted in Mark McKenna, *An Eye for Eternity: The Life of Manning Clark*, Melbourne: Miegunyah Press, 2011, p. 444.
13   Peter Ryan, interviewed by John Farquarson, 10–11 October 2000 (p. 37 of typescript), NLA, ORAL TRC 4631.
14   John McManners, 'Creeds in the Cradle', *Nation*, 20 October 1962, pp. 19–21. McManners (1916–2006) became regius professor of ecclesiastical history at the University of Oxford in 1972.
15   A.G.L. Shaw, 'Clark's History of Australia', *Meanjin Quarterly*, vol. 22, no. 1, 1963, pp. 117–19; Graeme Davison, 'Alan George Lewers Shaw, 1916–2012', *Annual Report 2012*, Canberra: Australian Academy for the Humanities, 2012, pp. 36–38, for quotation see p. 37, available at: www.humanities.org.au/about-us/annual-reports/.
16   Noel McLachlan, 'Manning Clark's Australian History', *Arena*, vol. 60, 1982, pp. 172–75. Such obsequience contrasts with McLachlan's typically acrid book reviews. For example, McLachlan, review of *Imperial Control of Colonial Legislation, 1813–1865*, by D.B. Swinfen, *New Zealand Journal of History*, vol. 7, no. 1, 1973, pp. 85–88, available at: www.nzjh.auckland.ac.nz/docs/1973/NZJH_07_1_09.pdf.
17   Robin W. Winks, review of Volume 1, *American Historical Review*, vol. 69, no. 4, 1964, pp. 1067–68, doi.org/10.2307/1842969; Robert Kubicek, review of Volumes 1–4, *Pacific Affairs*, vol. 53, no. 2, 1980, pp. 378–80, doi.org/10.2307/2757518; see also McKenna, *An Eye for Eternity*, p. 759 n.26.

were far less enamoured.[18] Sometimes it was sheer bewilderment as to what he was on about. Writing to Geoffrey Blainey about Volume 2, Melbourne historian Kathleen Fitzpatrick felt as if she

> were being swept along in a whirlwind, going dizzily around one of the lower circles of the Inferno. I don't know what to make of it, only what it makes of me. I wonder if you can keep your head better and form an opinion?[19]

To further complicate the picture is a lengthy and unqualified defence by historian Bede Nairn (1917–2006), proclaiming Volume 1 a work of great scholarly and literary merit. His article is a detailed rebuttal of the critical reviews, especially Ellis's 'History without Facts', and he does say that 'if [the critics] are right, I am absurdly wrong'.[20] What is interesting is the background to Nairn's publication in a special issue on 'Historical Approaches' in the Sydney-based Catholic journal *Manna*. It happened that its editor was Nairn's fellow Catholic and departmental colleague at the University of New South Wales, Patrick O'Farrell (1933–2003). Four years earlier, Clark, in his capacity as an examiner, had prevented O'Farrell's PhD thesis from being failed. O'Farrell went on to write highly favourable reviews of the first two volumes of the *History*, and Clark wrote equally favourable referee's reports on behalf of O'Farrell, one of which proclaimed:

> O'Farrell is something more than the academic historian. He is a man who has something essential to say. About the great issues of his day. This has helped to endow everything he has written with a liveliness and indeed a suggestion of grandeur.[21]

---

18   For example, D.K. Fieldhouse, review of Volume 1, *History*, vol. 49, no. 165 (1964), pp. 133–34 ('Its eccentricity, coupled with its readiness to attach emotional significance to routine matters … is likely to prevent it from becoming a standard work.'); 'Currency lads and lasses', review of Volume 2, *Times Literary Supplement*, 2 January 1969, p. 11 ('This is, indeed, a strange history by a strange historian').
19   Quoted in Geoffrey Blainey, *Before I Forget: An Early Memoir*, Melbourne: Hamish Hamilton, 2019, p. 156. Fitzpatrick (1908–1990) spent her working life in the history department at the University of Melbourne. Although she and Clark were initially adversaries (with Clark referring to her as 'Auntie Katie'), they later became close friends and confidants. Susan Davies (ed.), *Dear Kathleen, Dear Manning: The Correspondence of Manning Clark and Kathleen Fitzpatrick, 1949–1990*, Melbourne: MUP, 1996.
20   Bede Nairn, 'Writing Australian History', *Manna*, vol. 6, 1963, pp. 107–30, for quotation see p. 109.
21   Len Richardson, 'Patrick O'Farrell and the Making of *Harry Holland: Militant Socialist*', *Labour History*, no. 115, 2018, pp. 27–46, specifically 40–41, doi.org/10.5263/labourhistory.115.0027; O'Farrell to Clark, 15 September 1963, Manning Clark Papers, NLA, MS 7750, Series 18, Box 156, Folder 2; Patrick O'Farrell, review of Volume 1, *Irish Historical Studies*, vol. 15, no. 57, 1966, pp. 93–95, doi.org/10.1017/S0021121400035045; O'Farrell, review of Volume 2 (1822–38), *Irish Historical Studies*, vol. 17, no. 66, 1970, pp. 289–90, doi.org/10.1017/S0021121400111551; Clark to Frank Crowley (University of New South Wales), 24 April 1970, Manning Clark Papers, NLA, MS 7550, Series 7, Box 42, Folder 390.

O'Farrell had a clear motive in publishing a defence of Clark's work, and he provides an example of the networks of loyalty and obligation that to a certain extent shielded Clark.

There were also hidden expressions of sympathy. Max Harris, the editor of the *Australian Book Review* (and the victim of the Ern Malley hoax), was so incensed that he considered arranging a debate '*but only among historical scholars of some repute* [emphasis in original]'.[22] He was unable to bring the idea to fruition. And in 1965, historian Samuel McCulloch (1916–2013), an Australian who made a career in the United States and with whom Clark was on friendly terms, commissioned Douglas Pike to write an article for the *Journal of British Studies* once Volume 2 had appeared. This too fell by the wayside but, again, the motive was to give favourable publicity to Clark's *History*.[23] Clark had both supporters and detractors so there is no merit in asserting, as does Ryan, that the historical profession was uniform in its allegedly favourable assessment of the *History*.

* * *

The complex dynamic of the historical profession's attitude to Clark is further illustrated by a second series of episodes, in 1978, shortly before the publication of the fourth volume of the *History*. By this time, the *History* was becoming a national saga and Clark was becoming something of a household name. His just published *In Search of Henry Lawson* provoked a hostile review in the *Sydney Morning Herald* by his old adversary Colin Roderick, whose PhD thesis Clark had recommended be failed some 20 years earlier.[24] Roderick followed up by demanding Clark resign from the Australia Council, resulting in a flurry in the *Australian* that underscored the divide between the defenders and detractors of Manning Clark.

---

22 Harris to Clark [undated but probably September 1962], Manning Clark Papers, NLA, MS 7550, Series 18, Box 156, Folder 2.
23 McCullough to Pike, 30 April 1965, Pike Papers, NLA, MS 6869, Box 8, Folder 4. Pike (1908–1974) was appointed foundation general editor of the ANU-based *Dictionary of Australian Biography* in 1962.
24 Colin Roderick, 'Is this Lawson?', *Sydney Morning Herald*, 12 May 1978, pp. 7–8; Manning Clark, *In Search of Henry Lawson*, Melbourne: Macmillan, 1978; McKenna, *An Eye for Eternity*, p. 747 n.1. Roderick (1911–2000) was a foremost (and highly proprietorial) scholar of Henry Lawson and foundation professor of English at James Cook University.

The first salvo came from an unlikely quarter—Bob Ryan, an MA student at Macquarie University, who anticipated many of Peter Ryan's later strictures in deploring Clark's factual errors ('Surely we expect more rigorous writing of history from one so eminent') and in asserting that Clark was a holy cow and beyond criticism by the profession. He hopefully opined that Roderick's 'outright condemnation' had spelt Clark's death-knell 'as Australia's leading historian'.[25] Such temerity towards an elder and better generated a number of letters to the editor, the gist of which was that 'the business of criticism must be more than the finding of small errors'. One such letter came from a group of Monash University historians (including A.G.L. Shaw) who put the young whippersnapper in his place by saying that his pettifogging only served to obscure the fact that Clark was

> concerned to express, on a grand scale, a vision of Australian history, and indeed to see it as part of the human predicament in a more general sense … Whether one agrees with it or not, it is an enterprise of courage and scale, and Mr Ryan would be better served in examining it in those terms.[26]

That same issue of the *Australian* also carried a pairing of commissioned articles, pro- and anti-Clark. In the latter, Max Harris reversed his earlier pronouncement—'how vast, original and readable the great Manning Clark History is going to be'—and was now saying that 'the man writes ghastly prose'.[27] In Clark's defence his former student, Ian Turner (1922–1987) of Monash University, pointed out that 'the eager accumulation of minor error may bring joy to the critic's ego but it does not touch the centre of the historian's work', and, further, that disagreement with the *History*'s approach 'is not to challenge the integrity of Clark's intent'.[28] The battle lines remained firmly drawn between accuracy and factuality as against imaginative insight and a broader vision, and in ways that would be played out in future debates.[29]

---

25 Bob Ryan (presumably no relation of Peter), 'Is this the beginning of the end for Manning Clark?', *Australian*, 18 May 1978, p. 9; Stephen Holt, *A Short History of Manning Clark*, Sydney: Allen & Unwin, 1999, p. 190.
26 A.G.L. Shaw, J.D. Legge, J.D. Rickard and Ian Turner, 'In praise of Manning Clark' (letter), *Australian*, 25 May 1978, p. 6.
27 Max Harris, 'The issue—he writes ghastly prose', *Australian*, 25 May 1978, p. 7.
28 Ian Turner, 'Humbling talent is the national sickness…', *Australian*, 25 May 1978, p. 7; see also Geoffrey Fairbairn, 'Prophet not scapegoat', *Weekend Australian*, 27–28 May 1978, p. 10.
29 The special pleading for the factual errors in the *History* never quite ceased. For example, George Parsons, review of Volume 5 (1890–1915) and *Manning Clark and Australian History*, by Stephen Holt, *Journal of Australian Studies*, vol. 7, no. 13, 1983, pp. 95–96, doi.org/10.1080/14443058309386877; Humphrey McQueen, review of Volume 6 (1916–35), *Continuum: Journal of Media & Cultural Studies*, vol. 1, no. 2, 1988, pp. 134–40, specifically pp. 137–38, doi.org/10.1080/10304318809359344.

A third episode involved John Molony (1927–2018), a former Catholic priest and recently retired history professor at ANU. He had been Clark's departmental colleague since the mid-1960s and he owed it to Clark for appointing him to an academic position, which he probably would not have secured otherwise. He was more than aware of Clark's foibles. They ultimately came to have little regard for each other, with Clark referring to Molony's 'past treacheries'.[30] One of those incidents was probably Molony being a member of the committee that decided to exclude anyone over the age of 55 from writing chapters for a bicentennial project, *Australians: A Historical Library* (1987). Outraged by the decision and succumbing to his sense of entitlement, Clark regarded the rebuff as 'my great wound'— another example of Clark's 'degree of paranoia' and 'hair trigger sensitivity' resulting in him falling out with friends and colleagues.[31] Molony, for his part, felt that Clark ought not to be diverted from completing the final volume of the *History* by bicentennial matters. Over the years, Molony had become increasingly disappointed with Clark, culminating in the latter's refusal in the late 1980s to lend support to the eventually successful attempts within ANU to fight off amalgamation with the Canberra College of Advanced Education.[32]

Immediately after the publication of Ryan's first *Quadrant* article, Molony confided to his diary, 'I agree with some of Peter's criticisms but he sounds like an embittered old man which is sad'. A few days later he noted that 'all this argument about Manning means so little to me. The bubble had to burst some day', and he passively resisted attempts to embroil himself in Clark's defence. He eventually wrote Dymphna a letter of commiseration, which may not have been sent, in which he praised her dignity under fire and deplored the 'dreadful attack on Manning's character', seeing it as

---

30   McKenna, *An Eye for Eternity*, pp. 9, 505, 533, 759 n.32, for quotation see p. 717 n.10.
31   Oliver MacDonagh, 'The Making of *Australians: A Historical Library*—A Personal Retrospect', in *Australians: A Guide and an Index*, Sydney: Fairfax, Syme & Weldon, 1988, pp. 1–9, specifically p. 3; McKenna, *An Eye for Eternity*, p. 716 n.10 ('my great wound'); A.W. Martin to Clark, 4 November 1982, Martin Papers, NLA, MS 9802, Series 1, Box 3, Folder 29; Brian Matthews, *Manning Clark: A Life*, Sydney: Allen & Unwin, 2008, pp. 151, 157, 236.
32   Barry Ninham, email to author, 13 February 2020 (Ninham was Professor of Applied Mathematics at ANU and a close friend of Molony); Sally Peters, 'The ANU–CCAE Merger: Why the Intended Amalgamation Failed', BA (Hons) thesis, La Trobe University, 1997; S.G. Foster and Margaret M. Varghese, *The Making of The Australian National University, 1946–1996*, Sydney: Allen & Unwin, 1996, pp. 343–47; Roger Scott, 'A Personal Memoir of Policy Failure: The Failed Merger of ANU and the Canberra CAE', *Australian Universities Review*, vol. 47, no. 1, 2004, pp. 10–20, available at: www.aur.org.au/archive/2000s.

part of a wider conservative conspiracy. He praised Clark's values but was non-committal about the worth of the *History*, saying that 'it speaks for itself and stands for itself'.³³

Whatever the personal-cum-professional issues involved in their falling out, Molony's attitude towards Clark's work is a barometer of diminishing regard for Clark within the historical profession. Upon the publication of Volume 1, Clark received several congratulatory letters from fellow historians. Their praise of 'the accomplishment of your task' may have been heightened by Ellis's review but their tone is sincere, even when in disagreement. Allan Martin's verdict was:

> This is the most distinguished work we have on Australia yet. Not that I always *understand* the vision, but it excites me, even in those places where I baulk at acceptance. Beyond that, we of this generation are not likely to see anything else as elegant as this, or so close to being History in the sense La Nauze used that word in his Anzaas address a few years ago. When I told you that you sometimes make me want to give it all away, I sincerely meant it.³⁴

If a generalisation can be made, it is that Clark's reputation among his peers rose appreciably with the publication of Volume 1 but faltered with the fluctuating quality of the later volumes; it is alarming to compare the readability and general control of Volume 1 with the travesty that is Volume 6. The other part of the equation was that Clark increasingly irritated or alienated people. The ruptures involved a combination of the political, the personal and the professional. Clark's ANU colleague, economist Heinz Arndt (1915–2002), who had progressively moved to the conservative side of politics, had liked Clark 'very much' when they

---

33   Molony, Diary, 27 August 1993, Molony Papers, NLA, MS 6634, Series 6, Box 35, Folder 28; Diary, 3 & 6 September 1993, Molony Papers, NLA, MS 6634, Series 6, Box 35, Folder 29; Molony to Dymphna Clark, 28 September 1993, Molony Papers, NLA, MS 6634, Series 3, Box 27, Folder 83. The letter is handwritten. There isn't a copy in the Dymphna Clark Papers, which leads to the suspicion that it was never sent.

34   Martin to Clark, 27 September 1962, Manning Clark Papers, NLA, MS 7550, Series 18, Box 156, Folder 2. The other letters are: John La Nauze to Clark, 21 September 1962 ('profoundly impressed by it'); Max Crawford to Clark, 25 September 1962; Douglas Pike to Clark, 17 October 1962; Michael Roe [undated], all in Manning Clark Papers, NLA, MS 7550, Series 18, Box 156, Folder 2. La Nauze's ANZAAS presidential address was published as 'The Study of Australian History, 1929–1959', *Historical Studies, Australia and New Zealand*, vol. 9, no. 33, 1959, pp. 1–11, doi.org/10.1080/10314615908595147. La Nauze (1911–1990) ended his career as professor of history, Institute of Advanced Studies, ANU. Forbidding in manner, austere in historical outlook, and an adversary of Manning Clark, he is chiefly remembered as Alfred Deakin's biographer and for his follow-up work on the making of the Australian Constitution.

first met at Oxford in 1938 but came to dislike him 'in proportion as he grew as a guru'.[35] And Bede Nairn was 'not upset—only sad' when the controversy erupted.[36] The same person who had staunchly defended Clark 30 years before was now beyond caring. He did send Dymphna a letter of commiseration, but it was a criticism of Ryan rather than a defence of the *History*.[37] Hence, the answer to whether Clark was being shielded from valid criticism by a defensive history profession is both 'Yes' and 'No'.

* * *

Another historian who tired of Clark was the gentle and self-deprecating Allan Martin, who pointed out to Ryan:

> Yes, you are right, most of us have kept quiet: I lost count of the number of times I turned down requests to review the volumes as they came out. You will, no doubt correctly, think of that as a kind of cop-out. I suppose it was partly because I wanted to get on with my own work and thought controversy in the clever-clever Oxbridge sense somewhat trivial beside doing some sound research, and partly because Manning seemed so vulnerable about things that didn't matter to others and were simply best left alone.[38]

Martin's statement about Clark's vulnerability identifies what confronted many potential reviewers of the *History*. One part of the equation is that Clark cultivated his reviewers, somewhat in the manner that resulted in the English novelist Hugh Walpole being lampooned in W. Somerset Maugham's *Cakes and Ale* (1930).[39] In that vein, Stuart Macintyre relates that Clark 'wrote to express his appreciation of my review of volume 4 … He was not alone in doing this, but the effect was to establish a relationship that inhibited criticism'.[40] Clark also co-operated with Rob Pascoe to ensure, as best he could, that the latter would say only nice things about him in the MA thesis that became *The Manufacture of Australian History*

---

35 Ryan, note of telephone conversation with Arndt, 3 May 1993, Ryan Papers, NLA, MS 9897, Series 6, Box 10, Folder 3.
36 Molony, Diary, 27 August 1993, Molony Papers, NLA, MS 6634, Series 6, Box 35, Folder 28.
37 Nairn to Dymphna Clark, 2 September 1993, Dymphna Clark Papers, NLA, MS 9873, Series 10, Box 35, Folder 1.
38 Martin to Ryan, 7 October 1994, Ryan Papers, NLA, MS 9897, Series 6, Box 10, Folder 6.
39 Robin Maugham, *Somerset and All the Maughams,* Harmondsworth: Penguin edn, 1975, pp. 160–69.
40 Stuart Macintyre, comment on draft of this book, 26 June 2018.

(1979). The favour was returned in a referee's report where Clark opined that 'Pascoe seems to be a man who has already stretched his capacity to the limit' and disparaged the book as 'a rather disastrous plunge into the murk of theory'.[41]

The resort to flattery and manipulation extended only so far. Others were outside Clark's orbit. Ryan seems to have forgotten the excoriating review of Volume 5 by one such independent, Tony Griffiths of Flinders University, in the *Age Monthly Review*, whose opening paragraph reads:

> Manning Clark's fifth volume of his *History* is a strange and charming work. It is an existential analysis, in which all criticism is disarmed in advance by the author's disclaimer (which appears to be correct here at least) that 'the story of Australia will probably always elude its narrators'. If the story of Australia is absent, the personality and values of Manning Clark are not, and his determination to avoid the airy, if not the fairy, gives the work of nearly 500 pages an earthiness which is aptly in tune with his approach to his craft, essentially that of a story-teller rather than a social scientist. For Manning Clark has, at last, achieved his aim of writing fiction. While *Disquiet and other stories* failed as dull pieces of contrived writing, volume five of his History of Australia is a classical example of historical fiction.[42]

In other words, the *History*'s weaknesses were repeatedly identified by academic reviewers—to the extent that a reviewer of Volume 5 was expressing concern that it was 'becoming fashionable in certain Australian circles to denigrate [Clark's] considerable achievement'.[43]

* * *

---

41 Clark to Academic Registrar, ANU, 30 May 1980, Manning Clark Papers, NLA, MS 7550, Series 1, Box 8, Folder 65; Rob Pascoe, 'The Making of Manning Clark', *National Times,* 27 May– 2 June 1978, pp. 18–20, 22–23, available at: core.ac.uk/download/pdf/10836119.pdf; Pascoe, *The Manufacture of Australian History,* Melbourne: Oxford University Press, 1979, pp. 74–92.
42 Tony Griffiths, 'A bitter history', *Age Monthly Review,* December 1981, pp. 21–22 (clipping in the Ryan Papers, NLA, MS 9897, Series 6, Box 10, Folder 4). Griffiths is the author of *Contemporary Australia,* London: Croom Helm, 1977.
43 F.G. Clarke, review of Volume 5 (1890–1915), *American Historical Review,* vol. 87, no. 5, 1982, pp. 1450–51, specifically p. 1450, doi.org/10.2307/1857052.

A few days after the controversy broke University of Adelaide historian Wilfrid Prest entered the fray with a letter to the *Australian*:

> Your leader of 28-29/8 endorses Peter Ryan's claim that a mixture of 'cowardice, professional complacency and critical complicity' has hitherto prevented academic historians from properly assessing— ie denouncing—Manning Clark and his history of Australia. The truth of the matter is that the reception of the successive volumes by reviewers in the professional historical journals was far from wholly adulatory or uncritical. Thus, in the case of Volume V, which according to Ryan 'escape(d) entirely apart from an attack by Edward Kynaston in *The Weekend Australian*', Duncan Waterson's review in the premier Australian journal, *Historical Studies* (vol 20, 1983) speaks of 'irritating errors', 'history from the perspective of the pulpit', a 'less than satisfying' treatment of the colonial bourgeoisie and an overall approach 'relatively unconcerned with the values, passions and lives of the great majority of the people'. At the same time Waterson praises the epic qualities of Clark's work and his readiness to see the history of Australia as part of the 'broad river of human experience'.[44]

Ryan claimed that he slightly moderated his stance in response to Prest, but in fact he engaged in sleight of hand. He states:

> an eminent historian who has abstained from the controversy directed me to a round a dozen articles and reviews. All these I have now read, and in greater or lesser measure, or in one particular or another, all make indubitable criticisms of Clark's six-volume *History* and of his other work as it appeared. Twelve critical articles over twenty-five years can hardly be called an excess (though there could be others of which I remain unaware). Their total practical effect was inadequate to apply to Clark the check and scrutiny he needed. Nevertheless it is not the case that all historians neglected their duty, and it gives me pleasure to acknowledge this.[45]

What Ryan avoids disclosing is that the 'eminent historian' was Geoffrey Serle of Monash University and, more to the point, that Serle had privately rebuked him. This happened when Serle had dropped by to give Ryan the manuscript of his biography of the architect Robin Boyd to read. As Ryan explains in a note to himself:

---

44   Wilfrid Prest, 'Don't let's just stop with Clark' (letter), *Australian*, 3 September 1993, p. 20.
45   Peter Ryan, 'The Charge of the Lightweight Brigade', in his *Lines of Fire*, pp. 222–34, specifically p. 224.

> *He* did not raise [the matter of] M. Clark—*I* did. He said I had done my credit great harm by (i) putting 'all that personal rubbish' about M.C. and (ii) attacking in general the work and attitude of Australian historians 'of which I knew absolutely nothing'.[46]

This reprimand from a long-standing friend, whose books Ryan had published, did nothing to stop Ryan from continuing his attacks on both Clark and the historical profession; and one does have to wonder why he retained such incriminating material in his own papers. Having taken pains to avoid disclosing such matters during the controversy, he leaves behind evidence that exposes his strategic silences.

During his conversation with Ryan, Serle pointed out 'he had turned up "at least six major articles" *contra* Clark'. Ryan had no idea about the existence of these so Serle provided him with a list of the relevant articles and reviews that he 'could recall or dig out quickly'. Among these was Macintyre's assessment of the reviews of the first five volumes of the *History*, which likens the reviewing of successive volumes of the *History* to a perpetual, if sporadic, duck-shooting season.[47] Ryan then asked George Thomas, the assistant editor of *Quadrant*, to locate and fax him copies of some of the reviews mentioned by Serle as well as Macintyre's article—evidence of whose existence he was quite unaware. From this material he made four pages of notes, mostly identifying passages critical of Clark's work.[48]

At one point Macintyre observed that Clark's 'critics seldom went into print', and Ryan underlines this passage. He then ignores Macintyre's following sentences:

> Some [of the critics] bore scars and shrank from further controversy; some were reluctant to become involved in a witch-hunt; but most were prepared to accept the validity of the enterprise on its own terms for the notion no longer prevailed that a general history must

---

46 Ryan, note to himself, 13 January 1994, Ryan Papers, NLA, MS 9897, Series 6, Box 10, Folder 2. Serle (1922–1998) was one of the ex-servicemen who commenced university studies (or in his case resumed his studies) after WWII. He graduated at the University of Melbourne before Ryan resumed his own studies there and then took the customary path to academic preferment involving a second degree at Oxford. See John Thompson, *The Patrician and the Bloke: Geoffrey Serle and the Making of Australian History*, Canberra: Pandanus Books, 2006.
47 Serle to Ryan [undated], Ryan Papers, NLA, MS 9897, Series 6, Box 10, Folder 4; Macintyre, 'Manning Clark's Critics', pp. 442–52.
48 Ryan to George Thomas, 21 July 1994, Ryan Papers, NLA, MS 9897, Series 6, Box 10, Folder 4. Ryan's notes from the reviews (which are headed 'Serle's List'), as well as the faxed copies of Macintyre's article and many of the reviews mentioned in 'Serle's List' are also in the Ryan Papers, NLA, MS 9897, Series 6, Box 10, Folder 4.

be all-inclusive in its coverage, strictly empiricist in its method and free of moral judgement. The historians' reviews of volume five were by no means uncritical, but the great majority accepted the shortcomings as part of the price paid for Clark's historical vision.⁴⁹

That Ryan, when confronted by such counter evidence, only marginally softened his accusation of a negligent historical profession is dishonest and shows an unwillingness to own up to the extent of his original error. One also wonders why Ryan unerringly unscored passages in the reviews that are critical of Clark yet persists in his belief that Clark got a free ride from the profession. And to say that there were only about 'twelve critical articles over twenty-five years', when Macintyre's round-up of the reviews indicates many times more, is outright falsification on Ryan's part.

There are further incongruities. That Ryan needed to have the reviews drawn to his attention in the first place is a question in itself: how could he have been unaware of their existence considering they likely crossed his desk when he was director of MUP?⁵⁰ And why did he not check his accuracy, when proclaiming so confidently on the reviews, before publishing his first *Quadrant* article? It may well have been a case of forgetting what he did not want to remember and suppressing anything contrary to what he wanted people to believe. One also wonders what Ryan would have thought of the 'soft' reviews of the *History* by Serle and Blainey, both of whom he held in high regard, had these also been pointed out to him.⁵¹

Despite such expressions of praise, by the time of Volume 5 (covering the years 1888–1915) many historians were becoming increasingly impatient with the ongoing faults of style and substance, with one reviewer referring to its 'striking mixture of archaisms, grotesquery and narrational irony'.⁵² Macintyre did say that 'it is possible to enter into the spirit of Clark's enterprise and retain certain misgivings'.⁵³ The latter predominated.

---

49 Macintyre, 'Manning Clark's Critics', p. 448.
50 MUP assiduously collected reviews of its books and placed them in scrapbooks alphabetically arranged by author surname. Records of Melbourne University Press (hereafter MUP Records), 2003.0134, UM992.
51 Geoffrey Serle, 'One Man's Window on Our Past: Manning Clark's Third Volume', *Meanjin Quarterly,* vol. 33, no. 1, 1974, pp. 86–88; Serle, 'Some Stirrers and Shakers of the 1950s and 1960s', *Overland,* no. 128, 1992, pp. 16–21; Geoffrey Blainey, 'Towards History', review of Volume 5 (1890–1915), *Hemisphere,* September–October 1982, pp. 98–99; Blainey, 'Speaking volumes of history', review of Volume 6 (1916–35), *Herald Sun,* 24 August 1987, p. 11; Matthews, *Manning Clark,* p. 348.
52 Chris Wallace-Crabbe, 'Manning Clark['s] Troubled Landscape, with figures', *Scripsi,* Summer/Autumn 1982, pp. 86–89, specifically p. 86.
53 Stuart Macintyre, 'Clark's epic history sweeps to new peak', review of Volume 5 (1890–1915), *Age,* 10 October 1981, p. 25.

Even then, opinions on the relative merits of the various volumes of the *History* vary. Some regard Volumes 3 and 4 as the strongest, whereas Macintyre told Geoffrey Bolton that Volume 5 was 'the best yet'.[54] Some historians also change their minds, with Robert Murray reversing his verdict on Volume 6; in 2001 he thought it 'a good, vivid account … provided you can forgive the increasing crankiness and it being about 100 pages too long', whereas in 2020 he was saying that Volume 5 and 6 are 'the worst' of the six volumes comprising 'waffle, harangues and adolescent personality attacks on tall poppies'.[55]

I would agree with the thrust of Murray's later verdict. By Volume 5, the grand and metaphysical theme of the clash of the three great European influences had degenerated into late nineteenth- and twentieth-century personality politics, emphatically nationalistic in tone. An offended non-academic reviewer of Volume 5 observed:

> Strange mixture of sarcasm, spleen and cliché, activated by prejudice. Manning Clark castigates politicians, any vice-regal representative as elitists and betrayers of the Australian dream, and then substitutes another elitism—what Manning Clark thinks is best. Those who don't agree are quickly labelled 'bourgeois' or worse.[56]

One of the castigated politicians was Alfred Deakin, which led Bolton to observe that Clark's 'niggling and belittling assessment' showed a troubling 'failure of empathy'.[57] Certainly, none of Deakin's biographers have bothered with Clark's depiction. Judith Brett's *The Enigmatic Mr Deakin*, the most significant biography since La Nauze, does not mention Clark or even cite him in her bibliography, despite her focus, like Clark's, being on the interior life.[58]

---

54 Geoff [Bolton] to Clark, 9 October 1981, Manning Clark Papers, NLA, MS 7550, Series 18, Box 158, Folder 20.
55 Robert Murray, 'Forty Years of Manning Clark', *Quadrant*, vol. 45, no. 10, November 2001, 46–53; Murray, 'The Punch and Sparkle of Peter Ryan', review of *Ryan's Luck: A Life of Peter Ryan, MM*, by John Tidey, *Quadrant*, vol. 64, no. 12, December 2020, pp. 91–93, specifically p. 92.
56 Patrick Coady, 'Manning's imagination transcends history', *Catholic Weekly*, 17 January 1982 (clipping provided by Clive Moore).
57 Geoffrey Bolton, 'Through a Glass Darkly', review of Volume 5 (1890–1915), *Australian Book Review*, no. 37, 1981, pp. 3–4, specifically p. 3.
58 Judith Brett, *The Enigmatic Mr Deakin,* Melbourne: Text Publishing, 2017.

Volume 6 is even more nationalistic, deploring Australia's self-inflicted political and cultural subordination to Britain, and is framed by the superficial dichotomy of the Old Tree Dead ('British colonial culture, conservative, bourgeois and philistine') and the Young Tree Green ('the native Australia struggling for a radical identity, a national voice and an authentic faith').[59] Along the way are the absurd representations of 'Joe Lyons, the genial gollywog from the Nut, [who] changed the apron strings of his aunts for the apron strings of his wife', and

> Jimmy Scullin … [who] spoke the language of the measurers and the money-changers. He spoke not as a man who believed Australians could steal fire from heaven, not as a man with fire in the belly for an Australians' Australia as distinct from the Imperial Firm of John Bull and Co. in which Bruce, Page and Bob Menzies placed their trust.

We also hear that 'Miles Franklin spluttered and spat as only she could splutter and spit', and so on.[60] The writer and activist Beatrice Faust, who had no stake in the controversy, considered the prose 'banal, diffuse, over-written, old-fashioned, sentimental and unsubstantial' and could not understand why Clark 'was thought well of'.[61]

Another person who was perturbed was Roslyn Russell, the research assistant for Volume 6 and at the time an MA student in Australian history at the University of Sydney:

> I had my doubts as to the narrow choice of sources at the time, and of course with the passage of over 30 years and my own practice of history, these doubts remain. I only wish that I could have saved him from himself a bit more, but as his research assistant I was in too humble a position to challenge either his choice of material or its interpretation.[62]

---

59   The definitions are provided by Helen Bourke, 'Above the Mainstream: Manning Clark's History of Australia', *Overland*, no. 109, 1987, pp. 21–24, specifically p. 22.
60   C.M.H. Clark, *A History of Australia*, Volume 6: *'The old dead tree and the young green tree', 1916–1935*, Melbourne: MUP, 1987, pp. 263, 315, 480 respectively.
61   Beatrice Faust, 'Making sense of the real Manning Clark', *Australian*, 3 September 1993, p. 21.
62   Roslyn Russell, email to author, 10 May 2018.

Figure 7. Roslyn and Katie Russell, 1981.
Roslyn started work as Manning Clark's research assistant in January 1982. She and her daughter Katie 'shared the Manning and Dymphna experience'. They were included in many events at the home of the Clarks, and Katie retains vivid memories of both Dymphna and Manning.
Source. Provided by Roslyn Russell (photographer unknown) and reproduced with the subjects' permission.

Indeed, Volume 6 reads like a long vendetta against R.G. Menzies, who had scarcely made his mark by Clark's cut-off date of 1935. Clark did not view Menzies through 'the eye of pity' but regards him instead as an imperial lackey. As with Deakin, Menzies's biographers give Clark short shrift. There is no reference to Clark in Allan Martin's two-volume biography and Brett, in *Robert Menzies' Forgotten People*, is curtly dismissive of Clark's notion that Menzies was 'a hollow man' bereft of an interior life.[63] Just as Clark very largely ignored existing scholarship, subsequent scholarship has returned the compliment.

Nor did Volume 6 get a free ride from the reviewers, although Ryan is justified in feeling that many of the assessments were muted and insufficiently severe. Many historians and non-specialists alike seem to have been carried away by the euphoria and media fanfare surrounding

---

63   A.W. Martin, *Robert Menzies: A Life*, 2 vols, Melbourne: MUP, 1993–96; Judith Brett, *Robert Menzies' Forgotten People,* Sydney: Macmillan Australia, 1992, pp. 195–96.

the culmination of the epic project that was C.M.H. Clark's *A History of Australia*. The sense of occasion was anticipated in a poem by historian-turned-novelist Peter Corris (1942–2018), the first stanza of which reads:

> Five vols down and one to go
> Clark puts on a mighty show.
> See—men of God and men of Mammon
> Make it through the years of famine
> Grow the wheat, the spuds and vino,
> Ride upon the great Merino.[64]

Part of the heightened reception was Volume 6 winning the inaugural Gold Banjo Award of the National Book Council for the Australian book of the year (but only, it transpired, because the judging panel's chairman, Clark's friend Geoffrey Dutton, exerted improper influence on his co-judges).[65] And behind the scenes a number of senior historians wrote privately to Clark, congratulating him on the accomplishment of bringing his project to fruition but avoiding any semblance of actual assessment.[66]

Many reviewers did subject Volume 6 to a degree of rigorous appraisal that stopped well short of denunciation, thus lending credence to Ryan's observation that Clark's *History* was 'measured by standards other than those applied to the work of "ordinary historians"'.[67] Certainly, no academic historian in the late 1980s, apart from Tony Griffiths, made a comment remotely similar to Mark McKenna's later statement that Clark's interpretations had 'become so fictitious as to bear little resemblance to the historical events and people described'.[68] Any other academic, writing as Clark did in Volume 6, would have been severely

---

[64] Peter Corris, 'A History of Australia (C.M.H. Clark)', in Geoffrey Lehmann (ed.), *The Flight of the Emu: Contemporary Light Verse,* Sydney: Angus & Robertson, 1990, p. 68.

[65] Matthews, *Manning Clark,* p. 384. Among his many other activities, Dutton (1922–1998) was a cofounder of Sun Books, which made fruitless efforts to secure the paperback rights of the *History.*

[66] For example, Hugh Stretton to Clark, 7 August 1987, Manning Clark Papers, NLA, MS 7550, Series 18, Box 158, Folder 27; Richard Boswell to Clark, 2 October 1987, Manning Clark Papers, NLA, MS 7550, Series 18, Box 159, Folder 31.

[67] Ryan, 'Manning Clark', p. 194. Reviews of a critical nature include: A.G.L. Shaw, 'Clark completes his history', *Age,* 5 September 1987, p. 12 (described by Clark as 'a wintry sneer'); Colin Roderick, 'Not quite the history of Australia', *Courier-Mail Weekend,* 26 September 1987, p. 5; Peter Cochrane, review in *Journal of the Royal Australian Historical Society,* vol. 74, no. 2, 1988, pp. 170–74; Bill Cope, review in *Labour History,* no. 55, 1988, pp. 92–94, doi.org/10.2307/27508902; Michael Roe, review in *Tasmanian Historical Research Association – Papers & Proceedings,* vol. 34, no. 4, 1987, pp. 131–32; Beverley Kingston, review in *Australian Historical Studies,* vol. 23, no. 91, 1988, pp. 204–5; John Lack, 'Manning Clark's History', *Arena,* no. 82, 1988, pp. 168–73.

[68] McKenna, *An Eye for Eternity,* p. 626.

dealt with by reviewers, academic or otherwise. But ultimately it was not the book being 'reviewed' so much as its celebrity author and the great moment of culmination.

* * *

The irony of the Ryan–Clark controversy is that many historians were defending the late Manning Clark, and yet the *History* had been increasingly disregarded during Clark's lifetime as serious scholarship. There were, certainly, some feelings of envy about the impressive sales of his *History* as well as disapproval of his public profile and his role as national prophet.[69] But there was a more deeply entrenched resentment because Clark scorned his fellow historians for being uninspired 'Dry-as-Dusts' and disparaged the academy while at the same time drawing his salary *and* authority from his senior university position.[70] Clark's future biographer Brian Matthews recalls how offended he was with Clark during their first encounter, at a conference in 1973, when Clark quoted with obvious relish Henry Lawson's putdown of his 'cultured friends':

> I leave you alone in your cultured halls
> To drivel and croak and cavil:
> Till your voice goes further than college walls,
> Keep out of the tracks we travel!'[71]

This sneer, to a perplexed Matthews, was tantamount to betrayal:

> I was very upset by this performance: angry at Clark, exasperated by … [Clark's] apparently easy rejection of much that he himself stood for and belonged with. [It was] immensely puzzling to me at the time; and discouraging, enraging.[72]

Clark, however, wanted it both ways, referring to the profession in slighting terms as 'Historical Industries Propriety Limited'. He resented the elite status of historians at the Institute of Advanced Studies at ANU who were unencumbered with undergraduate teaching, in contrast to his own department across campus in the School of General Studies (renamed

---

69   Humphrey McQueen, *Suspect History: Manning Clark and the Future of Australia's Past,* Adelaide: Wakefield Press, 1997, p. 126; McKenna, *An Eye for Eternity,* pp. 573, 598; Wallace-Crabbe, 'Manning Clark['s] Troubled Landscape', p. 86.
70   McKenna, *An Eye for Eternity,* p. 499.
71   Henry Lawson, 'The Uncultured Rhymer to his Cultured Critics', *Poemhunter.com,* available at: www.poemhunter.com/poem/the-uncultured-rhymer-to-his-cultured-critics/.
72   Gia Metherell, 'Skirmishes in cultured halls', *Canberra Times,* 14 June 1997, for quotation see p. C3; Matthews, *Manning Clark,* pp. 317–18, 508–09.

The Faculties). On one occasion he sarcastically asked a newly arrived historian at ANU, 'how are you getting on among those Great Minds in the Institute?'[73] The newcomer didn't have a clue what he was talking about. Sarcasm or not, Clark still craved the indulgence and adulation of the academy and took extreme umbrage at real and imagined slights of his work. At his behest, MUP sent out hundreds of review copies of the *History*,[74] but Clark made no attempt to address the reviewers' criticisms, much less to incorporate the latest scholarship into his work. Yet in later life he was hoping that future historians would not judge him harshly.[75]

Macintyre probably sums up best Clark's professional standing among his peers:

> Historians criticised the volumes of the *History* and by the 1980s they paid very little attention to it. The *Documents,* and to a lesser extent the early volumes of the *History,* had an appreciable effect on the understanding of Australian history: his view of the convicts, his attention to the religious dimension, his treatment of the explorers, his account of self-government, etc. But it was rare to find any reference to Manning in work published after the 1970s.[76]

Ryan would probably have agreed with these criticisms, but he misconstrues the *History* in other respects. Given that it was increasingly considered unsuitable as undergraduate reading, Ryan was being disingenuous as well as implausible in repeatedly stating that he was acting on behalf of 'the young and innocent'.[77] It is difficult to be precise about the extent to which the *History* was set reading for undergraduates, but my discussions indicate that students received less exposure to it as time went on.[78] Perhaps what happened at the University of Adelaide provides an accurate enough summation. In 1964 the discussion for history honours students in the first week of the course was 'Manning Clark's *History of Australia*, vol. 1—

---

73 Stephen Foster, email to author, 9 December 2018.
74 For example, Internal memo, 7 March 1968 [five pages], MUP Records, 2003.0129, Unit 20 (vol. 2); 'Review copies', 24 August 1987 [also five pages in length], MUP Records, 2003.0129, Unit 21 (vol. 6).
75 Michael Dargaville, 'Unasked questions killing the country', *Mercury* (Hobart), 29 August 1987, p. 23.
76 Stuart Macintyre, email to author, 3 April 2018; see also Bourke, 'Above the Mainstream'. An example of Clark being ignored, when he might justifiably have been noticed, is Deborah Gare, 'Britishness in Recent Australian Historiography', *Historical Journal,* vol. 43, no. 4, 2000, pp. 1145–55, doi.org/10.1017/S0018246X00001564.
77 Ryan, 'Manning Clark', p. 212; 'A Reply to my Critics', p. 214; 'The Charge of the Lightweight Brigade', for quotation see p. 234.
78 Brian Dickey, discussion with author, 31 July 2015; Maurice French, email to author, 26 July 2019.

success or failure?' A few years later, in 1968, the second-term tutorials in the second-year Australian history course were based on eight books, one of which was Volume 1 of Clark's *History*. The following year Clark's volumes of *Select Documents* were routinely prescribed, but the *History* was off the menu. In 1973 Clark's *Select Documents* continued to be on the reading list but, again, not the *History*. There was a similar pattern of diminishing exposure to the *History* at the University of Melbourne.[79]

There are good reasons for the increasing neglect of Clark's *History* as a teaching tool: both secondary and tertiary students were likely to be bemused. Besides, the *History* was never intended as 'a work of reference' and Ryan misunderstands its nature to describe it as such—just as Malcolm Ellis did before him in describing Volume 1 as a 'text-book'.[80] It was a dramatic grand narrative epic in the literary traditions of the great nineteenth-century historians, as Clark himself explains in his third volume of autobiography.[81] Ryan knew about the autobiography, having referred to it in his first *Quadrant* article[82] but had either not read those passages or they had slipped his mind.

Ryan also misunderstood, or chose not to understand, the unspoken etiquette that academic reviews are normally couched in reasonably courteous language. The image of the ideal review is one that focuses on the strengths of the work at hand and yet conveys its limitations. Rudeness, incivility and destructive negativity are generally frowned upon within the profession. In the 1960s and early 1970s, Humphrey McQueen believed that Australian historians' courteousness towards each other's work—'the gentility principle', as he called it—was inimical to 'the idea of the university as a clash of ideas', and he was going to put things to rights. Colleagues were disconcerted by his adversarial style, which ran counter to the tacitly accepted way of doing things.[83] There was certainly a perception in some quarters that historians wrote 'soft' reviews.[84]

---

79 The relevant course outlines and tutorial guides for Adelaide are in the Tregenza Papers, Special Collections, Barr Smith Library, University of Adelaide, MSS 0047, Series 4.1, and for Melbourne in the Archive of J.M. Main, Special Collections, Flinders University Library, PGp2/116A.
80 Ryan, 'Manning Clark', p. 206; Ellis, 'History without Facts', in Bridge, *Manning Clark*, p. 70.
81 Manning Clark, *An Historian's Apprenticeship*, Melbourne: MUP, 1992, pp. 31–35.
82 Ryan, 'Manning Clark', p. 209.
83 Frank Bongiorno, 'Two Radical Legends: Russel Ward, Humphrey McQueen and the New Left Challenge in Australian Historiography', *Journal of Australian Colonial History*, vol. 10, no. 2, 2008, pp. 201–22, specifically pp. 214–15. Contrast with Christopher Pearson, 'Standover Left axes debate', *Weekend Australian*, 6–7 September 2003, p. 20.
84 Adrian Merritt, 'Methodological and Theoretical Implications of the Study of Law and Crime', *Labour History*, no. 37, 1979, pp. 108–19, specifically p. 108 n.2, doi.org/10.2307/27508388.

Ryan did express his amazement that 'the emotional championship of Clark—instant, hot and angry—stands in strangest contrast to the reserved and embarrassed character of his intellectual support'.[85] The defence of the *History* was, indeed, highly qualified and it was noted at the time that 'if Clark could not cut the mustard in terms of historical scholarship then the Ryan case was more than half proved'.[86] To assert that Clark's work would outlive his critics was never going to make headway, and the claim that Clark had a vision for Australia is readily undermined if his methods and accuracy can be faulted. Neither would newspaper headings such as 'Forget the fairy floss, this is history writ large', 'Manning Clark will outlast most critics' and 'Clark's legacy undimmed' carry the day.[87] It was certainly easier to assert than to explain why Clark's imagining of Australia might be uplifting. The difficulty is summed up by Alan Atkinson. He expressed no doubts that Clark was 'a great historian' while still admitting that 'it is not easy to work out the elements of his greatness, taking account especially of the serious charges which are often laid against his scholarship'.[88] Neither were sweeping, but nebulous, statements that the *History* was a 'many-voiced epic of national life' or that it 'began to show Australians that they were as richly endowed with spirituality, tragedy and splendour as any other people' going to gain traction in the face of hard-nosed scepticism.[89]

Many years later, Ryan asserted that 'every one of the clear and specific criticisms made of Clark in *Quadrant* back in 1993 remains fudged but never refuted by his supporters'.[90] They did try, and often did effectively refute, but he was not listening. The problem for Clark's defenders was being thrown back on a relativist argument, or as Macintyre pointed out:

> Remarkable is Ryan's complaint that Clark intrudes his views into the history and hence distorts objective historical truth. This notion of a formed historical truth lying outside the historian's

---

85 Ryan, 'The Charge of the Lightweight Brigade', p. 223.
86 Peter Craven, 'The Ryan Affair', in Bridge, *Manning Clark*, pp. 165–87 (text), p. 224 (endnotes), specifically p. 182.
87 Steve Dow, 'Forget the fairy floss, this is history writ large', *Australian*, 30 August 1993, p. 9; 'Manning Clark will outlive most critics' (editorial), *Canberra Times*, 28 August 1993, p. 12; Michael Cathcart, 'Clark's legacy undimmed', *Sydney Morning Herald*, 27 August 1993, p. 11.
88 Alan Atkinson, 'A Great Historian?' in Bridge, *Manning Clark*, pp. 122–35 (text), pp. 220–21 (endnotes), specifically p. 122.
89 Peter Craven, 'Excerpts from Clark's rich and strange history', *Age*, 23 June 1994, pp. 12–13 (Green Recording Guide); Michael Cathcart, 'The sage under siege', *Age*, 27 August 1993, p. 13.
90 Peter Ryan, 'Hollow Man of Yesterday', review of *Manning Clark: A Life*, by Brian Matthews, *Quadrant*, vol. 53, nos 1–2, January–February 2009, pp. 126–28, specifically p. 126.

experience and framework of values, a truth that the historian simply apprehends and reproduces, is simply pre-Copernican. Ryan seems not to have grasped that the facts do not speak for themselves, and that every work of historical scholarship conducts a dialogue between past and present.[91]

Others also commented with some bewilderment on Ryan's arch-empiricist approach:

Ryan is one of those mildly totalitarian men who long for books which will reveal 'objective' truths about history, mainly final 'truths' fully in accord with set-in-concrete views they already hold.[92]

There is also a newspaper clipping in the Ryan Papers with a marked-up passage that reads: 'Theory can be no more than this: a trap set in the hope that reality will be naive enough to fall into it'; and another one, again marked up, where Clark is quoted as saying: 'Everyone's got a bias … I'm not very interested in being objective'.[93] Ryan was nothing if not an unreconstructed positivist but one who was challenged in getting his own facts right and in representing situations accurately—or, for that matter, being 'objective'.

Even so, Ryan won the round of the contest concerning his critics being unable to defend Clark's work wholeheartedly—for the simple reason that most of them had no desire to defend the *History* but, rather, were disturbed by the tenor of Ryan's attacks and the debasing of public debate. In any case, none of Ryan's criticisms of the *History* were original and he emphatically failed to demonstrate the intertwining of Clark's personal failings and the failings of the *History*; to which might be added his own failure to confront Clark about the fluctuating and eventually declining quality of the *History* during the latter's lifetime. He complains that 'there was not one occasion when Manning would discuss [his factual] errors simply on a matter-of-fact basis',[94] without seeming to realise that it was

---

91 Stuart Macintyre, 'Clark's work sure to outlive its detractors', *Age*, 28 August 1993, p. 17.
92 Andrew Field, 'Clark's editor: a paragon of infidelity', *Courier-Mail*, 15 September 1993, for quotation see p. 8; Michael Cathcart, 'The sage under siege', *Age*, 27 August 1993, p. 13; Maurilia Meehan, 'Spot the Invisible Man', *Australian Book Review*, no. 156, November 1993, pp. 34–37, specifically pp. 36–37.
93 Bryan Appleyard, 'Now the orgy is over', *Spectator*, 15 May 1993, p. 39; 'They said it', *Canberra Times*, 7 October 1989, p. 9, respectively (copies in the Ryan Papers, NLA, MS 9897, Series 6, Box 10, Folder 2).
94 Ryan, 'Manning Clark', pp. 193–94.

his responsibility as Clark's publisher to voice concerns about the quality of the *History*. In the absence of such complaints, Clark had every right to believe that he was performing to his publisher's satisfaction.

Ryan's silence raises another matter. The critics maintained that Ryan's posthumous attack on Clark was an act of base cowardice, which Robert Manne disputes in the light of Ryan's wartime record and his foreknowledge of 'the social ostracism which would be visited upon him by [Clark's] vast network of friends and admirers'.[95] Clearly, bravery comes in more than one guise. It is not necessary to take *Fear Drive My Feet* at face value to realise that Ryan fought for his country with distinction: his mention in despatches confirms that he did.[96] Yet he lacked the intestinal fortitude to confront Clark about the shortcomings of the *History* or to debate face-to-face with his critics on television or radio. Bismarck is on the mark in drawing a distinction, back in 1864, between military courage and *Zivilcourage*.[97]

---

95   Robert Manne, 'A holy cow called history', *Age*, 1 September 1993, for quotation see p. 16; Manne, comments on a draft of this book, 11 March 2019.
96   Enclosed in Ryan's Service file, NAA: B883, VX128541 (p. 35).
97   Richard Swedberg, 'Civil Courage *(Zivilcourage):* The Case of Knut Wicksell', *Theory & Society*, vol. 28, no. 4, 1999, pp. 501–28, specifically p. 501.

Part 3.
Ruminations

7

Deliberation: Manning Clark and the History Wars

> If Manning Clark had not existed, it would have been necessary to invent him—or so he convinced us all. He cast a role model for himself in his national drama, as 'an Australian voice ... in the great debate on what it has all been for, telling the story of who Australians were and what they might be'. So Clark invented himself in his own image.
>
> Marian Quartly (1994)[1]

> Manning Clark wrote Australia's future as much he did its past.
>
> Donald Wright (2015)[2]

Manning Clark increasingly became the *bête noire* of Australian conservatives as he embraced the triple role of nationalist historian, pro-ALP activist and History Warrior. Yet he did not start out as a Labor partisan and it tends to be forgotten that Clark was sceptical of the ALP in the 1950s. There is also his association with *Quadrant* in its earlier days—ironically in view of the later attacks—when he was recruited to the journal's inaugural editorial board in 1955 as a voice of a progressive

---

1   Marian Quartly, 'Reinventing Manning Clark', *Meanjin,* vol. 53, no. 1, 1994, pp. 175–78, specifically p. 175. The quotation within the quotation comes from *Manning Clark's History of Australia,* abridged by Michael Cathcart, Melbourne: Melbourne University Press (hereafter MUP), 1993, p. 550. Quartly is Emerita Professor of History at Monash University.
2   Donald Wright, *Donald Creighton: A Life in History,* Toronto, University of Toronto Press, 2015, p. 321.

Australian conservatism.³ Clark's position shifted and from at least the mid-1970s he increasingly became a Labor icon. With the aura and gravitas of an Old Testament prophet, he became, in the popular imagination, 'the wise old man with a unique insight into the state of his country's soul'.⁴ Such was his value that the ALP machine gave him encouragement to provide 'an ever-deepening statement of the grand themes about our nature and the purpose of the continent' on its behalf.⁵

The turning point in Clark's relationship with the ALP stemmed from his admiration for Gough Whitlam (1916–2014). His public support of Labor became more strident after The Dismissal of the Whitlam Government in 1975. As well as asserting that 'History will be kinder to Labor than the people', he characterised the 23 years of Liberal–Country Party rule as 'the years of unleavened bread', denounced The Dismissal of the Whitlam Labor government ('Are we a nation of bastards?') and made ill-considered public statements that appeared to condone violent revolution.⁶ He irked conservatives to the extent that members of the Fraser administration criticised the ABC's appointment of Clark to deliver the 1976 Boyer Lectures and unprecedented measures were taken to vet them.⁷ The final straw came with Clark's repeated espousal of Aboriginal rights during the lead-up to the bicentenary; at that point, 'in the eyes of conservatives Clark moved from being an apologist for the Labor Party to a traitor'.⁸ As well, in the early 1990s Clark was widely credited with being the inspiration for Paul Keating's 'Big Picture' republican nationalism. In these ways, Clark became a subject of the Australian History Wars as well as a participant.

* * *

---

3   Cassandra Pybus, *The Devil and James McAuley*, Brisbane: University of Queensland Press, 1999, p. 152; Mark McKenna, *An Eye for Eternity: The Life of Manning Clark*, Melbourne: Miegunyah Press, 2011, pp. 387–88.
4   Frank Bongiorno, *The Eighties: The Decade that Transformed Australia*, Melbourne: Black Inc., 2015, p. 247.
5   Graham Freudenberg, *A Figure of Speech: A Political Memoir*, Brisbane: Wiley, 2005, p. 194.
6   Manning Clark, 'History will be kinder to Labor than the people', *Australian*, 7 January 1976, p. 7; Clark, 'The Years of Unleavened Bread: December 1949 to December 1972', *Meanjin Quarterly*, vol. 32, no. 3, 1973, pp. 245–50; Clark, 'Are we a Nation of Bastards?' *Meanjin Quarterly*, vol. 35, no. 2, 1976, pp. 215–18.
7   Manning Clark, *A Discovery of Australia: The 1976 ABC Boyer Lectures and their 1988 Postscript*, Sydney: ABC Enterprises for the Australian Broadcasting Commission, 1991.
8   McKenna, *An Eye for Eternity*, p. 620.

Keating became prime minister in December 1991 and set about implementing his 'Big Picture'—a broad program that involved Aboriginal reconciliation, engagement with Asia and making Australia a republic. He had a vision, he was a man in a hurry and he needed no encouragement to trample over opponents. Part and parcel of republicanism, in Keating's mind, was a repudiation of the British link and associated Brit-bashing. He left his position in no doubt. In a stirring parliamentary delivery early in his tenure as prime minister, he brought up past grievances towards Britain as well as condemning the 'fogeyism of the fifties' and 'that awful cultural cringe under Menzies which held us back for nearly a generation'—the so-called 'golden age when vast numbers of Australians never got a look in'. Amid uproar in the House, he threw down the gauntlet with a rousing denunciation of the Opposition:

> You can go back to the fifties to your nostalgia, your Menzies, the Caseys and the whole lot. They were not aggressively Australian, they were not aggressively proud of our culture, and we will have no bar of you or your sterile ideology.[9]

And to think that only eight years earlier Clark considered Keating to be 'lacking in old-fashioned [?] moral passion, and indignation and anger'.[10]

A kindly Keating biographer has asserted:

> one of the responsibilities of national leaders is to clarify a country's rhetoric and define—or redefine—the way in which a country sees itself, and few would dispute that Australia in 1992 was a country in need of some redefinition.[11]

Clark, had he still been alive, would certainly have thought so. But there was insufficient electoral demand for a republic or for other aspects of the Big Picture, as Keating's advisers recognised.[12] It was Keating's misfortune that a recession focused people's attention on bread-and-butter issues and his support for the arts in straitened times was viewed askance. Neither

---

9 *Hansard* (House of Representatives), 27 February 1992, pp. 373–74, for quotation see p. 473; also available as a video clip at: australianpolitics.com/1992/02/27/keating-blasts-liberal-party-fogies.html.
10 Roslyn Russell (ed.), *Ever, Manning: Selected Letters of Manning Clark, 1938–1991,* Sydney: Allen & Unwin, 2008, p. 443 (Clark to John Molony, 28 May 1984).
11 Michael Gordon, *A Question of Leadership: Paul Keating, Political Fighter,* Brisbane: University of Queensland Press, 1993, p. 196; cf. Robert Manne, 'Paul Keating' (1996 and 2002), in Manne, *Left Right Left: Political Essays, 1977–2005,* Melbourne: Black Inc., 2004, pp. 335–41.
12 John Edwards, *Keating: The Inside Story,* Ringwood: Penguin Books, 1996, pp. 526–28; Don Watson, *Recollections of a Bleeding Heart: A Portrait of Paul Keating PM,* Sydney: Knopf, 2002, pp. 563, 587.

did Keating's tactics have appeal. Keating had been warned that, by making anti-British jibes the touchstone of his republican crusade would detract from his message and antagonise much of the electorate, as his abrasive style was already doing.[13] But he couldn't help himself. Keating's Brit-bashing and disparagement of Menzies was a sport, for the deliberate purpose of infuriating the opposition, who obligingly rose to the bait— or, to change the imagery, Don Watson likened it to a piece of cat fur being thrown to a pack of dogs.[14] It would come back to haunt him. The problem was that when he tried, after 1993, to articulate a more middle-of-the-road position on the republic, it was too late: he had already injected a Manning Clark faultline through the nation between 'young tree green' Labor nationalists and 'old dead tree' bootlicking Tories.[15] In the event, his 'Big Picture' was ultimately unrealised and all the while the History Wars were intensifying.

The question remains: to what extent was Keating a Clark acolyte? They first met in 1985. As Keating explains:

> I used to drop in on him not to draw any particular wisdom from him but simply because I liked him and enjoyed sharing the music with him. But we did share a lot of common ground. He despised the notion of the Austral Briton and its domination of the political debate, particularly after the First World War— where they imposed their values on society, never thinking of the Australian way and how Australia was entitled to be a society that gave expression to its own mores and values.[16]

---

13 James Curran and Stuart Ward, *The Unknown Nation: Australia after Empire*, Melbourne: MUP, 2010, p. 226; Stuart Ward, *Australia and the British Embrace: The Demise of the Imperial Ideal*, Melbourne: MUP, 2001, p. 1; Neal Blewett, *A Cabinet Diary: A Personal Record of the First Keating Government*, Adelaide: Wakefield Press, 1999, p. 100; Watson, *Recollections of a Bleeding Heart*, pp. 563–64 ('He was squandering his substance with his style').
14 James Curran, 'Ruled by Britannia', review of *Robert Menzies: The Art of Politics*, by Troy Bramston, *Weekend Australian Review*, 11–12 May 2019, p. 22.
15 James Curran, 'The "Thin Dividing Line": Prime Ministers and the Problem of Australian Nationalism, 1972–1996', *Australian Journal of Politics and History*, vol. 48, no. 4, 2002, pp. 469–86, specifically p. 485, doi.org/10.1111/1467-8497.00271.
16 Kerry O'Brien, *Keating*, Sydney: Allen & Unwin, 2015, for quotation see p. 520; David Day, *Paul Keating: The Biography*, Sydney: Fourth Estate, 2015, pp. 303–05; McKenna, *An Eye for Eternity*, pp. 609–11.

Peter Ryan certainly thought that Clark had a baleful effect on Keating and that the latter's 'republican drive was largely "underpinned" by Manning Clark's writings and philosophy'.[17] Ryan went on to say that 'it *matters*— because it affects things / e.g. Keating has been fed M. Clark & comes out with … anti-Brit nonsense'.[18] Ryan's was the prevailing view: friend and foe alike were deceived by appearances into magnifying the extent of Clark's influence over Keating.[19] Peter Craven disagreed, saying that to suggest that Keating's vision came out of Clark's *History* is 'a shade sillier than suggesting that Harold Wilson, say, derived his vision, if he had any such thing, from E.P. Thompson's *The Making of the English Working Class*'.[20] But his was a minority voice at the time.

Keating himself imparted the impression of a relationship that was closer than it actually was. He appropriated Clark's imagery and posited a struggle between progressive 'enlargers' like himself and the stick-in-the-mud 'straiteners' and museum pieces who infested the Opposition benches. As Don Watson recalled, this distinction did not come from Keating actually having read Clark's *History*:

> The PM was himself responsible for the 'punishers and enlargers' rhetoric in the [1993] election campaign. On a plane back from Adelaide he was telling me how he saw the world and how his opponents seemed to see it. I simply told him he had divided people into the categories Manning Clark often used. Thereafter nothing could stop him using them.[21]

Keating did have a high regard for Clark. As well as delivering a eulogy in parliament when Clark died, Keating came out swinging on Clark's behalf when the Ryan controversy broke out.[22] He also opened the Manning

---

17   Ryan, notes of telephone conversation with Brian Millership, 6 March 1995, Ryan Papers, National Library of Australia (hereafter NLA), MS 9897, Series 6, Box 10, Folder 8.
18   Ryan, undated note to himself, Ryan Papers, NLA, MS 9897, Series 6, Box 10, Folder 5.
19   *Hansard* (Senate), 7 September 1993, pp. 1120–23 (C.R. Kemp); Geoffrey Bolton, 'Oedipus Clark for the Nineties', *Editions,* no. 17, August–September 1993, p. 9; Bolton, 'Don't smash the icon', *Bulletin,* 12 October 1993, pp. 42–43, specifically p. 43; 'Campbell not expecting to be expelled', *Canberra Times,* 27 November 1993, p. 6; Barry Jones, *A Thinking Reed,* Sydney: Allen & Unwin, 2006, p. 302.
20   Peter Craven, 'Clark cacophony revisited', *Australian,* 25 May 1994, p. 29.
21   Mark McKenna, '"I wonder whether I belong" Manning Clark and the Politics of Australian History, 1970–2000', *Australian Historical Studies,* vol. 34, no. 122 (2003), pp. 364–83, for quotation see p. 380, doi.org/10.1080/10314610308596260.
22   *Hansard* (House of Representatives), 28 May 1991, p. 4032; Scott Henry and Robert Garran, 'Keating lauds Clark's gift of imagination', *Weekend Australian,* 28–29 August 1993, p. 4; Karen Middleton, 'Manning Clark's critics bitchy: PM', *Age,* 28 August 1993, p. 3; 'PM backs historian', *Canberra Times,* 28 August 1993, p. 1.

Clark Centre at ANU in late February 1994, where he said that he regarded Clark as 'a great Australian'.[23] He hastened to add that they were by no means close friends—only that they shared a vision about Australia's future. What the press picked up on was his wish that Clark were still alive to see such changes as the republican push and the passage of the Native Title legislation, thus giving more weight to their relationship than it warranted.[24]

Rather, Clark merely reinforced the anti-British, pro-Asia strain in Keating's thinking. Since at least the 1950s Clark saw that Australia's future as part of Asia was impeded by the White Australia policy, whereas the rationale for Keating's engagement with Asia came from a different direction: it was to accommodate global political and economic realignments following the collapse of the Soviet Union.[25] As a cultural nationalist, Clark wanted a more 'distinctive' national culture rather than one that was derivative of and deferential to Britain and being governed by people he was pleased to describe as 'the sycophants and career men of the Menzies circus'.[26] Clark's anti-British strain independently dovetailed with Keating's views:

> The fall of Singapore and Australia's place in Asia did not come from the *History*. They were reference points that Paul Keating drew from his own [Irish working class] childhood, distilled from Labor lore and conjured from his convictions.[27]

A specific and significant source of political inspiration, from the early 1960s, stemmed from the nationalist fervour of his mentor, Jack Lang.[28] Donald Horne put it more starkly in saying:

> Keating's own experience of Australian history seems to be confined to a few scraps of Labor myth he picked up out of Jack Lang's recycle bin when, as a young acolyte, he used to visit the old demagogue—although behind Lang some have divined the evil spirit of Clark.[29]

---

23 'Speech by the Prime Minister the Hon P.J. Keating, MP – Opening of the Manning Clark Centre, ANU, Canberra 22 February 1994', available at: pmtranscripts.pmc.gov.au/release/transcript-9126.
24 'Changes would please Clark: PM', *Canberra Times,* 23 February 1994, p. 3.
25 McKenna, *An Eye for Eternity,* pp. 350–54; Watson, *Recollections of a Bleeding Heart,* pp. 70–72, 77–78.
26 Quoted in McKenna, *An Eye for Eternity,* p. 383.
27 Stuart Macintyre and Anna Clark, *The History Wars,* 2nd edn, Melbourne: MUP, 2004, p. 63.
28 James Curran, *The Power of Speech: Australian Prime Ministers Defining the National Image,* 2nd edn, Melbourne: MUP, 2006, pp. 190–235.
29 Donald Horne, 'How Manning made his enemies', *Weekend Australian,* 31 August–1 September 1996, p. 18.

Nevertheless, the received wisdom was that Clark was the intellectual sorcerer and Keating his apprentice. They certainly formed a mutual admiration society. When British journalists entered the fray, they wanted to throw The Paul & Manning Show into disarray and bring down the curtain on what they regarded as an odious double act.

* * *

Despite the angst it caused, the Ryan–Clark controversy was dismissed at the time as a little local difficulty: 'The whole wretched affair was a nine-day wonder' is one description, referring to how long it lasted as a media sensation.[30] Both Ryan and the columnist Peter Craven wrote it off as parochialism of the sort that only Australia could accomplish.[31] Not so. Far from being a parish pump affair that was largely confined to Melbourne and Sydney, the controversy was given a new lease of life when English journalists Bryan Appleyard and Paul Johnson, both of whom were visiting Australia at the outbreak of hostilities, triggered a commotion in the British press, thus drawing in another audience. Their attacks were as much a contribution to Australia's History Wars as they were an assault on Clark.

Writing for the *Independent,* an English national broadsheet, Appleyard threw the proverbial kitchen sink at Clark and Keating. The occasion was provided by Keating's upcoming audience with the Queen at Balmoral to declare his intention that Australia become a republic. Drawing much of his information from Ryan's first *Quadrant* article, Appleyard described Clark as a discredited 'monster' whose *History* was 'the Bible of the Labor Party … in that it provided a long tale of bitter struggle against the colonial master'.[32] Repeating Ryan's assertion that Clark was 'an imposition on Australian credulity', Appleyard linked Clark to the Ern Malley hoax. Both were frauds:

> [Each] arose because of an excessive enthusiasm for a specifically Australian authenticity, a narrative or a voice that could be found nowhere else and would, therefore, advertise Australia's real

---

30 Stuart Macintyre, 'Why do the Tories hate Manning Clark?' in ('Symposium Defending Manning Clark'), *Evatt Papers,* vol. 1, no. 2, 1993, pp. 17–20, specifically p. 17.
31 Peter Ryan, 'A Reply to my Critics', in his *Lines of Fire: Manning Clark & Other Writings,* ed. A.K. Macdougall, Binalong, NSW: Clarion Editions, 1997, pp. 214–22, specifically p. 214; see also Peter Craven, 'The Ryan Affair', in Carl Bridge (ed.), *Manning Clark: Essays on his Place in History,* Melbourne: MUP, 1994, pp. 165–87 (text), p. 224 (notes), specifically p. 179.
32 Bryan Appleyard, 'The dinkum Aussie? Strewth!' *Independent* (London), 8 September 1993, p. 21.

presence as opposed to shadowy existence as a thinly populated offspring of white Europe. Mr Keating's political route to this authenticity is via republicanism.

Now in full stride, Appleyard taunted the republican ideal as simply the expression of an insecure and 'insanely politic nation'—a somewhat pitiful and distant outpost whose inhabitants were

> as burdened with identity as any nation on earth. If it remains implicit rather than explicit, that is a problem, but it will not be solved by bloody, historical lies and certainly not by Canberra politicos who think they know what the nation 'must' become.

Keating's Brit-bashing, in other words, was being countered by a retaliatory dose of Aussie-bashing, and Appleyard does provide an indication of the offence caused by Keating's denigration of Australia's British links—such as 'the British bootstraps stuff' and 'the awful cultural cringe under Menzies'.

Appleyard's studied insults added little of value to the debate about republicanism or about Clark. Predictably enough, his swingeing attack affronted Clark's friends and supporters in Britain, and the *Independent* published some of their responses. Neither were these particularly helpful; a case in point was the reaction of historian David Fitzpatrick of Trinity College Dublin (and a family friend of the Clarks) who asserted, 'If Clark's earlier volumes received no searching reviews from "heavyweight academic historians" in his field, this was because there were none. He was the pioneer—ploughing his own furrow'.[33] This is a stark example of the all-too-prevalent hyperbole from Clark's defenders. It was as though other Australia historians of Clark's generation—Geoffrey Blainey, Geoffrey Bolton, Frank Crowley, Ken Inglis, John La Nauze, Allan Martin, A.G.L. Shaw and Geoffrey Serle spring to mind—never existed. It was as though Fitzpatrick's own father, the radical historian Brian Fitzpatrick (1905–1965), had written nothing of consequence on Australian history.[34] Neither was it a case of Clark ploughing his lonely furrow so much as a different furrow. Clark was no different, say, to John

---

33 David Fitzpatrick, 'In defence of Australia and its influential historian' (letter), *Independent*, 10 September 1993, p. 21. Fitzpatrick (1948–2019) also made the point that 'nobody with Irish experience would credit [Appleyard's] claim that "Australia had a monopoly on political insanity"'. Fitzpatrick was Professor of History at Trinity College, Dublin.
34 See Don Watson, *Brian Fitzpatrick: A Radical Life,* Sydney: Hale & Iremonger, 1978.

La Nauze or Allan Martin, who ploughed their own lonely furrows during the lengthy research and writing of their political biographies of Alfred Deakin and Henry Parkes, respectively.[35]

More was to come a week later with another broadside of Keatingesque ferocity by Paul Johnson, a journalist, prolific popular historian, former speechwriter for Margaret Thatcher and 'all-round verbal pugilist'.[36] Johnson also played to the gallery, dubbing Clark as Australia's 'fraudulent historian'. Writing for the *Spectator*, he dismissed Keating as a 'street-wise bruiser of Irish descent, who left school at 14 and has educated himself while eye-gouging his way to the top of Canberra politics'.[37] His real venom, however, was directed at Clark ('the founder of the Pom-bashing industry, at least in its modern, pseudo-academic form') and his 'inflated reputation'. His strictures against Clark were all drawn from Ryan's first *Quadrant* article, which were accepted as gospel truth and which, in Ryan's words, he plundered 'to the point of plagiary'.[38] Such was Johnson's dependence on Ryan that Axel Clark expressed doubts whether he had actually read a word of the *History*.[39]

Only once does Johnson go beyond Ryan, and that is the allegation that Clark was the kingmaker and master puppeteer of the Australian historical profession: 'His pupils found their way to top jobs in the university history departments where they wage a ferocious warfare against scholars who disputed the Clark line'.[40] He also linked Clark and Keating with the comment that Ryan's exposé of the *History* and its author as being 'fraudulent' placed a big question mark over the Australian republican movement 'since it shows that the school of history on which it rests is fundamentally bogus'. It is absurd to claim that there was a Manning

---

35   J.A. La Nauze, *Alfred Deakin: A Biography*, 2 vols, Melbourne: MUP, 1965; A.W. Martin, *Henry Parkes: A Biography*, Melbourne: MUP, 1980.
36   Elizabeth Grice, 'Paul Johnson: "After 70 you begin to mellow"', 4 June 2010, available at: www.telegraph.co.uk/lifestyle/7800902/Paul-Johnson-After-70-you-begin-to-mellow.html.
37   Paul Johnson, 'The Queen, Mr Keating and the case of the fraudulent historian', *Spectator*, 16 September 1993, p. 22. An abridged version appeared as 'Bloody Poms and uppity Aussies', *Age*, 4 October 1993, p. 14.
38   Peter Ryan, 'The Charge of the Lightweight Brigade', in his *Lines of Fire*, pp. 222–34, specifically p. 229.
39   Axel Clark to Jim Griffin, 6 September (should be October) 1993, Dymphna Clark Papers, NLA, MS 9873, Series 10, Box 35, Folder 2.
40   The notion of Clark being the godfather of Australian history was reasserted in 'Editorial: 'Manning Clark's blinkered view', *Courier-Mail*, 31 May 1997, p. 22. Austin Gough put his own spin on it, alleging that Clark was a 'prosy old icon looming over the mastersingers and apprentices of the highly politicised craft of Australia Studies'. Gough to Ryan, 6 September 1993, Ryan Papers, NLA, MS 9897, Series 6, Box 10, Folder 3.

Clark school of Australian history whose adherents ran a closed shop.[41] For one thing, Clark was unclonable. He was an inspirational teacher and was blessed with a group of very able students at the University of Melbourne in the late 1940s, who went on to distinguished careers in history and political science. They were everlastingly grateful to their former teacher but none sought to emulate his type of history or his style of writing. Neither did any of his PhD students. John Barrett, as we have seen, publicly repudiated him.

Johnson's so-called analysis was none other than 'a construct spun from fairy floss', to use one of Ryan's phrases about the *History*,[42] but it was altogether too much for Noel McLachlan of the Melbourne University history department. McLachlan had been one of Clark's former students in the late forties and, like many of the others, he held his old teacher in high esteem—although he might have thought differently had he realised that Clark had recommended against the publication of his PhD thesis by Clarendon Press.[43] He made it his single-handed mission to refute the infamies about Clark in sections of the English press. A man of the left, although his patrician manner suggested otherwise, McLachlan's first career was in Fleet Street journalism before becoming an academic historian. He placed great store in his connections and influence and would have expected that he could orchestrate a defence of Clark in the English media.[44]

He went about it in a way that was never going to win the hearts and minds of the educated British public, such was his immoderate and belittling language in accusing the British of patronising Australians—while in the same breath patronising them. His first salvo was targeted at the *Guardian*: 'Surely the time has come to discuss the Australian-English connexion a little less emotively', and then he proceeded to disregard his own injunction:

---

41   See Macintyre and Clark, *The History Wars,* p. 62, for a rebuttal.
42   Peter Ryan, 'Manning Clark', in his *Lines of Fire,* pp. 179–214, specifically p. 180.
43   Peter Spicer to Clark, 14 September 1959, Manning Clark Papers, NLA, MS 7550, Series 1, Box 3, Folder 23: 'The original contribution … does not seem of sufficient importance to warrant the great deal of labour that would eventually be involved in putting the manuscript in a publishable condition'. I have not been able to locate Clark's letter to the Clarendon Press.
44   Charles Sowerwine, 'Noel David McLachlan, 1927–2006', *History Australia,* vol. 4, no. 1, 2007, pp. 15.1–15.2, doi.org/10.2104/ha070015; Stuart Macintyre, email to author, 3 September 2018. McLachlan later involved himself from the sidelines in the *Courier-Mail* business: 'Manning's mauling raises a storm' (letter to editor), *Weekend Australian,* 31 August–1 September 1996, p. 16.

> I was abroad (comparing all the gilt vulgarity of Buckingham Palace and the Barnes and other U.S. collections for a study of New world nationalism) when Peter Ryan's peevish attack on our mutual teacher, sage and friend, Manning Clark, was published, and I find Bryan Appleyard's piece in the *Independent* and Paul Johnson's in the *Spectator* even more extraordinary—and disgraceful.[45]

McLachlan then provides a tedious catalogue of specific rebuttals and clarifications and concludes by saying that 'ignorant Anglocentric contempt' is still alive and well: 'Understanding your ex-colonies seems as hard for some of you as understanding your children—and the psychological hang-ups labyrinthine'. Unsurprisingly, the letter was spiked.

His numerous other emotionally charged letters to editors deploy the same intemperate language and they mostly fell by the wayside, including one to Robert Manne at *Quadrant*.[46] As McLachlan admitted to Dymphna Clark, his efforts were bearing little fruit.[47] But he did, on his second attempt, place a letter in the *Spectator* and he also managed to publish a rebuttal when Johnson reviewed the Cathcart abridgement of the *History* in the *Times Literary Supplement*, where he (McLachlan) concluded that 'Ryan, like Johnson, exhibits all the unctuous and peevish recklessness of the ageing, lapsed radical—both finding (posthumous) radical-baiting now the best and safest of blood sports'.[48] It was another of those interventions that saw the dialogue deteriorate into insults and that provoked Peter Craven into an effective rebuttal in the *Australian*.[49] Not to be left out, Ryan got his own back by describing McLachlan as 'Dr "Maudlin" McLachlan'.[50]

---

45   McLachlan to Peter Preston (editor of the *Guardian*), 30 September 1993, attached to McLachlan to Dymphna Clark, 6 October 1993, Dymphna Clark Papers, NLA, MS 9873, Series 10, Box 35, Folder 3.
46   McLachlan to Manne, 30 January 1994, copy in Dymphna Clark Papers, NLA, MS 9873, Series 10, Box 35, Folder 3.
47   McLachlan to Dymphna Clark, 1 February 1994, Dymphna Clark Papers, NLA, MS 9873, Series 10, Box 35, Folder 3.
48   McLachlan, 'Over Manning' (letter), *Spectator*, 15 January 1994, p. 24; Johnson, 'Smart Alecs' (rejoinder to McLachlan), *Spectator*, 22 January 1994, p. 22; Johnson, 'Blood on the wattle', review of Michael Cathcart, *Manning Clark's History of Australia*, abridgement, *Times Literary Supplement*, 13 May 1994, p. 25; McLachlan, 'Manning Clark's History of Australia' (letter), *Times Literary Supplement*, 3 June 1994, for quotation see p. 17.
49   Peter Craven, 'Clark cacophony revisited', *Australian*, 25 May 1994, p. 29.
50   Ryan, 'The Charge of the Lightweight Brigade', p. 230.

The overlay of personal abuse in the wars of words between McLachlan and his English opponents clouded the issues at stake in Australia's History Wars. Yet the British reaction did show that linking republicanism with Brit-bashing only served to provoke an equally unseemly Aussie-bashing. Little was accomplished by rubbishing the other, except to show that feelings ran high on both sides. But the dispute did illustrate some of the fault lines surrounding the Australian History Wars. One was the notion, forcefully expressed by Ryan (following Véliz), that Volume 5:

> portray[ed] an Australia teetering on the brink of bloody social revolution, groaning under the yoke of immoral British imperialism, sinking into a repulsive embourgeoisement, and finally in danger of vanishing beneath a dustbowl created by the rapacious squatters and their introduced allies the rabbits.[51]

Such a depiction was at odds with the countervailing notion, espoused by conservatives, that Australia was remarkably free of turmoil and had a history to be proud of. To suggest otherwise was to own up to a history of abject failure, and this was a charge that Johnson (as well as Ryan) pressed home. With Johnson, the implication was that only Australians could be so hopeless as to have so thoroughly fouled their own nest. At the same time, the stark us-or-them sentiments expressed by Keating precluded the possibility that one could be unequivocally Australian and yet retain a regard for British heritage—a point identified by Kenneth Minogue (1930–2013), a conservative Australian political scientist based at the London School of Economics.[52] In Britain, as in Australia, allegiances in the History Wars were defined in ideological partisan terms.

Whatever else it was or was not, the exposure of the Ryan–Clark controversy in the English press demonstrated that it was more than a parochial Australian affair. It reached well beyond Australia's shores and had a two-hemisphere dimension. Appleyard and Johnson made sure of that.

* * *

---

51   Ryan, 'Manning Clark', pp. 199–200.
52   Kenneth Minogue, 'Whingeing on about Aussies and Poms', review of Michael Cathcart, *Manning Clark's History of Australia,* abridgement, *Times,* 28 March 1994, p. 39.

Closer to home, the ghost of Clark continued as a *bête noire* of the right long after the dust had settled on the Ryan affair. On 24 August 1996 the Brisbane *Courier-Mail* caused a furore by (falsely) alleging that the Soviet Union had awarded Clark the Order of Lenin for knowingly serving its Australian operations or, at the very least, being an 'agent of influence'.[53] The *Courier-Mail*'s campaign backfired, precisely because it was so obviously a vindictive beat-up, but it showed the lengths that some were prepared to go in attempting to destroy Clark's credibility. The Order of Lenin allegations flared up again the following year when journalist Peter Kelly, who had instigated the stoush, resumed hostilities in the pages of the *Australian*.[54] The war of words gained extra imputus a few weeks later with the publication of Humphrey McQueen's rebuttal of the *Courier-Mail*'s allegation in his book *Suspect History*.[55] Ryan was no passive bystander but, rather, had foreknowledge that the original *Courier-Mail* attack was afoot.[56] Dymphna recalled that the *Courier-Mail* affair was

> very, very difficult [for me]; very, very disturbing; very distressing. But I'd had, in a way, a sort of rehearsal three years earlier when *Quadrant* started this rampage against Manning by publishing that great long article by Peter Ryan, so I'd [already] been through the mill.[57]

The *Courier-Mail*'s beat-up was but a continuation of the serial denigration of Clark. Six weeks earlier, Alexander Downer (the new minister for foreign affairs) entered the lists, at least symbolically, by refusing to present a boxed set of Clark's *History* to Georgetown University in Washington, DC; instead, he gave a copy of an (unspecified) biography of Sir John Monash.[58] Soon after, John Howard, by then the prime minister, declared his 'less than rapturous view of the Manning Clark view of Australian

---

53   *Courier-Mail*, 24 August 1996, pp. 1, 4–5 and *Courier-Mail Weekend*, 24 August 1996, pp. 1–4, with considerable follow-up over the next fortnight.
54   Peter Kelly, 'Manning, Marx and the medals', *Weekend Australian*, 1–2 March 1997, p. 26.
55   Humphrey McQueen, *Suspect History*, Adelaide: Wakefield Press, 1997; see also John McLaren, 'When hysteria becomes history', *Sydney Morning Herald*, 31 May 1997, 'Spectrum Books' section, p. 9s; Robert Manne, 'Battle for history's high ground', *Weekend Australia*, 7–8 June 1997, p. 23; Stephen Holt, 'The third man', Gerard Henderson, 'Get real, Clark was soft on the Soviet Union', and Andrew Field, 'Rampant ideology must be challenged', all in *Courier-Mail Weekend*, 20 September 1977, p. 9.
56   McKenna, *An Eye for Eternity*, 691. There are two files of newspaper clippings on the subject in the Ryan Papers, NLA, MS 9897, Series 6, Box 11, Folders 10 and 11.
57   Dymphna Clark, interviewed by Heather Rusden, 13 February 1997 (starting at 23.00 minutes), NLA, ORAL TRC 3548, available at: nla.gov.au/nla.obj-217338911/listen.
58   Don Watson, 'History according to Alexander Downer' (letter), *Weekend Australian*, 15–16 June 1996, p. 20; David McNicoll, 'Opinion', *Bulletin*, 25 June 1996, p. 26.

history'; insisting that 'the balance sheet of our history is one of heroic achievement'.[59] Howard and Clark were at one on a fundamental issue in dismissing 'any suggestion of Australian subservience' to Britain, but in every other respect they diverged.[60] In retirement, Howard wrote a massive and laudatory history of the Menzies era.[61] Although there was little chronological overlap in their accounts, given that Volume 6 of the *History* went little beyond 1935, Howard is diametrically at odds with Clark's views of Menzies, as he was with Clark trying 'to generate a sense of pessimism about Australia'.[62]

In referring to 'the balance sheet of our history', Howard was echoing Geoffrey Blainey's 1993 Latham Lecture, which deprecated what he termed the 'black-armband' view of Australian history and its association with Clark. Blainey's exact wording was:

> My friend and undergraduate teacher, Manning Clark, who was almost the official historian in 1988, ha[s] done much to spread the gloomy view *and also* the compassionate view with his powerful prose and his Old Testament phrases [my emphasis].[63]

The published version of the lecture in *Quadrant* had little impact until appropriated by Howard, who had just been elected prime minister. As Blainey recalled, the phrase 'black-armband history' then 'took off like a rocket'.[64] But it was a selective appropriation because Howard concentrated on Clark's gloom and simply ignored what Blainey had said about his compassion. As the 1990s unfolded, it became increasingly evident that two visions of Australia were in conflict. Both had their prime minister—Keating and Howard—and each was identified with an historian (Blainey and Clark, respectively).

---

59 Quoted in Anna Clark, 'Politicians using History', *Australian Journal of Politics and History*, 56:1 (2010): pp. 120–31, specifically p. 120, doi.org/10.1111/j.1467-8497.2010.01545.x; Macintyre and Clark, *The History Wars*, p. 50.
60 Stuart Ward, 'Fellow Britons?' *Meanjin Quarterly*, vol. 63, no. 3, 2004, pp. 56–64, specifically p. 56.
61 John Howard, *The Menzies Era: The Years that Shaped Modern Australia*, Sydney: HarperCollins Publishers, 2014.
62 Quoted in Craig Johnstone, 'Howard raps Clark's "negative" history', *Courier-Mail*, 31 August 1996, p. 1.
63 Geoffrey Blainey, 'Drawing up a Balance Sheet of Our History', *Quadrant*, vol. 37, nos 7–8, July–August 1993, pp. 10–15, specifically p. 11.
64 Quoted in Richard Allsop, *Geoffrey Blainey: Writer, Historian, Controversialist*, Melbourne: Monash University Publishing, 2019, p. 191; Macintyre and Clark, *The History Wars*, p. 132.

Figure 8. Paul Keating and John Howard squaring off.

Two visions of Australia were in conflict during the 1990s. Both had their prime minister, and each was identified with an historian—Manning Clark and Geoffrey Blainey, respectively.

Source. © Peter Nicholson (Rubbery Figures Pty Ltd) 2003 (nicholsoncartoons.com.au/). Reproduced with permission.

Howard's view of history largely prevailed because he was able to represent Keating's social engineering as a 'heist'—an 'attempt to rewrite history in the service of a partisan political cause'[65]—and he proceeded to appeal to a political constituency himself. Both Howard and Blainey embrace the notion of 'the balance sheet of history' because it gives the impression of judiciously weighing the pros and cons of a given situation, thereby occupying a moderate middle ground. But as historical geographer Alan Lester points out, the balance-sheet approach needs to be discarded because it 'makes "benefits" that worked very unevenly seem universal, while it reduces "costs" to specific episodes rather than systematic features of imperial rule'.[66] Notwithstanding, Howard emerged as the defender of the nation and its values and in this he was aided and abetted by 'a genuine hunger in the community for an uncomplicated and positive historical narrative that could serve as a source of national communion'.[67] His 'battlers', many of whom had previously voted Labor, displaced

---

65 Quoted in Ben Goldsmith, 'A question of inference', *Brisbane Review*, September 1996, pp. 3–4 (I owe this reference to Clive Moore).
66 Alan Lester, 'Time to Throw Out the Balance Sheet', *Snapshots of Empire*, 26 January 2016, accessible at: blogs.sussex.ac.uk/snapshotsofempire/2016/01/26/time-to-throw-out-the-balance-sheet/. I owe this reference to Nicholas Hoare.
67 Mark McKenna, 'The History Anxiety', in Alison Bashford and Stuart Macintyre (eds), *The Cambridge History of Australia*, Melbourne: Cambridge University Press, 2013, vol. 2, pp. 561–80, specifically p. 579.

Keating's 'true believers' in the hustings. At the same time, Howard appropriated concepts of the left, such as mateship, to further his own agenda.[68] He was also the only extant Australian prime minister not to attend the apology to Indigenous Australians for the Stolen Generations in 2008. His attitude, as Ann Curthoys puts it, was that 'anything bad that happened was long ago ... has little or nothing to do with us now'.[69] The argument here is that contemporary white Australians had nothing to do with injustices towards Aboriginal peoples personally and therefore they bear no *individual* responsibility. But if those same people extol the virtues of British civilisation and see themselves as heirs to this tradition, as does Howard, then they bear a measure of *inherited* responsibility to address those past injustices. To put it another way, the 'three-cheers' view of Australian history is a means of evading any sort of culpability.

The irony is that during the 1950s the radical nationalist historians of left-wing persuasion had propagated a 'rosy' view of Australian history, which Clark had challenged in his ANU inaugural lecture.[70] By the early 1960s, the landscape had changed and calls for a more overtly critical view of Australian history were coming from the political right. An influential collection of essays (*Australian Civilization*), covering a broad spectrum of Australia life and affairs, appeared in 1962. Clark was one of the contributors. The editor was Peter Coleman (1928–2019), a prominent journalist (including stints as editor of the *Bulletin* and *Quadrant*), social critic and later a Liberal Party politician, who concluded his introductory chapter by saying that 'signs of real maturity are ... clearly apparent in the growing willingness to criticize Australian life frankly and firmly, to see it clearly and wholly with all its limitations'.[71] By the 1980s there had been another about-turn in political alignments over the country's past, and conservatives were now taking the rosy view and condemning the left for tarnishing the Australian achievement with its pessimism and recriminations.

---

68   Judith Brett, 'Relaxed and Comfortable: The Liberal Party's Australia', *Quarterly Essay*, no. 19, 2005, pp. 1–79, specifically pp. 35–36; Allsop, *Geoffrey Blainey*, p. 202.
69   Ann Curthoys, 'History in the Howard Era', talk to the Professional Historians' Association of New South Wales, 19 July 2006 (p. 7 of typescript), available at: www.phansw.org.au/wp-content/uploads/2012/11/CurthoysHistoryintheHowardEra.pdf.
70   Manning Clark, 'Re-writing Australian History', in T.A.G. Hungerford (ed.), *Australian Signpost: An Anthology*, Melbourne: F.W. Cheshire, 1956, pp. 130–43.
71   Peter Coleman, 'Introduction: The New Australia', in Coleman (ed.), *Australian Civilization: A Symposium*, Melbourne: F.W. Cheshire, 1962, pp. 1–11, specifically p. 11; see also Allsop, *Geoffrey Blainey*, pp. 191–92.

Figure 9. John Howard on history, facts and dates, 5 July 2006.
Source. © Peter Nicholson (Rubbery Figures Pty Ltd) 2006 (nicholsoncartoons.com.au/). Reproduced with permission.

In reclaiming the ideological high ground and regaining ownership of the national narrative, as well as dismantling much of Keating's legacy, Howard continued to express his scorn at Clark being the darling of the cultural left and to condemn his pernicious influence in the propagation of black-armband history—which was to exaggerate Clark's role and reach.[72] Howard's counter-revolution has aptly been described as the work of 'the cultural traditionalist as populist',[73] which enabled him to give the impression of occupying a moderate and righteous middle ground. Keating did have a vision, if clumsily applied in places, whereas Howard weighed into the History Wars with an insular and rigid chauvinism. His counter-revolution involved a mindless and cloying patriotism in which a whitewash of the nation's past and a defence of the nation's honour were one and the same. It carried the clear implication that all decent people and responsible citizens subscribed to his complacent brand of patriotism. The rest were beyond redemption. Keating was just as intolerant in his own way, even though his Big Picture was presented as a discourse of national unity. In Don Watson's words, 'If you couldn't see the big picture, you didn't belong'.[74] Such is the stuff of History Wars anywhere, and not just the Australian variety; they are about politics rather than about history with each side attempting to imprint its own ideological stamp, often by whatever means.

---

72   The considerable literature on Howard's part in the Australian History Wars includes: Sean Brawley, '"A comfortable and relaxed past": John Howard and the "Battle for History": The First Phase–February 1992 to March 1996', *Electronic Journal of Australian and New Zealand History*, 1997, pp. 13–25, available at: webarchive.nla.gov.au/awa/20070904044916/http://www.jcu.edu.au/aff/history/articles/brawley.htm; Andrew Bonnell and Martin Crotty, 'Australia's History under Howard, 1996–2007', *Annals of the American Academy of Political and Social Science,* vol. 617, no. 1, 2008, pp. 149–65, doi.org/10.1177/0002716207310818.
73   Paul Kelly, *The March of Patriots: The Struggle for Modern Australia,* Melbourne: MUP, 2009, pp. 328–40.
74   Watson, *Recollections of a Bleeding Heart,* p. 92; see also Brett, 'Relaxed and Comfortable', pp. 20–21.

8

Reflection: Peter Ryan's Motives

> My essay arose from a troubled, deep concern about the survival of historical truth in my country. Only an advanced victim of *paranoia politica* could find there any political motivation.
>
> Peter Ryan (1994)[1]

> We all know of examples … of people who could scarcely rise from their beds in the morning were it not for the energy given to them by their hatreds and the political activities which express them.
>
> Raimond Gaita (1992)[2]

Peter Ryan attacked Manning Clark for a variety of reasons, each adding its weight to the others. As well as sheer vindictiveness, there was professional jealousy, feelings of marginalisation and the insecurity that goes with it, a corresponding desire to restore his public profile, political differences and a need to renounce his part in bringing out successive volumes of the *History*. Ryan launched his attacks in the most public manner possible and in ways that would maximise the damage to Clark.

---

1   Peter Ryan, 'The Charge of the Lightweight Brigade', in his *Lines of Fire: Manning Clark & Other Writings*, ed. A.K. Macdougall, Binalong, NSW: Clarion Editions, 1997, pp. 222–34, specifically p. 225.
2   Raimond Gaita, 'The Political Responsibilities of Intellectuals: Intellectual Combatants', *Quadrant*, vol. 36, no. 6, June 1992, pp. 23–25, specifically p. 25. Gaita came to Australia with his family as one of Hitler's émigrés in 1950 as a three-year-old. He is a prominent Australian philosopher and public intellectual. Of his many books, *Romulus, My Father*, Melbourne: Text Publishing, 1998, breaks the mould in that an autobiography-cum-family-history seldom enters the canon so promptly. The book has also been made into a film.

Some of Ryan's grievances stemmed from Clark not being an 'easy' author. He was unpunctual and in the later stages of the *History* Ryan was justifiably concerned that Clark's heavy schedule of speaking commitments was distracting him from completing Volume 6.[3] When manuscripts did finally arrive, they had 'every technical blemish known to the editorial craft … strewn thick upon his pages', requiring expensive editorial input.[4] Clark then resisted suggestions for textual changes.[5] There were also Clark's frequent requests for cash advances in the early years, although Ryan might also have mentioned that he declined to take 'full advantage' of Clark's offer to forego royalties on the money-losing commemorative edition of the *History*.[6] To cap it off was Clark's 'duplicity' in entering into informal but unauthorised discussions with other publishers concerning their acquiring the paperback rights of the *History*.[7] Ryan was within his rights to be annoyed on that score, even if they did provide an opportunity to off-load the *History*.

On quite another level, Clark's emotional neediness meant that he required constant mollycoddling: 'He seemed deeply, at times almost incapacitatingly insecure', remarked Ryan.[8] Shortly before the publication of Volume 1, Ryan had an early taste of how petulantly demanding Clark could be. He was 'caught rather off balance' by an 'agitated' phone call from a distraught and angry Clark, demanding to know why he had not received an advance copy. It turned out that Clark had been misinformed by another publisher that Volume 1 was already in print. He kicked up an inordinate fuss and was not easily mollified, thus providing an early warning that he was going to be a high-maintenance author.[9]

* * *

---

3   Peter Ryan, 'Manning Clark', in his *Lines of Fire,* pp. 179–214, specifically p. 203; see also Tim Curnow to Ryan, 5 November 1984, Records of Melbourne University Press (hereafter MUP Records), 2003.0129, Unit 21 (vol. 6). For an idea of Clark's schedule of engagements, see Brian Matthews, *Manning Clark: A Life,* Sydney: Allen & Unwin, 2008, p. 389.
4   Ryan, 'Manning Clark', p. 195.
5   Ryan, 'Manning Clark', pp. 195–96.
6   Ryan to Clark, 17 September and 24 September 1987, and Clark to Ryan, 21 September 1987, all in MUP Records, 2003.0129, Unit 21 (vol. 6); Mark McKenna, *An Eye for Eternity: The Life of Manning Clark,* Melbourne: Miegunyah Press, 2011, p. 614.
7   For example, Ryan to Clark, 25 June 1969, MUP Records, 2003.0129, Unit 20 (vol. 2); Peter Ryan, *Final Proof: Memoirs of a Publisher,* Sydney: Quadrant Books, 2010, p. 135.
8   Ryan, 'Manning Clark', p. 201.
9   Ryan to Halstead Press, 22 August 1962; Halstead Press to Ryan, 23 August 1962; all in MUP Records, 2003.0129, Unit 20 (vol. 1); Ryan to Clark, 27 August 1962, Manning Clark Papers, National Library of Australia (hereafter NLA), MS 7550, Series 18, Box 156, Folder 2.

Ryan had gripes of a more personal nature and these stemmed from another of his quirks of character—namely, his admiration for practical, self-made people like himself. In this regard he presents a contrast to Clark, who had never been other than a student, a school teacher and an academic. Ryan prided himself on his own 'can do' attitude and the 'will do' bustle of Melbourne University Press (hereafter MUP), and he was justly proud of his war service record. Ryan warmed to other ex-servicemen and he could be judgmental towards those who hadn't been in uniform.[10] That was the case with Clark, whose grand mal epilepsy precluded him from being enlisted. It is not surprising that Ryan was put out by Clark's seeming indifference to his singular war record.[11] He was also horrified by Clark's depictions of WWII in one of his popular books, but gave him no credit for visiting Gallipoli and other WWI battlefields with a view 'to do the impossible—to evoke Ypres, the Somme & Pozieres'.[12]

There were also Ryan's increasingly negative feelings about academic life and academics generally. His varied background in the school of hard knocks helps explain his disdain for 'the sheltered workshop mentality and habit of Australian academics',[13] whom he considered had 'no notion of the glory of soaring in the real world, nor of its perils'.[14] It was anathema to Ryan that anyone could spend their lives in 'the leisurely corridors of academe' as a member of a 'narrow priesthood of the professionals', bereft of 'experience in worldly affairs', insulated from 'the gritty world of real work', revelling in the 'blackberry thicket of academic sniping and spite', and reduced to shuffling papers rather than 'actually *making* something'.[15] The irony is that Ryan's hostility towards academia may, in part, have been the resentment at his own dependence on the academy and its occupants.[16] He fulminated against university presses for being what he described as '"thesis mills" serving academic ambitions for promotion and

---

10   Ryan, *Final Proof*, pp. 52, 60–61, 116–17, 124–25, 155–57, 166.
11   Ryan, 'Manning Clark', p. 185.
12   McKenna, *An Eye for Eternity*, p. 294 ('Only when Clark saw the lie of the land could he begin to understand its past'), pp. 468, 690; Stephen Holt, *A Short History of Manning Clark*, Sydney: Allen & Unwin, 1999, for quotation see p. 209; Tom Griffiths, *The Art of Time Travel: Historians and their Craft*, Melbourne: Black Inc., 2016, pp. 11–12.
13   Peter Ryan, 'A Reply to my Critics', in his *Lines of Fire*, pp. 214–22, specifically p. 220.
14   Ryan, 'The Charge of the Lightweight Brigade', p. 233.
15   Ryan, *Final Proof*, pp. 37, 45, 72.
16   That said, some academics place more stress on Ryan's positive qualities and still hold him in good regard—e.g. Robert Wallace, email to author, 4 May 2016; John Poynter, 'Peter Ryan the Publisher', *Quadrant*, vol. 60, no. 3, March 2016, pp. 58–59; Brenda Niall, *Life Class: The Education of a Biographer*, Melbourne: MUP, 2007, pp. 149–50.

a sort of extravagant public relations adjunct to their universities'.[17] A pet hate was being approached to publish revised (and sometimes unrevised) PhD theses:

> How many dutiful young doctors, theses limp in hand, have waited in the ante-rooms of publishers, hoping to learn that alchemy can convert their academic goose into a swan—preferably one winged between hard covers. Persistence and departmental subsidy swings it with awful oftenness. Awful? Ask any bookseller, any librarian; any general reader.[18]

In his view, academic historians had 'turned history into a private game for salaried professionals'[19] and he was apt to treat them in a belittling fashion. When Peter McPhee was working on his biography of scientist R.D. Wright (1907–1990), McPhee sought explicit approval for quotation rights from everyone he had interviewed. The only one to decline was 'that self-important cockerel Peter Ryan'.[20] On an earlier occasion he was approached by Geoffrey Gray for information on the role of anthropologists within DORCA (the Directorate of Research and Civil Affairs) during WWII. Without warning, Ryan launched into 'an unasked for' and irrelevant tirade against the University of Melbourne anthropologist Donald Thomson (1901–1970) that shocked his unsuspecting listener.[21] Even when being helpful to researchers, Ryan could still be disconcerting—on one occasion by his curious combination of anti-intellectualism *and* deference to academic status when being interviewed in 2004 by Sylvia Martin for her biography of librarian Ida Leeson (1885–1964). Ryan thought highly of Leeson, who had been his colleague at DORCA; without Leeson's intercession *Fear Drive My Feet*

---

17 Ryan to Tony Eggleton (press secretary to the prime minister), 8 February 1968, Ryan Papers, NLA, MS 9897, Series 1, Box 1, Folder 1.
18 Peter Ryan, 'Young historians wasting their time trying to milk the bull', *Age*, 14 July 1990, p. Extra 2 ('As I Please' column).
19 Peter Ryan, 'As Lost as Burke and Wills', *Quadrant*, vol. 44, nos 1–2, January–February 2000, pp. 119–20, specifically p. 120.
20 Peter McPhee, discussion with author, Melbourne, 7 December 2015, and email to author, 11 June 2016; McPhee, *'Pansy': A Life of Roy Douglas Wright*, Melbourne: MUP, 1999. McPhee held a personal chair in history at the University of Melbourne and ended his career as provost.
21 Geoffrey Gray, emails to author, 30 July 2018 and 14 August 2018. At the time, Gray had a grant from the Australian War Memorial to study DORCA. He is now an adjunct professor of history at the University of Queensland.

might never have been published.²² The interview was conducted in the company of John Legge, an old friend of Ryan's from their days at DORCA, and Martin went away with decidedly ambivalent feelings:

> [Ryan] was friendly, if slightly obsequious, rather pointedly calling me Dr Martin all the time. I now wonder whether he was being mockingly deferential. His talk was full of racy stories about life at the Directorate—all a bit sleazy. John Legge was a quiet man who tried to tone Peter down and I didn't feel he was trying to impress me, unlike Peter. That said, he did give me his time and was generous with it.²³

The wonder is that he stuck with his job as a university publisher for 25 years when he deplored its *raison d'être* and harboured such an obvious prejudice against academics as a group, which was fully reciprocated. Symptomatic of Ryan's anti-academic attitudes are the pointed references to some of his favourite MUP authors being non-academics.²⁴

That Clark and Ryan were not cut from the same cloth only served to fuel Ryan's growing disenchantment, especially when he (Ryan) had capacities for unqualified friendship and deadly enmity in equal measures, with little sign of a middle ground. He was loyal to his friends, about whom he wrote with great affection,²⁵ and Clark's insulting remarks about W. Macmahon Ball, whom Ryan revered but whom Clark dismissed as a yesterday's man, were intolerable.²⁶ Yet despite his qualms, Ryan locked himself into a deadly embrace and never discussed with Clark his concerns about the *History*, resulting in 25 years of largely suppressed resentments finally coming to the boil and overflowing onto the pages of *Quadrant*. Ryan did say that Clark's *History* 'could, without gross exaggeration, be called a daily preoccupation of my life' at MUP.²⁷

---

22 Sylvia Martin, *Ida Leeson: A Life: Not a Blue-Stocking Lady*, Sydney: Allen & Unwin, 2006, p. 158; Peter Ryan, 'Preface' (2000), to *Fear Drive my Feet*, Melbourne: Text Classics, 2015, pp. 7–10. Ryan's esteem for Leeson—'the essential "bigness" of this tiny women', as he put it—is heart-warmingly expressed in his book *Brief Lives*, Sydney: Duffy & Snellgrove, 2004, pp. 139–52.
23 Sylvia Martin, email to author, 22 June 2018. J.D. Legge (1921–2016) was Foundation Professor of History (later Emerita Professor) at Monash University.
24 Peter Ryan, 'Elsie Webster, Scholar' (1994), in his *Lines of Fire*, pp. 91–94; Ryan, *Final Proof*, pp. 85, 130–31, 152, 156–64, 169.
25 See his selection of essays on such 'Men of Character', in his *Lines of Fire*, pp. 119–76; and Ryan, *Brief Lives*, passim.
26 Ryan, 'Manning Clark', p. 183; see also Manning Clark, *The Quest for Grace*, Ringwood: Viking, 1990, pp. 22–25. Clark was not alone among contemporaries in feeling that Ball had failed to realise his academic potential. See Ai Kobayashi, *W. Macmahon Ball: Politics for the People*, Melbourne: Australian Scholarly Publishing, 2013, pp. 197–99.
27 Ryan, 'Manning Clark', p. 181.

It became an increasingly disagreeable preoccupation. It bears mentioning that Ryan stayed away from the launch of Volume 6 'and an association of fifty years came to an end'.[28] 'Manning was quite upset about that', recalled Dymphna, adding that this was one of a number of episodes that led to a cooling of Clark's friendship with Ryan. 'There were many indications', she remarked in retrospect, that Ryan was becoming 'very sour' towards Manning.[29]

* * *

A further set of reasons why Ryan turned on Clark—namely, a mixture of personal grievances, professional insecurities and political antagonisms—were shrewdly identified by Brian Matthews in a newspaper interview:

> I think he is a very disappointed man. He never did satisfactorily answer the question of why he blew the whistle so late. Ryan was a man who fought for his country. He wrote a very good book about it. But he didn't write anything comparable again. He's a man who always moved in intellectual, academic circles. But it was always somehow in reflected glory.
>
> Then Clark dies and has this enormous funeral. And where is Ryan? No longer director of Melbourne University Press. No longer has his column in 'The Age'. He is, as he might see it, rejected by a society which looks like being ruled by the Labor Party until the millenium, a party whose philosophies he does not like in a country he fought famously for, which no longer seems to acknowledge him but which seems to have established Clark as an icon.[30]

---

28 Ryan, *Final Proof,* p. 139.
29 Dymphna Clark, interviewed by Heather Rusden, 13 February 1997 (74.04 minutes), NLA, ORAL TRC 3548, available at: nla.gov.au/nla.obj-217338911/listen; Sebastian Clark, telephone discussion with author, 14 July 2020.
30 Quoted in Fiona Capp, 'London Calling', *Age,* 2 July 1994, p. 8. Ryan threatened to sue when Matthews branded him a frustrated and embittered one-trick pony. See Ryan's annotations (12 September 1994) on Matthews to Ryan, 4 August 1994; see also Christopher Sexton to Ryan, 11 July 1994 and Ryan to Sexton, 14 July 1994, all in Ryan Papers, NLA, MS 9897, Series 6, Box 10, Folder 5. Matthews and Ryan had a 'history'. Ryan had published Matthews's first book, *The Receding Wave: Henry Lawson's Prose* (1972). Matthews had promised Ryan first right of refusal for his next book, a factionalised biography of Lawson's mother, and refuse it he did: '[Ryan] was rather scathing and "wondered" what I would think of it in years to come (i.e. by implication, when I'd "matured" a bit)'. Matthews, emails to author, 26 July 2014 and 4 July 2018. The manuscript was not only published, as *Louisa,* by McPhee Gribble in 1987, but won literary prizes and was twice republished. The editors of the *Australian Book Review* 'liked *Louisa* so much' that they reprinted its opening pages: 'And Now, the Book…', *Australian Book Review,* no. 97 (December 1987–January 1988), pp. 8–10.

As Matthews implies, Ryan could hardly have been indifferent to the honours bestowed in abundance upon Clark. In 1975 Clark became a Companion of the Order of Australia and in 1980 was Australian of the Year. As well, his books won several literary awards,[31] and he had honorary doctorates from Melbourne, Newcastle and Sydney universities—ironically given his increasing disdain of the academy. He was also one of the writers whom Louis Kahan sketched for *Meanjin Quarterly*.[32] A symposium was held in Melbourne in 1979 to discuss Volume 4 of the *History*, and the year after his death Carl Bridge organised a full-scale seminar on his life and work at the University of New England, the proceedings of which were also published.[33] There are biographies of Clark by Stephen Holt (1999), Brian Matthews (2008) and Mark McKenna (2011) and the quasi-biography by Humphrey McQueen (*Suspect History*, 1997), not to mention Holt's earlier intellectual biography (*Manning Clark and Australian History, 1915–1963*, 1982). He and Brian Fitzpatrick are joint subjects of an edited collection (*Against the Grain*, 2007). Two collections of his correspondence have appeared—*Dear Kathleen, Dear Manning* (1996) and *Ever, Manning* (2008). He has an entry in *The Oxford History of Australia* and several brief appearances in *The Cambridge History of Australia* (whereas Ryan is mentioned in neither publication).[34]

At ANU, a chair of history was named in his honour as well as a building: the Manning Clark Centre. The structure was demolished in a major redevelopment of the Copland area of ANU in 2017 but the name has been perpetuated with the erection of the imposing Manning Clark Hall in the adjacent Kambri Precinct of the campus.[35] In 2015, a Manning Clark Centenary seminar honoured 'Manning Clark's contribution and legacy as a publicly engaged historian'. Elsewhere in Canberra, he and Dymphna

---

31 Volume 1 shared the Ernest Scott Prize and Volume 2 was the outright winner. It was the same for the Barbara Ramsden Award with Volume 3 sharing the prize and Volume 4 having it all to itself. As well, Volume 2 won the Rothman's Moomba Festival Award for Australian Literature and the Australian Literary Society Gold Medal; Volume 3 shared *The Age* Book of the Year Award; Volume 4 won the New South Wales Premier's Award, 1979; and Volume 6 took out the Gold Banjo Award.
32 Louis Kahan [sketch of Manning Clark], *Meanjin Quarterly*, vol. 32, no. 3, 1973, p. 244; Kahan, *Australian Writers: The Face of Literature,* Melbourne: MUP, 1981, portrait 7.
33 Ailsa McLeary (ed.), 'Manning Clark and Australian Historiography', *Australia 1888,* vol. 3, 1979, pp. 4–73; Carl Bridge (ed.), *Manning Clark: Essays on his Place in History,* Melbourne: MUP, 1994.
34 Carl Bridge, 'Manning Clark', in Graeme Davison, John Hirst and Stuart Macintyre (eds), *The Oxford Companion to Australian History,* Melbourne: Oxford University Press, 1998, pp. 128–29; Alison Bashford and Stuart Macintyre (eds), *The Cambridge History of Australia,* Melbourne: Cambridge University Press, 2013, vol. 1, pp. 179, 244 and vol. 2, pp. 180, 573, 574, 575.
35 'Manning Clark Hall officially opened at ANU', 12 March 2019, available at: www.anu.edu.au/news/all-news/manning-clark-hall-officially-opened-at-anu.

share a plaque on the Australian Capital Territory Honour Walk; a street has been named after him in the northern suburb of Franklin; and the family home has been converted into Manning Clark House, a non-profit organisation to promote Australian culture and history. One of its events is an annual Manning Clark Lecture.

By contrast, the honours bestowed on Ryan amount to a thoroughly merited Military Medal (and four service medals) as well as being Mentioned in Despatches for his wartime service in New Guinea; sharing *Quadrant*'s George Watson Essay Prize (with Geoffrey Partington), in 1987, for the best published essay on a political subject by an Australian citizen or resident of Australia;[36] and the short biography by John Tidey (*Ryan's Luck*, 2020). The 143-word note on Ryan in *The Australian Companion to Literature* is overshadowed by the 995-word essay on Clark in the same volume.[37] It is not as though Ryan's life was bereft of achievement—far from it—but more honours had come Clark's way and it clearly irked Ryan that he had contributed to Clark becoming something of a national celebrity. It got to the stage that, in 2009, Ryan just wished that Clark would disappear from sight and mind, and he beseeched his readers, 'Now could we all forget about Manning Clark? Anything more "yesterday" can hardly be imagined'.[38]

* * *

At the time, people did state that Ryan was politically motivated: 'I can only believe', said historian and family friend of the Clarks, David Fitzpatrick, 'that the whole thing is "political" & that Manning's place in it is merely "useful" but otherwise accidental [incidental?]'.[39] In the fraught History Wars setting, politicians on both sides entered the fray, reinforcing the polarised and divisive setting that the Ryan affair reflected.

---

36   'Announcement: The George Watson Essay Prize 1987: A Tie', *Quadrant*, vol. 32, nos 1–2, January–February 1988, p. 5; Peter Ryan, 'True Journalists' (1996), in his *Lines of Fire*, pp. 137–40, specifically p. 140; John Tidey, *Ryan's Luck: A Life of Peter Ryan MM*, Melbourne: Arcadia, 2020, pp. 92–93.
37   William Wilde, Joy Hooton and Barry Andrews (eds), *The Oxford Companion to Australian Literature*, 2nd edn, Melbourne: Oxford University Press, 1994, pp. 167–68 (Clark), p. 668 (Ryan).
38   Peter Ryan, 'Hollow Man of Yesterday', review of *Manning Clark: A Life*, by Brian Matthews, *Quadrant*, vol. 53, nos 1–2, January–February 2009, pp. 126–28, specifically p. 128.
39   For example, David [Fitzpatrick] to Dymphna Clark [September 1993], Dymphna Clark Papers, NLA, MS 9873, Series 10, Box 35, Folder 3; see also Humphrey McQueen, 'Manning Clark Revisited', *ABC Radio 24 Hours*, March 1994, pp. 55–58.

Paul Keating, by then prime minister, intervened on the very evening that Ryan's first *Quadrant* attack appeared in the bookshops, dismissing Clark's critics as being 'bitchy' and deploring their small-mindedness.

Lindsay Tanner of the Labor left faction put it explicitly in saying that Ryan's intervention:

> Was essentially a politically motivated attack which comes from what I would describe as the old Right within the Australian community, which has for a long time felt very keenly the lack of intellectuals in the literary and the historical arena on the right of the political spectrum. That part of the community has been keen to ensure that people such as Manning Clark, who has been seen to have essentially Left-oriented perspectives on Australian history in society, should be denigrated and torn down.[40]

Ryan strongly denied accusations of being politically motivated,[41] but the evidence says otherwise, especially when the environment at the time and his own politics are taken into account. He started as a 'young leftie' in the University of Melbourne Labour Club. Whether he was ever *really* a man of the left may be doubted in view of the fact that he was an ASIO snitch during the 1950s—he informed on Max Crawford, the history professor at Melbourne—which Ryan made light of when he was outed in 1999 in the *Age*.[42] He attributed his shift in political allegiance to the follies of the Whitlam Government, especially the granting of independence to the Territory of Papua New Guinea in 1975, and by 1986 he was referring to his 'total change of [political] outlook'.[43]

---

40   *Hansard* (House of Representatives), 1 September 1993, for quotation see p. 702; Fred Chaney to Dymphna Clark, 27 August [1993], Dymphna Clark Papers, NLA, MS 9873, Series 10, Box 35, Folder 2.
41   Ryan, 'The Charge of the Lightweight Brigade', p. 225.
42   Fay Anderson, *An Historian's Life: Max Crawford and the Politics of Academic Freedom*, Melbourne: MUP, 2005, pp. 295–96, 316 n.113. Ryan's cover was blown because his name was not redacted in Crawford's ASIO file. See Stuart Macintyre, 'Max Crawford: A Casualty of the Cold War', *Overland*, no. 155, 1999, pp. 19–22, specifically p. 22. The first volume of Ryan's ASIO file (NAA: A6119, 2616), shows that he was under surveillance from 1952, available at: recordsearch. naa.gov.au/SearchNRetrieve/Interface/ViewImage.aspx?B=3901342. Its later contents suggest a tacit understanding that Ryan would provide information, when asked, in return for ceasing to be a person of interest to the organisation.
43   Peter Ryan, 'End of the Dreamtime' (1986), in his *Lines of Fire*, pp. 101–11, for quotation see p. 105: Ryan, 'Humanity's Crimes', *Quadrant*, vol. 43, no. 3, March 1999, pp. 87–88, specifically p. 87; Ryan, 'Curtin, Chifley and Whitlam', *Quadrant*, vol. 59, nos 1–2, January–February 2015, pp. 143–44, specifically p. 144; Tidey, *Ryan's Luck*, p. 83.

Ryan's shift of allegiances happened when Clark was becoming more politically prominent in the wake of The Dismissal. There may well have been an element of jealousy as Clark stumped the countryside making a name for himself with what Ryan regarded as a pernicious message. Added to this was Clark's theatricality and his increasingly eccentric attire, worn in order to draw attention to himself in his contrived persona as the nation's sage.[44] Ryan sneered at Clark's studied façade, including the matching attire of Akubra hat, three-piece suit replete with pocket-watch and chain, boots and wide belt. The beard and the walking stick completed the picture. Wherever he appeared, everyone knew who he was. The trademark hat was a necessity as well as an affectation—to prevent sunburn and to avoid getting more cancer spots—but he also kept it on his head in quite unnecessary situations, such as dinner parties and at conference presentations.[45]

The attire added to Clark's messiah image. Frank Bongiorno has an explanation for his 'extraordinary career as national prophet and preacher from the early 1970s through to his death in 1991', while acknowledging that there does remain 'something odd about it all':

> How was it that in a country seen as secular-minded, egalitarian, democratic, informal and even anti-intellectual, Manning Clark—withhis searching spirituality, his well-honed biblical language and his cryptic allusions to the writings of Dostoyevsky and Lawrence—came to achieve this strange celebrity status? My own feeling is that the national stereotype itself is flawed; that many Australians of the 1970s and 1980s possessed a remarkably old-fashioned hunger for a dignified symbolism of nationhood that could be taken seriously by 'old' countries. How convenient to have found a man of such bearing and eloquence. Clark looked and sounded like many people's idea of an Old Testament prophet and yet under a famous hat that seemed glued to the bald dome of his head, he also cultivated the unlikely image of a simple boy from the Australian bush. Here was evidence that after the British Empire, Australia had a conscience and a soul. And his books showed it had a history.[46]

---

44   Ryan, 'Manning Clark', pp. 196–97.
45   Katerina and Axel Clark, interviewed by Susan Marsden, 19 June 2001, NLA, ORAL TRC 4770 (p. 6 of transcript); Carl Bridge, 'Manning Clark and the Ratbag Tradition', *Journal of Australian Studies*, vol. 21, nos 54–55, 1997, pp. 91–95, specifically p. 92, doi.org/10.1080/14443059709387341; Richard J. Evans, email to author, 26 August 2018.
46   Frank Bongiorno, review of *An Eye for Eternity*, by Mark McKenna, *Britain and the World*, vol. 6, no. 2, 2013, pp. 291–93, specifically p. 292.

The content of Clark's message both as an historian and as a public intellectual seriously annoyed Ryan, who loved his country,[47] and here was Clark telling him, or so he thought, that it was not worthy of his love. It never seemed to occur to Ryan that Clark also loved Australia, if in a different way. He had clearly forgotten that Clark, in 1964, had told him that Australia is 'the country I go on loving to distraction'.[48] Clark's Menzies-bashing offended Ryan in equal measure to his black-armband, gloom-and-doom view of Australian history, including that of Aboriginal dispossession, and what Ryan described as his 'glum depiction of [Australia as] a mob of born losers'.[49] Black-armband history was, in Ryan's view 'nationally insulting bunkum'.[50]

This is where Ryan's point of attack shifted from the person-cum-professional and locked into the History Wars. Ryan considered Clark's depiction of history as part and parcel of a 'sour revisionism' that Australia had a shameful past, and he disagreed with Clark's glorification, as he saw it, of radicalism.[51] As Ryan later remarked:

> My objection to much recent ideology-driven history is that it tends to leach away our self-respect. You and I are portrayed as guilty successors to generations whose lives were devoted to doing little but harm, ancestors for whom no good word can be found … This depressing and debilitating presentation of our history leads to nowhere, except perhaps to some great southern wailing wall.[52]

Or take Ryan peddling the view that there had not been 'a single race riot' in Australian history, quite forgetting Clark's description of the 1861 Lambing Flat riots in Volume 4 of the *History*, which he claimed to have read on at least three occasions.[53]

---

47 Ryan, 'Manning Clark', p. 186.
48 Roslyn Russell (ed.), *Ever, Manning: Selected Letters of Manning Clark, 1938–1993*, Sydney: Allen & Unwin, 2008, p. 201 (Clark to Ryan, 10 February 1964); see also McKenna, *An Eye for Eternity*, p. 557.
49 Ryan, 'A Reply to my Critics', p. 214.
50 Ryan, 'A Reply to my Critics', p. 214.
51 Ryan, 'Manning Clark', pp. 199–200, 212–13; Ryan, 'The Charge of the Lightweight Brigade', pp. 229–30.
52 Peter Ryan, 'Geoffrey Blainey's History' (1995), in his *Lines of Fire*, pp. 87–90, for quotation see p. 89.
53 Peter Ryan, 'Immigration', *Quadrant*, vol. 42, no. 5, May 1998, pp. 87–88, specifically p. 87; Ryan, 'Manning Clark', p. 213; C.M.H. Clark, *A History of Australia*, Volume 4: *The Earth Abideth Forever, 1851–1888*, Melbourne: MUP, 1978, pp. 128–34, 143, 350–52 278–82.

Ryan's bland and sanitised view of Australian history precluded any meaningful acknowledgment of the darker episodes in the country's past. Not for him the notion that 'there is, of course, much to be bleak about'.[54] Yet Ryan had his own version of black-armband history, except that it worked in reverse. He saw a meritorious past but surmised that the country was going to the dogs in a deplorable present—the standard conservative language of cultural and moral decline. The paradox with Clark, as Peter Coleman observed, was 'a gloom-and-failure-sodden view of the Australian past, while often holding a simple opportunistic "Progressive" view of our future'.[55] Ryan's unease only deepened when confronted, in 1981, by ALP attempts to have Volume 5 associated with the party by way of joint ventures and launches on Labor premises.[56] None of this excuses Ryan's attempt, in his capacity of director of MUP, to arrange a hostile article in the *Age*, based on the proofs of Volume 5.[57] It was an explicit act of disloyalty to both his author *and* employer that undermines Ryan's claim that 'I was … paid to do my damnedest for the Press, and I did'.[58] For his part, Clark was becoming concerned, yet professed to remain mystified, about Ryan's political repositioning and his anti-intellectualism.[59]

Ryan's distaste for Clark's politics, and the growing public stature that accompanied his public appearances, together with his contempt for Clark's view of Australian history, were integral to the *Quadrant* attacks. Ryan, the aggressor, then clothes himself in the garb of victimhood, never ceasing to complain that his 'polite' observations received a veritable flood of abuse. But there is another way of looking at it. Far from being

---

54 Michael Sexton, 'It's war, and the rest is history', review of *The History Wars*, by Stuart Macintyre and Anna Clark, *Sydney Morning Herald Spectrum*, 6 September 2003, p. 15, available at: www.smh.com.au/entertainment/books/the-history-wars-20030906-gdhcbm.html.
55 For example, Ryan, 'End of the Dreamtime' (1986), in his *Lines of Fire*, pp. 101–11; Ryan, 'A Better Place', *Quadrant*, vol. 47, nos 1–2, January–February 2003, pp. 119–20; John McLaren, *Free Radicals on the Left in Postwar Melbourne*, Melbourne: Australian Scholarly Publishing, 2003, for quotation see p. 218.
56 Ryan to Clark, 9 February 1981; David Combe (National Secretary of the ALP) to Ryan, 9 June 1981, and Ryan to Combe, 15 June 1981, in MUP Records, 2003.0129, Unit 21 (vol. 5).
57 McKenna, *An Eye for Eternity*, pp. 596–97.
58 Ryan, 'A Reply to my Critics', p. 217. It transpires that Ryan cost MUP sales in the mid-1970s, at a time of credit squeeze, by insisting on 30-day terms with booksellers, who then declined to stock MUP books. See Frank Bongiorno, 'The Road from Preston: *The Australian Colonists* and Ken Inglis's Explorations in Social History', in Peter Browne and Seumus Spark (eds), *'I Wonder': The Life and Work of Ken Inglis*, Melbourne: Monash University Publishing, 2020, pp. 216–39, specifically p. 227.
59 Susan Davies (ed.), *Dear Kathleen, Dear Manning: The Correspondence of Manning Clark and Kathleen Fitzpatrick, 1949–1990*, Melbourne: MUP, 1996, p. 113 (Clark to Fitzpatrick, July 1987).

8. REFLECTION

an act of 'civic courage', his increasingly strident *Quadrant* articles were written with the deliberate purpose of causing offence and distancing himself even further from the 'loquacious Left'. He needed to atone for being Clark's publisher. By vilifying his former author and the *History* so publicly and vehemently, Ryan confirmed where his political loyalties lay and contributed to the demolition of Clark's credibility in the eyes of the political right.

In short, Ryan's attack on Clark was a decidedly political intervention that can be explained by his change of allegiances and his need to reaffirm where his loyalties now lay; by his embrace of the 'three-cheers' school of history; and by a desire to absolve himself of responsibility for being Clark's publisher, along with the claim that his hands were tied in the matter. Perhaps he was even angling to become a columnist for *Quadrant*.

* * *

A final consideration is Ryan's need for notoriety and notice. He was not so much a prophet without a cause as a preacher without a pulpit. Like Clark, he had a 'passion to be a public figure',[60] but in 1993 he lost his audience upon the termination of his fortnightly by-line column in the *Age* ('As I Please'). This stemmed from the fallout from a potentially libellous column Ryan had written three months earlier about the incumbent prime minister's financial involvement in a piggery.[61] Much earlier, he had provided the 'Spy' column in the fortnightly magazine *Nation* and a restaurant column in the *Australian Financial Review*; he was not named as its author but that was known among the circle whose approval he valued.[62] He had also written for the *Australian*. His qualifications for these gigs were literary facility, an opinionated outlook and a determinedly independent stance on life and affairs. His employment with the *Age* stemmed from a need to 'balance' its progressive tone, and probably to stir up the readership for good measure, thus giving scope to the personalised

---

60 Ryan, 'Manning Clark', p. 202.
61 Ryan, 'Answers please, Mr PM!', *Age*, 16 January 1993, p. 2; see also Michael Baume (interjection), *Hansard* (Senate), 7 September 1993, p. 1120; Bruce Anderson to the editor, *Australian* [undated; not published], attached to Anderson to Dymphna Clark, 18 August 1995, Dymphna Clark Papers, NLA, MS 9873, Series 10, Box 35, Folder 3; A.K. Macdougall, 'Introduction' to Ryan, *Lines of Fire*, pp. 6–18, specifically p. 17; Peter Ryan, 'The Year of the Swine', *Quadrant*, vol. 43, no. 10, October 1999, pp. 87–88; and especially Tidey, *Ryan's Luck*, pp. 103–4.
62 Tidey, *Ryan's Luck*, pp. 82–83. His first contribution to *Nation* was an insightful book review of *Orr*, by W.H.C. Eddy, *Nation*, vol. 69, no. 20, May 1961, pp. 20–21.

and often nasty edge that was never far beneath the surface.⁶³ The *Age* had employed a number of contrarian columnists, and Ryan was made to order. But he was now out of that line of work and bereft of public platform. Obscurity beckoned.

Ryan extracted himself from his predicament via Clark. While the precise dates of ensuing events cannot always be ascertained, a time line can nonetheless be established. Ryan's last column in the *Age* was in late April 1993.⁶⁴ A little later he enquired whether Robert Manne was still interested in an article on Manning Clark for *Quadrant* and was assured that this was the case.⁶⁵ Freed from the treadmill of writing for the *Age*, Ryan then set about composing his attack on Clark, which appeared nominally in September but in fact in late August. Around this time—exactly when is uncertain—Manne went a step further and offered Ryan an ongoing column in *Quadrant*.⁶⁶ In this way Ryan's public profile was restored with the added advantage of a platform from which to continue sniping at Clark.

Ryan insisted, implausibly, that he attacked Clark 'without relish'⁶⁷ and without bitterness.⁶⁸ The poet Bruce Anderson, a family friend of the Clarks, was having none of this, telling Dymphna:

> When you think about it … that remark of Peter's ['You never hear Manning Clark mentioned today'] is very sick. What he is saying is, 'Look at me. I have wiped someone out. What an achievement! How powerful I am! You may think it is some kind of intellectual sadism or you might wonder what accounts in my psyche for such a compulsion but I did it out of a great sense of public duty. I have struck down a mighty from his seat, and oh, how I am enjoying the fame!'⁶⁹

---

63 For example, Peter Ryan, 'Constitution is not the problem', *Age*, 2 January 1993, p. Extra 2.
64 Peter Ryan, 'In memory of a unit ahead of its time [DORCA]', *Age*, 24 April 1993, p. 20.
65 Robert Manne, 'A holy cow called history', *Age*, 1 September 1993, p. 16.
66 Robert Manne, email to author, 20 March 2019.
67 Ryan, 'Manning Clark', p. 182; Ryan, 'The Charge of the Lightweight Brigade', p. 233.
68 Ryan to Max Suich, 23 August 1993, Ryan Papers, NLA, MS 9897, Series 6, Box 10, Folder 4; Ryan to J.P. Parsons, 16 December 1993, Ryan Papers, NLA, MS 9897, Series 6, Box 10, Folder 5.
69 Anderson to Dymphna Clark (postscript), 18 August 1995, Dymphna Clark Papers, NLA, MS 9873, Series 10, Box 35, Folder 3.

8. REFLECTION

The statement to which Anderson so objected was quoted in the *Weekend Australian Magazine* and shows that Ryan was nothing if not unrepentant. As reported by the journalist in question:

> Scathing and harsh though Ryan's criticisms were, he rejects they were in any way an outburst, nor were they malicious. He re-read all of the historian's published works in the three years before the article. 'Manning created a phoney Australian ethos. I felt I had to redress the balance. It was not an easy moral position; I'd been his publisher, I'd been his friend. But I felt it had got out of hand.' Many people never spoke to him again. 'It didn't trouble me much because when I reflected [about his critics] I thought yes … yes, you have been getting pretty wishy-washy a bit of late, and you've been a professional for 30 years and you've written f…-all, and said f…-all and probably done f…-all work, too.'[70]

---

70   *Weekend Australian Magazine*, 29 July 1995, p. 17.

9

Aftermath: The Dissembling Publisher, *Quadrant* and the History Wars

The public debate over Australian history has been conducted for the most part in terms of truth and falsehood. While the motives and integrity of participants are part of that debate, there is surprisingly little attention to the ethical dimensions of historical scholarship. If it is a fundamental duty of the historian to tell the truth, then that hardly exhausts the obligations that arise when we work with the past. The choice of subject, the engagement with the sources, respect for the evidence, fair dealing with the work of others, attention to context, humility in the exercise of judgement and recognition of what cannot be known—these are just some of the responsibilities a researcher incurs. The mediation between past and present is a profoundly moral activity. Of all the faculties of the historian, a good conscience is indispensable. Technical virtuosity will disguise many faults, but not bad faith.

Stuart Macintyre (2004)[1]

Quadrant maintained its onslaught against Manning Clark—to the extent that, when launching Mark McKenna's *An Eye for Eternity* in 2011, novelist Tom Keneally cheekily remarked on the number of friends of Clark in attendance and the 'under-representation from *Quadrant*, who

---

1 Stuart Macintyre, 'Introduction' to Macintyre (ed.), *The Historian's Conscience: Australian Historians on the Ethics of History*, Melbourne: MUP, 2004, pp. 1–16, specifically pp. 4–5.

take such a passionate interest in his work'.[2] Since 1994, the journal has published numerous articles, in addition to those by Peter Ryan, dealing wholly or partly with Clark (see Appendix 4). Some constitute fair comment, but the majority are one-sidedly hostile. It seems that many of the History Warriors thought they were settling something important about understandings of the national past by continuing to debase Clark's character.

Quadrant had given Ryan a new lease of journalistic life and an audience, although not nearly as good as a column in a major metropolitan daily given that he now lacked a broadly based readership and was preaching to the converted. He had a roving commission to write about whatever he liked, and he often did so with tacky commentary and cruel invective. There was no doubting his likes and dislikes as he roamed freely, sometimes reviewing a book but mostly engaging in wider commentary. Military history, educational issues and Papua New Guinea were frequently on the menu, as were a long list of pet hates—including the chattering classes, organised sport (i.e. team games), animal libbers, the peace movement, school teachers, tree-huggers (although he didn't use that term) and other environmentalists, the notion of the Stolen Generation, republicanism, academics generally, beards, feminists, exposed belly-buttons and pierced navels.[3] Such commentary led Geoffrey Serle to record the 'distress' of Ryan's old friends that the person who once 'burned with radical idealism' had transformed into 'a standard elderly, misanthropic newspaper columnist'.[4]

From his pulpit, he could smite his enemies and praise his friends, as well as pronounce on the decaying state of the nation. Such interventions, when he went into attack mode, could be venomous. Mirroring his *Age* columns, his tactics were disparagement, insult, ridicule and put-downs. Take the opening sentences of his first *Age* column for 1993:

> One of the happier notes struck during this festive season was inaudible: The Australian republican movement was silent, like Sherlock Holmes's dog that did not bark at night. No theatricality

---

2   Tom Keneally, at the launch of *An Eye for Eternity*, Sydney, 19 May 2011 (starting at 4.44 minutes), available on 28 November 2011 at: www.mup.com.au/page/92 (no longer available on the MUP website).
3   A selection of his *Quadrant* articles is in Peter Ryan, *It Strikes Me: Collected Essays, 1994–2010*, Sydney: Quadrant Books, 2011.
4   Geoffrey Serle, *Robin Boyd: A Life*, Melbourne: MUP, 1995, p. 103; see also Paul Bourke 'Ryan is playing with the "pornography of power"', *Canberra Times*, 28 August 1993, p. 4.

from those old self-promoters Tom Keneally and Donald Horne; Patrick White and Manning Clark are quiet forever; Paul Keating pondered the resurrection of John ('Lazarus') Hewson. All in all a good Christmas.[5]

Further down the column he writes:

> Consider: among our prime ministers we have endured drunks, hysterics, barnyard roosters, gays, near-cretins, sires of illegitimate children and persons with fingers so sticky that you oughtn't to let them near the fowlhouse, let alone the Treasury.

Not without reason did an acquaintance from their University of Melbourne days describe Ryan's *Age* columns as having 'a certain idiosyncratic, sometimes amusing, point of view, but always very negative … and sometimes quite grotesque, full of bitterness and self-righteousness'.[6]

As well, Ryan became a regular reviewer for the *Australian*, which gave him added scope for sledging the historical profession.[7] He continued writing for *Quadrant* until shortly before his death in late 2015. His last two columns are thoroughly unpleasant personal attacks on the historian Brian Fitzpatrick.[8]

But what inspired Ryan to write with such bitterness and ill-feeling? A possible answer is that he was psychologically scarred during wartime service in the New Guinea campaign; he certainly went through terrifying ordeals in that perilous theatre of war. Service records are often detailed but Ryan's is thin and it neither confirms nor denies torments that would

---

5   Peter Ryan, 'Constitution is not the problem', *Age*, 2 January 1993, p. Extra 2.
6   Bruce Anderson to Dymphna Clark, 28 August 1993, Dymphna Clark Papers, NLA, MS 9873, Series 10, Box 35, Folder 2.
7   For example, Peter Ryan, 'All hail the unlikely saviour', review of *The Fabrication of Aboriginal History*, by Keith Windschuttle, *Australian*, 10 January 2003, p. 11 (where he rails against Windschuttle's opponents in the academy); Ryan, 'Tyranny of the trivia', review of *The Fuss That Never Ended: The Life and Work of Geoffrey Blainey*, ed. Deborah Gare, Geoffrey Bolton, Stuart Macintyre and Tom Stannage, *Weekend Australian*, 15–16 March 2003, p. 10; Ryan, 'Fighting words', review of *The History Wars*, by Macintyre and Clark, *Australian*, 6–7 September 2003, pp. R10–11.
8   Peter Ryan, 'The Unforgotten Brian Fitzpatrick', *Quadrant*, vol. 59, no. 9, September 2015, pp. 111–12; Ryan, 'In the Neighbourhood of Brian Fitzpatrick', *Quadrant*, vol. 59, no. 10, October 2015, pp. 110–12. He was still managing to make factual errors. At the time of her marriage in 1932, Kathleen Fitzpatrick was not 'soon to be Professor of History at [the University of] Melbourne', as Ryan stated in 'The Unforgotten Brian Fitzpatrick', p. 111. She was eventually promoted to associate professor 16 years later, in 1948, and she declined to be considered to fill the newly created second chair of history within the department in 1955.

have had lasting effects on his mental state. He contracted malaria in late 1943 and suffered lifelong recurrences, but in November 1945 his medical classification was 'A1'.[9] During his time in the University of Melbourne Labour Club in the late 1940s, pugnacity was the dominant characteristic,[10] but was this a function of his wartime experiences? Given the paucity of information in Ryan's service file, it is impossible to say whether his capacity for unpleasantness was pre-existing or related to his war service. All the same, it is hard not to wonder whether all the pieces were working together properly. There is more than just eccentricity or crankiness in motion.

Yet Ryan was more than capable of writing in a constructive vein, providing there was no axe to grind. But this was not in evidence when he turned his gaze to Clark, contributing to *Quadrant*'s continued denigration of the deceased historian (Appendix 3). The majority of Ryan's 19 articles simply deliver a passing swipe—for example:

> Serious history had vanished under the fog of Manning Clark's fantasies, until our national story virtually ceased either to be taught or to be learned; Australia's strong and self-respecting sense of self was evaporating.[11]

In several instances he revisits the 1993 affair, defending his position and repeating his attacks on Clark. Here, he reverts to type in saying that his politely expressed views exposing 'the hollowness of Manning Clark drew abuse, but did not draw even an attempt to answer any of the clear questions I had asked'.[12] In fact, he didn't ask any 'clear questions' and he said nothing new about the *History* despite claiming to have read all six volumes 'not merely once throughout, but three times, and some parts

---

9   Ryan's Service file, NAA: B883, VX128541 (pp. 24–25, 35).
10 Stuart Macintyre, email to author, 22 August 2019 (based on Macintyre's research in the Records of the Labour Club).
11 Peter Ryan, 'A Better Place', *Quadrant*, vol. 47, nos 1–2, January–February 2003, pp. 119–20, specifically p. 119.
12 Peter Ryan, 'A Reply to my Critics', in his *Lines of Fire: Manning Clark & Other Writings*, ed. A.K. Macdougall, Binalong, NSW: Clarion Editions, 1997, pp. 214–22, specifically p. 217; Ryan to J.P. Parsons, 16 December 1993, Ryan Papers, National Library of Australia (hereafter NLA), MS 9897, Series 6, Box 10, Folder 5; Ryan, 'Kokoda in Perspective', *Quadrant*, vol. 50, no. 6, June 2006, pp. 95–96, for quotation see p. 96; Ryan, 'Manning Clark's second coming', *Australian*, 10 February 2007, p. 29; Ryan, 'Hollow Man of Yesterday', review of *Manning Clark: A Life*, by Brian Matthews, *Quadrant*, vol. 53, nos 1–2, January–February 2009, pp. 126–27; Ryan, 'My Life as a Leper', *Quadrant*, vol. 55, nos 1–2, January–February 2011, pp. 127–28; Ryan, 'The Only Justifiable End of Eloquence', *Quadrant*, vol. 57, no. 9, September 2013, pp. 111–12, specifically p. 111.

oftener'.[13] That he was unable to come up with ideas of his own in his critique of Clark the historian led Frank Bongiorno to question Ryan's intellectual capacities:

> He might have had literary skills but I'm not aware of any work of genuine insight or originality by Ryan. He seems a shallow thinker, capable of clever literary allusion but without any interest in sustained research or difficult analysis.[14]

Indeed, presenting new factual details to illustrate wider issues that others had rehearsed many times over is not the same thing as originality or profundity.

Ryan's often denunciatory and combative column is a microcosm of *Quadrant*'s worsening habits of ideological aggression and personal abuse. Some of this can be put down to *Quadrant* always having seen itself as anti-communist and oppositional to the left-leaning journals such as *Meanjin* and *Overland*.[15] *Quadrant* had also reinvented itself in the late 1980s; now seeing itself as a bastion against the new ideologies—'radical feminism, gay liberationism, anti-nuclearism, extreme environmentalism, multi-culturalism, animal liberationism'—which it perceived as having replaced communism as the major threats to cultural freedom.[16] Just as Clark's *History* generally deteriorated with successive volumes, *Quadrant* has not improved with age, although it does from time to time publish articles contrary to its own party line.[17] Its second editor, Peter Coleman (1967–1988), was a courteous enough conservative, although he moved further to the right as the History Wars progressed. Robert Manne, who took over the editorship in 1990, had no intention of turning

---

13 Peter Ryan, 'Manning Clark', in his *Lines of Fire*, pp. 179–214, specifically p. 213.
14 Frank Bongiorno, comment on earlier version of this book, 29 July 2018.
15 James McAuley, 'The First 15 Years', *Quadrant*, vol. 15, no. 10, October 1971, pp. 13–16; Jim George and Michael Hutchinson, 'Culture War as Foreign Policy in the US and Australia', in Jim George and Kim Huynh (eds), *The Culture Wars: Australian and American Politics in the 21st Century*, Melbourne: Palgrave Macmillan Australia, 2009, pp. 37–56, specifically pp. 47–52; Norman Abjorensen, 'The Culture Wars Down Under', in Jim George and Kim Huynh (eds), *The Culture Wars: Australian and American Politics in the 21st Century*, Melbourne: Palgrave Macmillan Australia, 2009, pp. 59–74, specifically p. 62; Phillip Edmonds, *Tilting at Windmills: The Literary Magazine in Australia, 1968–2012*, Adelaide: University of Adelaide Press, 2015, pp. 149–52, doi.org/10.20851/windmills; and, more generally, David Carter and Roger Osborne, 'Periodicals', in Robyn Sheahan-Bright and Craig Munro (eds), *Paper Empires: A History of the Book in Australia, 1946–2005*, Brisbane: University of Queensland Press, 2006, pp. 239–57.
16 'Editorial: A Short Way with Dissenters', *Quadrant*, vol. 33, no. 3, March 1989, p. 7.
17 For example, S.G. Foster, 'Contra Windschuttle', *Quadrant*, vol. 47, no. 3, March 2003, pp. 25–28. A measured assessment of *Quadrant* is by Don Aitkin, 'Why Do I Read *Quadrant*', *Australian Quarterly*, vol. 79, no. 1, 2007, pp. 9–16.

Quadrant into 'an Australian Thatcherite magazine, socially conservative and economically dry'. Manne did give the journal renewed intellectual substance but his relations with *Quadrant* colleagues became increasingly fraught. His critique of economic rationalism and neoliberal policy in 1992 resulted in the first major rupture.[18] His espousal of Aboriginal concerns, which included articles on Mabo by Raimond Gaita, caused further consternation, as did his refusal to buy into the spy-of-the-century nonsense played out in the *Courier-Mail* in which *Quadrant*'s literary editor, poet Les Murray (1938–2019), alleged he had seen Manning Clark wearing the Order of Lenin.[19] The parting of the ways came in 1997 because his accumulated differences with the editorial board had become insurmountable.[20] Even then Clark was in the mix because Manne's refusal to publish a submission by Hal G.P. Colebatch, which fingered Clark as an anti-Semite, helped to catalyse the revolt.[21] Symbolic of the advent of a new order at *Quadrant* was the publication of an article, in opposition to Manne's views, supporting the allegations of the Brisbane *Courier-Mail* that Clark was the recipient of the Order of Lenin and an agent of Soviet influence.[22] The parting of the ways was acrimonious and Manne has since had to field repeated brickbats from the journal he once edited, not least from Peter Coleman who was very bitter about Manne's 'virtuous trajectory' and where this had taken the journal.[23]

---

18 John Carroll and Robert Manne (eds), *Shutdown: The Failure of Economic Rationalism and How to Rescue Australia*, Melbourne: Text Publishing, 1992.
19 Robert Manne, 'On the Manning Clark Affair' (1996), in his *Left Right Left: Political Essays, 1977–2005*, Melbourne: Black Inc., 2004, pp. 81–91; Peter F. Alexander, *Les Murray: A Life in Progress*, Melbourne: Oxford University Press, 2000, pp. 276–78; Raimond Gaita, 'Mabo (Part One)', *Quadrant*, vol. 37, no. 9, September 1993, pp. 36–39; Gaita, 'Mabo (Part Two)', *Quadrant*, vol. 37, no. 10, October 1993, pp. 44–48. In the interest of open discussion, Manne published a retort to Gaita—namely Ron Brunton, 'Shame about Aborigines', *Quadrant*, vol. 41, no. 5, May 1997, pp. 36–39.
20 Robert Manne, 'Why I have Resigned', *Quadrant*, vol. 41, no. 12, December 1997, pp. 3–4. Cf. Frank Devine, 'Welcome changing of the guard for a journal of debate', *Australian*, 5 January 1998, p. 11.
21 Andrew Bonnell and Martin Crotty, 'Australia's History under Howard, 1996–2007', pp. 156–57, *Annals of the American Academy of Politics and Social Science*, vol 617, no. 1, 2008, pp. 149–65, doi.org/10.1177/0002716207310818; Stuart Macintyre and Anna Clark, *The History Wars*, 2nd edn, Melbourne: MUP, 2004, pp. 145–46; Alexander, *Les Murray*, p. 283. *Quadrant* later published Colebatch's 'Manning Clark's Anti-Semitism', *Quadrant*, vol. 52, no. 5, May 2008, pp. 92–97. Colebatch (1945–2019) was a journalist, university lecturer and historian of reactionary persuasion whose broadsides against Manning Clark verged on the paranoid.
22 Wayne Smith, 'Manning Clark and the *Courier Mail*', *Quadrant*, vol. 42, no. 9, September 1998, pp. 40–43. Cf. Robert Manne, 'Christ and Lenin', *The Australian's Review of Books*, October 1996, pp. 6–8.
23 For example, Peter Coleman, 'All that Swagger: Robert Manne's Virtuous Trajectory', review of *Left Right Left: Political Essays, 1977–2005*, by Robert Manne, *Quadrant*, vol. 49, no. 9, September 2005, pp. 82–84, available at: www.the-rathouse.com/PC_Manne.html; Keith Windschuttle, 'A Cribber and a Fibber', *Quadrant*, vol. 52, no. 5, May 2008, pp. 98–103; and numerous more recent swipes on the *Quadrant* webpage, available at: quadrant.org.au/.

* * *

Beyond his *Quadrant* column, Ryan's obsession with Clark was demonstrated when approached by researchers. During an interview in 2007, McKenna observed that 'talking about Clark seemed to animate [Ryan's] whole being'.[24] Much the same emerged when Sylvia Martin interviewed Ryan for her biography of Ida Leeson. In his second volume of autobiography, Clark told the blatantly sexist story that he and other young researchers had a daily competition at the Mitchell Library: they would request books on the high shelves and the prize would go to the first to identify the colour of the garters under Leeson's skirts as she ascended the ladder. That Ryan kept repeating the story during the interview is further evidence of his obsession with Clark. Ryan then spent one-third of his review of the Leeson biography on the garters scenario. He ended by saying that her book was not 'enhanced' by relating such information despite Martin concluding that the story was probably apocryphal.[25] This is not to excuse Clark, any more than the occasion in the late 1940s when he described his departmental colleague Kathleen Fitzpatrick to Ryan as 'the Unsatisfied One'—a tasteless remark about a divorcée who had not remarried and in fact never did. Ryan 'said he was appalled by the comment when Clark made it, and was still appalled by it now', but there is no evidence of any remonstrance from Ryan at the time.[26]

Ryan continued to chisel away at the reputation of Manning Clark, but, on a broader front, one senses an ambiguity in conservative circles in dealing with Clark's legacy and reputation. The reaction alternated between denunciation and cold-shouldering, which happened at *Quadrant*'s fiftieth anniversary celebrations in 2006. One of the speakers was John Howard, who denounced Clark as an example of 'the philo-communism that was once quite common in Australia in the 1950s and 1960s'.[27] He was evidently unaware that Clark had been actively recruited on to *Quadrant*'s foundation editorial board, and equally oblivious to the fact that Clark

---

24 Mark McKenna, *An Eye for Eternity: The Life of Manning Clark,* Melbourne: Miegunyah Press, 2011, p. 690.
25 Sylvia Martin, *Ida Leeson: A Life: Not a Blue-stocking Woman,* Sydney: Allen & Unwin, 2006, pp. 187–88 (and email to author, 4 July 2016); Manning Clark, *The Quest for Grace,* Ringwood: Penguin Books, 1991, pp. 167–68; Ryan, 'Woman of letters', review of *Ida Leeson,* by Sylvia Martin, *Weekend Australian Review,* 15–16 July 2006, pp. 14–15.
26 Elizabeth Kleinmetz, *A Brimming Cup: The Life of Kathleen Fitzpatrick,* Melbourne: MUP, 2013, pp. 156, 292 n.63.
27 John Howard, 'A Tribute to *Quadrant*', *Quadrant,* vol. 50, no. 11, November 2006, pp. 22–24, specifically p. 22.

had long since expressed his dismay at 'the intransigence and the bullying of the Soviets'.²⁸ Peter Coleman also spoke that evening and he certainly knew about Clark's early association with *Quadrant*, having helped to coopt him onto the original editorial board, but he left Clark out of his address altogether.²⁹

Clark's critics were handed ammunition when it was revealed, in 2007, that Clark had not been in Germany at the time of *Kristallnacht* in late 1938, as he had repeatedly claimed, when Nazi storm troopers went on their state-sanctioned rampage against Jewish persons and property. He actually arrived in Germany a fortnight later, but in subsequent years he appropriated the account in Dymphna's letters and made their content his own, claiming that what he witnessed the night after *Kristallnacht* was an epiphany.³⁰ Discovery of the subterfuge caused a brief flurry—nothing of the magnitude of the *Courier-Mail* episode—with assertions that Clark was indeed a fraud, as he was on that occasion.³¹

There was, however, a countervailing unease in right-wing circles that exposés of Clark perpetuated the unworthy legacy of someone best forgotten—the feeling that the ghost of Manning Clark be allowed to slink back to the obscurity from which it should never have emerged. Both Ryan and Colebatch, in reviewing the big biographies of Clark, encapsulated this ambivalence by trumpeting Clark's unlikeable qualities and then asking: why bother with him at all?³² Journalist Paul Kelly, in 2009, took the latter course and was utterly dismissive, declaring:

---

28   Roslyn Russell (ed.), *Ever, Manning: Selected Letters of Manning Clark, 1938–1993*, Sydney: Allen & Unwin, 2008, p. 444 (Clark to Lyndall Ryan, 19 August 1984).
29   Peter Coleman, 'Fifty Years in the Front Line', *Quadrant*, vol. 50, no. 11, November 2006, pp. 26–27.
30   Mark McKenna, 'Being There: The Strange History of Manning Clark', *The Monthly*, no. 21, March 2007, pp. 22–37.
31   For example, David Marr, 'The man who wasn't there: Manning Clark's fraud exposed', *Sydney Morning Herald*, 5 March 2007, p. 1; 'Clark's biographer speaks about historian's past' (Mark Colvin interviewing Mark McKenna), 5 March 2007, available at: www.abc.net.au/reslib/200703/r129612_427103.mp3 (audio); www.abc.net.au/pm/content/2007/s1863641.htm (typescript).
32   Peter Ryan, 'Hollow Man of Yesterday', review of *Manning Clark: A Life*, by Brian Matthews, *Quadrant*, vol. 53, nos 1–2, January–February 2009, pp. 126–28; Hal G.P. Colebatch, 'Sins of omission', review of *An Eye for Eternity*, by Mark McKenna, *Spectator Australia*, 25 June 2011, available on 17 June 2013 at: www.spectator.co.uk/australia/7049633/australian-books-sins-of-omission/ (no longer available on the publisher's website).

> Lawson and Clark said Australians had to choose between the old dead tree and the young tree green. But the Australian people, wisely, decided this was a false choice. They repudiated Clark and Lawson.[33]

John Howard also seems to have got the message. During his prime ministership he frequently criticised Clark for disparaging the Australian achievement but reduced the object of his previous ire to a solitary passing mention in his autobiography—on a matter that had nothing to do with the History Wars.[34]

In any case, Clark's public profile had long been on the wane, despite the continued white-anting in *Quadrant*. As a public intellectual, he was a man of the moment. By the turn of the century, he had passed his use-by date. Clark's biographer McKenna acknowledged in 2011 that Clark would, by then, be 'laughed out of court', but in the 1970s and 80s

> Australians wanted someone, or needed someone, to talk, or point to [their] identity, their future—who were we as a people?— [whereas today we are] standing solidly behind a more conservative and less critical view of ourselves.[35]

So, Clark is no longer the public presence that he once was, especially as the History Wars have taken different turns. In what might be a temporary respite, the History Wars no longer held centre stage in national life as in the early to mid-2000s when the print media would likely be reporting that yet another front had opened up.[36] As Frank Bongiorno remarks:

> There's continuing interest in Clark, but inevitably, the caravan's moved on somewhat. I'm more than ever struck by his importance as a cultural icon of post-imperial Australia—that is, the world of the mid-to-late 1960s, 1970s and climaxing in the Bicentenary of 1988. As soon as the post-imperial moment turned into the mixture of globalisation and cultural warfare that we've had since the mid-1990s, Clark was of little use to either the left or right. Perhaps the Ryan affair was [a late] gasp of the old order.[37]

---

33 Paul Kelly, *The March of Patriots: The Struggle for Modern Australia,* Melbourne: MUP, 2009, p. 71.
34 John Howard, *Lazarus Rising: A Personal and Political Biography,* Sydney: Allen & Unwin, 2010, p. 73.
35 'Making History: Mark McKenna on Manning Clark' (interviewed by Michael Cathcart), Wheeler Centre, Melbourne, 6 June 2011 (starting at 11.20 minutes), available at: www.wheelercentre.com/broadcasts/making-history-mark-mckenna-on-manning-clark/.
36 Luke Trainor, review of *The History Wars,* by Macintyre and Clark, *New Zealand Journal of History,* vol. 38, no. 2, 2004, pp. 308–9 , specifically p. 308, available at: www.nzjh.auckland.ac.nz/docs/2004/NZJH_38_2_14.pdf.
37 Frank Bongiorno, email to author, 9 May 2018.

Clark's reputation as an historian is also in decline, which would have horrified him. Michael Cathcart has put it with eloquence in suggesting:

> Manning lived in a state of existential agitation—that he feared that a great nothingness lay beyond death and that he was terrified by the loneliness of that prospect. It was appalling to him that life—especially *his* life—should end in nullity ... At a deep level, I think that Manning was in search of immortality ... *A History of Australia* is his attempt to write his life onto the great wilderness of Australia so that its very history becomes his mausoleum.[38]

Yet his eclipse is hardly a cause for surprise considering that historians typically have short shelf lives, even those who were well known and widely read during their lifetimes. When G.M Trevelyan's biographer presented a paper on Trevelyan (1876–1962) at the University of Cambridge in the late 1980s 'the majority of graduate students [in the audience] admitted to never having read him', or even heard of him, despite Trevelyan's prolific published output, his public profile and his long association with Cambridge.[39] This was less than 30 years after Trevelyan's death. In similar fashion, almost all members of an honours class in Australian historiography at the University of Melbourne in 2018 had no prior knowledge of Clark.[40] The paradox is that, despite his diminished reputation and his probably being little read by the general public anymore, Clark retains a cultural presence and continues to be discussed in the context of academic discourse. It is more than a cottage industry. Ironically, Clark ignored the profession in the *History*, but the profession is by no means ignoring his cultural influence, and this despite his fading professional and historiographical reputation. He remains by far the most discussed of all Australian historians (Appendix 4). Events thus far have confirmed Stuart Macintyre's 1994 prediction that Clark's 'position as a writer and influential figure in Australian cultural life is assured'.[41]

---

38   Michael Cathcart, email to author, 20 October 2017.
39   David Cannadine, *G.M. Trevelyan: A Life in History*, London: Fontana Press, 1993, p. xii.
40   Stuart Macintyre, comment on earlier version of this book, 3 April 2018.
41   Stuart Macintyre, '"Always a pace or two apart"', in Carl Bridge (ed.), *Manning Clark: Essays on his Place in History*, Melbourne: MUP, 1994, pp. 17–29 (text), pp. 212–13 (endnotes), specifically p. 29; see also John Reeve, 'Masters of History: Three Students of Trinity College', *Victorian Historical Journal*, vol. 80, no. 1, 2009, pp. 76–90.

Clark's continuing cultural profile confounds Ryan's 1993 pronouncement about 'the imminent and inevitable crumbling of Clark'.[42] As if to make a wish come true, Ryan repeatedly white-anted his former author. In 1994 he noted that Clark was missing from a line-up of 30 prominent Australians in an issue of the *Australian* commemorating its first 30 years—proof in Ryan's eyes of the early eclipse of Manning Clark.[43] And in 2005 Ryan wrote:

> it is now more than 10 years since Australia's historical charlatan-in-chief, Manning Clark, was toppled from his pedestal ... It is today most unusual to hear Clark quoted as an historical authority on anything at all.[44]

The latter point is true enough, but in what *ways* are Manning Clark's *History* likely to have an afterlife? My own prediction is that what is now a secondary source will probably become a primary source in future contexts. Ryan had his own view about this from the vantage point of 1993:

> What, then, has preserved the existence, and even the influence, of this immense and odd cultural artefact? Perhaps it survives as a relic, a product of the sixties and seventies which an aging generation still clutches as a security blanket? Perhaps, deep in many an unconscious, it retains vague but comforting associations with Woodstock and Vietnam protests and nice Mr Whitlam who, on the very point of establishing the kingdom of heaven upon earth, was 'crucified' by the 'forces of Mammon' [as Clark put it]? Perhaps ... who knows.[45]

Along with Macintyre, I would venture to suggest that, far from being an ephemeral relic, Clark's *History* will continue as an important cultural artefact. Perhaps historian James Griffin was a little too grudging when predicting in 1995 that the *History* 'will stand on the shelves as a curiosity of historically based literature and nationalist polemics'.[46] Like Edward Gibbon and Thomas Babington Macaulay before him, Clark's *History of Australia* will retain value, for all its idiosyncrasies, as an indicator

---

42 Peter Ryan, 'A Reply to my Critics', p. 222.
43 Peter Ryan, 'The Charge of the Lightweight Brigade', in his *Lines of Fire*, pp. 222–34, specifically p. 223; see also the *Australian*, 16 June 1994, p. 1 (Special Commemorative Edition).
44 Peter Ryan, 'Apologise to Blainey', *Australian*, 15 December 2005, p. 10.
45 Ryan, 'Manning Clark', pp. 213–14.
46 James Griffin, 'The historiographer Clark unravelled', review of *Manning Clark*, ed. Carl Bridge, *Australian*, 1 February 1995, p. 26.

of a selection of political and social assumptions at its time of writing, and the extent to which underlying assumptions shifted with successive volumes. In those respects, the *History* will live on whereas the more academically respectable monographs from the period will bite the dust and join the great unread, if they have not done so already. Paul Bourke added a further dimension when the controversy erupted:

> Clark's [*History*] was a special kind of historical enterprise, much like the work of the 19th century American writer George Bancroft or the English G.M. Trevelyan. These authors who wrote multi-volume histories of their countries, have not been read for their access to an uncontroversial body of fact; these writers have had the function of assisting a wide range of people in their societies to think about their origins, their identities and their common life. Historians rarely have such audiences.[47]

Whether Clark's *History*, with its repetitive clichés and overwrought prose, will be read as literature, in the manner that Gibbon and Macaulay are to this day, is a moot point. The exception might be his set piece narratives where story-telling ability really matters. Otherwise, in the words of Norman Etherington, 'the current scholarly consensus [is] that [Clark] did not come within cooee of greatness as a writer of history'.[48]

And what of Peter Ryan? Predictions are hazardous but the attempt must be made here too. As already mentioned, Bruce Anderson said in 1995:

> [Ryan] claims, 'You never hear Manning Clark mentioned today'. Whether that is the case or not, one thing is certain, Peter Ryan would not be mentioned if it were not for Manning Clark.[49]

That is to overstate one's case, but not by much. Frank Bongiorno suggests that 'Ryan really had two great stories in him. He'd offered one many decades before, in his war memoir. The other was his relationship with the country's most famous historian'.[50] To be sure, Ryan was largely identified as the publisher of Clark's *History*, a twinning that he clearly

---

47   Paul Bourke, 'Ryan is playing with the "pornography of power"', *Canberra Times*, 28 August 1993, p. 4.
48   Norman Etherington, 'The Spectre of Manning Clark', review of *An Eye for Eternity*, by Mark McKenna, *Australian Book Review*, vol. 337, December–January 2011–12, pp. 12–14, specifically p. 12.
49   Anderson to the Editor, *Australian* (undated; not published), attached to Anderson to Dymphna Clark, 18 August 1995, Dymphna Clark Papers, NLA, MS 9873, Series 10, Box 35, Folder 3. Anderson was responding to what Ryan was quoted as saying in an untitled article in the *Weekend Australian Magazine*, 29 July 1995, p. 17.
50   Frank Bongiorno, email to author, 4 April 2018.

disliked despite persisting in being its publisher. But with Clark gone, Ryan developed a literary life of his own with, successively, his *Age* and *Quadrant* columns. Whether his legacy will rival Clark's is improbable: this book (and John Tidey's *Ryan's Luck*) may prolong his afterlife, but his supporters are old and few and he will largely fade away. Ask current readers of the *Age* who Peter Ryan is, and they will more likely identify his namesake, who joined the newspaper in 2017 as a senior sports reporter—a sublime irony given that our Peter Ryan so detested team sports. Ryan's *Nation, Age* and *Quadrant* columns, taken in their entirety, may coalesce into a cultural artefact and might even capture the attention of a postgraduate student in search of a thesis topic—in other words to become fodder for the 'thesis mills' he so despised.

Ryan might have made an early contribution to the ongoing Clark industry had he availed himself of an unexpected opportunity. In response to his first attack in *Quadrant*, the English publishing house of Andre Deutsch enquired whether he would be interested in writing a biography of Clark. Although gratified by the offer, Ryan declined, explaining that his post-retirement job as clerk of the Supreme Court of Victoria left him with limited opportunity for his own writing 'in the short time left to me'.[51] It was a wise decision from all points of view. Ryan would not have been able to spend the necessary time in Canberra consulting the papers of Manning Clark. Even had he done so, his three *Quadrant* articles suggest that any such biography would have been an extended and intellectually uninformed diatribe. As Peter Craven remarked, Ryan's depiction of his relationship with Clark in his first *Quadrant* essay

> reads like a portrait of Hamlet as an old goat written by an aging Horatio who seems to have spent half his time wishing he could run through the crazy bastard with his sword ... There is a sense in which the face which stares back at us from Ryan's essay, by virtue of the power of his writing and his willingness to persevere with his own contradictions, is the face of Manning Clark (transfigured as he could never have done deliberately himself in his writings) into a comic character.[52]

---

51 T.G. Rosenthal to Ryan, 19 October 1993, and subsequent correspondence, in Ryan Papers, NLA, MS 9897, Series 6, Box 10, Folder 4. Ryan suggested the journalist and writer Michael Duffy as an alternative, but the latter 'didn't think he would have time, so he declined with very great regret'.
52 Peter Craven, 'The Ryan Affair', in Bridge, *Manning Clark,* pp. 165–87 (text), p. 224 (endnotes), specifically p. 175.

Ryan's life of Clark, had he written it, might have bolstered his reputation as a 'master of anecdote and caricature' but the eventual book would not have remotely approached the standard of Stephen Holt's short biography of Clark, published in 1999.[53]

* * *

Despite the difficulties he experienced as Clark's publisher, I believe that Ryan behaved badly and was culpable in his many misrepresentations of events; he emerges from the episode with little credibility. That said, I am not faulting Ryan for expressing disapproval of Manning Clark per se. Nor am I sure that I subscribe to the view that a publisher has a confidential relationship with an author; if so, then historians breach this confidentiality every time they discuss publisher–author interactions, as I have in this book. One might also argue that if Ryan praises those whom he considers virtuous authors, then he is entitled to express dissatisfaction with the miscreants, as he does in his autobiography.[54] But if the publisher–author relationship is seen as one of mutual trust and support, then Ryan clearly transgressed. Louise Adler, then director of Melbourne University Press (hereafter MUP), entertained no doubts on the matter and made her views abundantly clear at the launch of *An Eye for Eternity* in 2011. Reminding the audience that 'Manning Clark and MUP ... had a complex history', she went on to say:

> MUP profited immeasurably from publishing his six-volume *History of Australia.* Some might say that the Press's Director during that time made his own reputation as a consequence, on the back of Manning Clark ... no one here today will be unaware that that same publisher would, much later on, make his own highly pejorative views of his author known. My own personal view is that the publisher's first loyalty is to one's author. We publishers can actually choose to take on a book or not, we can share the author's views or not, but we actually in the end owe both the book and the author enduring loyalty and advocacy of their work.[55]

---

53 Peter Craven, 'Veil of death draws to a close several artistic eras', *Australian,* 18 January 1995, for quotation see p. 28; Stephen Holt, *A Short History of Manning Clark,* Sydney: Allen & Unwin, 1999.
54 Peter Ryan, *Final Proof: Memoirs of a Publisher,* Sydney: Quadrant Books, 2010, pp. 170, 180–82.
55 Louise Adler, at the launch of *An Eye for Eternity,* Sydney, 19 May 2011, starting at 2.36 minutes, available on 28 November 2011 at: www.mup.com.au/page/92 (no longer available on the MUP website).

Directly after his first attack on Clark, a newspaper correspondent asserted:

> Peter Ryan must, through his academic experience over 26 years as the supremo at Melbourne University Press, and his intimate knowledge of the man and of the massive six-volume work, be accepted as an 'expert witness'.[56]

Ryan was an unreliable witness, and in ways that undermine his version of events: 'frivolous and vexatious' might be a better legal expression to describe Ryan's testimony. What he says about Clark as a person, although largely correct, fails to capture his complexity. It is also irrelevant and should have been 'struck off the record'. His criticisms of the *History* are wholly unoriginal. To continue with legal jargon, Ryan perjures himself by saying that he inherited an open-ended contract, and he creates a quite false impression by not revealing that he resisted all opportunities to terminate Clark's project, or else to shuffle it on to another publisher. His assertion that Clark was shielded by a duplicitous historical profession does not stand up to scrutiny. He suppressed information that discredits his argument, and his denial that he was politically motivated is an outright falsehood.

But why are there so many mistakes and distortions? One reason might be that Ryan was writing largely from memory, and another that Ryan was loath to admit that he might have been wrong or mistaken. Having burned his bridges with MUP, he no longer had access to his former employer's records. He still had his own papers (which were purchased by the National Library of Australia in 2003) but these contain little material concerning the publication of the *History*. To compound the problem, once Ryan got something in his head, it was entrenched and assumed the status of truth personified. I was alerted to this when reading his statement that A.E. Housman's *A Shropshire Lad* was an instant commercial success, which I knew was not the case at all.[57] What happened was that Ryan misunderstood the relevant passages in Richard Perceval Graves's biography of Housman and the mistake carried through over time; over 30 years later he repeats

---

56   Bob Morrow, 'Emperor's new clothes' (letter), *Daily Mail* (Sydney), 2 September 1993, p. 8; see also 'Editorial: 'Manning Clark's blinkered view', *Courier-Mail*, 31 May 1997, p. 22.
57   Peter Ryan, 'A Shropshire Lad of Genius' (1988), in Ryan, *Lines of Fire,* pp. 48–51, specifically p. 49; see also A.E. Housman, *The Works of A.E. Housman,* Hertfordshire: Wordsworth Poetry Society, n.d., p. ix; Norman Marlow, *A.E. Housman: Scholar and Poet,* London: Routledge & Kegan Paul, 1958, p. 9; Richard Perceval Graves, *A.E. Housman: The Scholar-Poet,* London: Routledge & Kegan Paul, 1979, pp. 111, 113, specifically p. 119.

the initial misapprehension in his autobiography.[58] It is a common enough phenomenon, as evidenced by historian Lewis Namier (1880–1960) whose frequent retellings of his reminiscences elevated their inaccuracies to gospel truth in his own mind.[59] On another occasion Ryan claimed that a series that MUP intended publishing on Asian contract law was terminated after the first volume, on the grounds that the series was receiving the financial backing of the CIA (as had *Quadrant* in its earlier years). One of the series editors offered the correction that CIA funding had long ceased, but Ryan persists with his mistaken version in his autobiography.[60]

Being captive to the idée fixe may also explain why he continued to believe that he inherited an unsatisfactory contract with regard to Clark's *History*; and why he was so reluctant to back down from the idea that academic reviewers gave the *History* a free ride. It may also explain why Ryan kept insisting that *The Musical* 'was a ghastly flop, rushed red-faced off the stage after a run of a few days', a point he reiterates in 1999 when disputing Stephen Holt's more accurate assertion that it limped on for 'some six weeks' (mid-January to late February 1988).[61] Ryan repeats his own mistakes even when offering correction to others.

Another feature is Ryan's lack of self-perception. In the light of the false representations, strategic omissions and outright errors of fact in his three *Quadrant* articles, it is oddly out of place that he approvingly paraphrases Eric Hobsbawm's argument:

> That facts exist, and are the starting point of history; that the truth can be found and is not merely the plaything of subjectivist intellectuals; that historians must not bend facts and history for

---

58 Ryan, *Final Proof*, pp. 178–79.
59 D.W. Hayton, *Conservative Revolutionary: The Lives of Lewis Namier*, Manchester: Manchester University Press, 2019, p. 5.
60 Peter Ryan, 'Throw the book' (letter), *Australian*, 26 January 1999, p. 12; David E. Allen, 'Clear funds for new book', *Australian* (letter), 4 February 1999, p. 12; Ryan, *Final Proof*, p. 166. *Quadrant* was just one of a number of journals worldwide that, knowingly or unknowingly, received CIA money through front organisations. John Leonard, 'It's not the gift, it's the thought behind it', *New York Times*, 8 October 1972, p. BR47, available at: www.nytimes.com/1972/10/08/archives/its-not-the-gift-its-the-thought-behind-it.html.
61 Peter Ryan, 'Folk Memory v History', *Quadrant*, vol. 43, no. 10, October 1999, pp. 70–71, specifically p. 70; Ryan, 'Manning Clark's second coming', *Australian*, 10 February 2007, for quotation see p. 29 'Manning Clark', pp. 203–4; Peter Fitzpatrick, '"History—The Musical": A Review and a Retrospect', *Australian Historical Studies*, vol. 23, no. 91, 1988, pp. 171–79, specifically p. 171, doi.org/10.1080/10314618808595802; Holt, *A Short History of Manning Clark*, p. 220; John Bell, *The Time of My Life*, Sydney: Allen & Unwin, 2002, pp. 157–81; Sophie Cunningham, *Melbourne*, Sydney: NewSouth, 2011, p. 96.

ideological purposes; and that historians must stand aloof from the passions of national identity politics. For me, a canon of historiographical integrity is established on such principles, and Manning Clark sinned against every one of them.⁶²

Peter Ryan also sinned against every 'canon of historiographic integrity' if it comes to that. His wont of self-perception is also illustrated by his reaction to 'a personal account' he was commissioned to write for *Australians: A Historical Library* (1987) being rejected. What started as a moving description of Depression-time Australia degenerates into a tirade about the woeful state of the nation and the idiot politicians trying to run the show. It is amazing that Ryan, himself an academic publisher, could never see why it had to be rejected out of hand—not on grounds of political correctness as he claimed but because a rant of that nature had no place in a scholarly collection.⁶³

Yet Ryan called for 'a little honest introspection by Australian historians',⁶⁴ and goes on to say that history in Australia 'has been "professionalised", if not out of existence, then beyond relevance to ordinary people'.⁶⁵ There is no recognition that he takes a share of the responsibility given that MUP published many such books under his watch, and he overlooks the fact that his decision to bring out paperback editions of the *History* 'was instrumental in steering Clark's work towards an even more popular audience'.⁶⁶ It escapes him entirely that the work he particularly regrets having published subverted the insidious professionalisation of the historical discipline, since it was written for a general readership and was snapped up by its tens of thousands by 'ordinary people'. Ryan also derides Clark's 'passion to be a public figure',⁶⁷ despite his own ambitions in that direction and the fact that Clark's public profile increasingly enhanced the sales of the *History*. And, to repeat, neither does he explain why he never confronted Clark with his concerns, despite promptings from his critics, including an early (and unanswered) enquiry from a correspondent on that very point:

---

62 Ryan, 'The Charge of the Lightweight Brigade' p. 233; see also Eric Hobsbawm, 'Fact, fiction and historical revisionism', *Australian*, 8 December 1993, p. 21.
63 Peter Ryan, 'End of the Dreamtime' (1986), in his *Lines of Fire,* pp. 101–11. Ryan's biographer is equally uncomprehending as to why the essay was unpublishable in an academic outlet. John Tidey, *Ryan's Luck: A Life of Peter Ryan MM,* Melbourne: Arcadia, 2020, pp. 92–93.
64 Ryan, 'A Reply to my Critics', p. 221.
65 Ryan, 'The Charge of the Lightweight Brigade', p. 232.
66 McKenna, *An Eye for Eternity,* p. 588.
67 Ryan, 'Manning Clark', p. 202.

> As I read [your 28 August article in the *Australian*], one question came to my mind and I anxiously read on expecting an answer. It was not there. To satisfy my curiosity I must ask—'why did you not express these criticisms while Clark was alive?'. Was it your friendship?[68]

There was ample opportunity to raise such matters with Clark, but Ryan had long given up discussing 'editorial problems' with Clark, even via their correspondence. He should not then lay the blame on Clark for the lack of frank discussion between author and publisher.

There are also the false claims. In a 2007 article in the *Australian*, Ryan maintained that 'My *Quadrant* essays (September and October 1993, October 1994) cover the whole of Clark's career and all his published books'.[69] In fact, Clark's two volumes of *Select Documents in Australian History* (1950, 1955), his *Meeting Soviet Man* (1960) and *A Short History of Australia* (1963) are only mentioned in passing, while *Sources of Australian History* (1957) and *In Search of Henry Lawson* (1978) are not mentioned at all. And the three *Quadrant* articles, even in their entirety, add up to a very patchy and lopsided account of Clark's career. One has to ask how far Ryan's version enhances our understanding of Clark and his work, and the temptation is to apply A.G.L. Shaw's assessment of Volume 1, that 'the inaccuracies taken together are irritating, and add up to create a sense of mistrust in the work as a whole'.[70]

Some of these errors and misconceptions can be put down to the honest mistakes that we all make from time to time, but their frequency suggests Ryan was unconcerned about whether he was right or wrong so long as he was persuasive and beguiling. The most charitable interpretation is that he did not take reasonable steps to ensure the accuracy of his information. He did not seem to care whether he was caught out—he would ignore or else deny the charge and go on the counterattack. In a word, he was dissembling. Instead of writing to further 'the survival of historical truth',[71] his attacks on Clark were malicious and politically motivated,

---

68   Cyril White to Ryan, 21 September 1993, Ryan Papers, NLA, MS 9897, Series 6, Box 10, Folder 2. Ryan claimed to have received many abusive letters in the wake of his September 1993 *Quadrant* article. None of these is in his papers so presumably he threw them away in disgust. Cyril White's is the only letter in the Ryan Papers containing criticism.
69   Peter Ryan, 'Manning Clark's second coming', *Australian*, 10 February 2007, p. 29.
70   A.G.L. Shaw, 'Clark's History of Australia', *Meanjin Quarterly*, vol. 22, no. 1, 1963, pp. 117–19, specifically p. 119.
71   Ryan, 'A Reply to my Critics', p. 225.

enabling Ryan to get back at Clark and in the same breath to perpetuate his own public profile. He was simply not interested in telling the truth any more than he was in checking his facts and avoiding distortions. When accused of being ungrateful for the Clarks' hospitality, for example, his response was that it amounted to 'one scratch lunch to me and my friend Gerry Gutman'—a slanderous statement given Dymphna and Manning's renowned hospitality, whether at their Canberra home or their beach house at Wapengo on the southern New South Wales coast.[72]

The broadsides on Clark were in keeping with the common tactic during the History Wars of impugning the character of a target. But until then there had not been such a sustained attack on an individual, apart from the hue and cry surrounding Geoffrey Blainey's criticisms of immigration policy and, by implication, multiculturalism—and even then Blainey stoked the flames rather than allowing the controversy to subside.[73] As well, Ryan was also the first to inject such a personal element. It was a full-scale assault citing personal and professional dealings. Linked to it was a splenetic but unoriginal denunciation of the *History*. He purported to set the record straight but instead engaged in wide-ranging dishonesty, especially in denying that he was politically motivated. His contribution also involved systematic misrepresentation and vilification. Ryan himself asked:

> Is it a disreputable national trait of us Australians to mangle and distort the characters of the dead? To twist them recklessly in any way which current ideology or particular literary purpose needs? My own answer is Yes.[74]

---

72 Peter Ryan, 'Fighting words', review of *The History Wars*, by Macintyre and Clark, *Australian*, 6–7 September 2003, p. R11. The hospitality of the Clarks is ubiquitously documented: Nicholas Gruen, 'On Reading Mark McKenna's Biography of Manning Clark', 25 August 2011, available at: staging.insidestory.org.au/on-reading-mark-mckennas-biography-of-manning-clark/; Bob Reece, '"Don't accept any lifts from professors to Wagga": Some Personal Recollections of Manning Clark', *Australian Historical Association Bulletin*, vol. 83, 1996, pp. 86–92, specifically p. 89; Katerina and Axel Clark, interviewed by Susan Marsden, 19 June 2001, NLA, ORAL TRC 4770 (p. 47 of transcript); Roslyn Russell, email to author, 25 May 2020; McKenna, *An Eye for Eternity*, pp. 269, 312, 508, 544.
73 H.W. Dick, 'The Immigration Debate Revisited', *Asian Studies Review*, vol. 9, no. 2, 1985, pp. 150–56, doi.org/10.1080/03147538508712398; Richard Allsop, *Geoffrey Blainey: Writer, Historian, Controversialist*, Melbourne: Monash University Press, 2019, pp. 142–43, 160; Eric Richards, *Destination Australia: Migration to Australia since 1901*, Sydney: UNSW Press, 2008, pp. 284–88; Frank Bongiorno, *The Eighties: The Decade that Transformed Australia*, Melbourne: Black Inc., 2015, p. 64; Macintyre and Clark, *The History Wars*, p. 82.
74 Peter Ryan, 'Problems with the Truth', *Quadrant*, vol. 48, no. 9, September 2004, pp. 95–96, specifically p. 95.

Such a claim is borne out by his treatment of Clark. The fraudulence that he saw in the *History* and the dishonesty that he detected in Clark repose in himself.[75]

Ryan was a contradictory and perplexing individual in whom the elements were strangely mixed. Energetic and resourceful, he was a fine writer who wasted his talents on invective, both in word and in print. He deplored Paul Keating's studied insults,[76] but he more than matched Keating in that department. He was intensely loyal to friends and hateful towards those who aroused his ire. Indeed, one might wonder how Ryan, who claimed to have had an 'amazingly happy life',[77] could have been so combative and embittered. An arch empiricist and a stickler for accuracy in others, he was indifferent to the truth when it came to himself. He berates Clark for his 'unreliability with mere facts', but his own writings are replete with errors and misrepresentations. His deceit and deception point to something else—namely, the element of the hypocrite, starting with his insincere flattery of Clark. He was also two-faced. As a publisher, Ryan inveighed against Literature Board grants and other forms of subsidising authors,[78] while happily taking advantage of the book bounty, the indirect subsidy provided by his monopoly of campus book sales, and MUP's tax-free status as a result of being part of the University of Melbourne. He did at least acknowledge the latter.[79] Neither did Ryan object to MUP publications being subsidised, whether from private monies or the public purse (the CSIRO subsidised *The Insects of Australia*).[80] As Stuart Macintyre remarked, 'Peter Ryan has been very good at having his cake and eating it too'.[81] How much of this can be attributed to emotional damage during the war is unknown, but probably that had a bearing on his approach to life and affairs.

---

75 Ryan, 'Manning Clark', pp. 200–1 and 'The Charge of the Lightweight Brigade', pp. 228–29.
76 Tidey, *Peter Ryan*, pp. 102–3.
77 Ryan, 'End of the Dreamtime', p. 111.
78 Peter Ryan, 'A Shropshire Lad of Genius' (1988), and 'A.D. Hope: A Memoir' (1992), in his *Lines of Fire*, pp. 50, 153–76, 167 respectively; Ryan, 'Writer's spat over the public purse', *Age*, 13 February 1993, p. Extra 2 ('As I please' column); Ryan, 'Ingrate Writers of Our Times', *Quadrant*, vol. 44, no. 4, April 2000, pp. 87–88; Stuart Glover, 'Literature and the State', in Robyn Sheahan-Bright and Craig Munro (eds), *Paper Empires: A History of the Book in Australia, 1946–2005*, Brisbane: University of Queensland Press, 2006, pp. 165–73, specifically p. 168.
79 Ryan, *Final Proof*, p. 121.
80 Ryan, *Final Proof*, pp. 101, 107–8.
81 Quoted in Louise Carbines, 'Publisher pays out on Manning Clark's "fairy floss"', *Age*, 26 August 1993, p. 1.

Let Ryan have the last word in a summation of Clark that is a mirror image of himself: '*Why* did he behave so? He was a wilful sinner, in my opinion; he *knew* he was doing wrong, and he went on doing it, and profiting from it'.[82]

* * *

But not quite the last word. Clark's adversary Colin Roderick recognised from the outset that the controversy

> is likely now to turn into a political dogfight—left v. right. Unhappily almost all social questions in Australia today seem to have descended to this, so seriously are we 'polarized'.[83]

The irony is that Roderick was actively in touch with Ryan and egging him on, but his instinct about the course of the controversy was correct. Indeed, a feature of History Wars is that what starts as a noisy debate, ostensibly about issues, quickly degenerates into personal abuse and finger-pointing, as Anna Clark discovered. Her discussion of the history curriculum for school children as an aspect of the History Wars drew some disconcerting attacks on the spurious grounds that she was Manning Clark's granddaughter and therefore had a conflict of interest when in fact she has always avoided coat tailing on the reputation of the grandfather she loved as a child. Questioning the integrity, credibility and competence of participants becomes the order of the day. It usually continues to the point of no return as the belligerents paint themselves into a corner in the fashion of Ryan's first *Quadrant* article, which had no hope of creating genuine dialogue given the atmosphere of the early 1990s. What it did do was to turn up the heat, resulting in complaints from both sides that national debate was being reduced to 'an endless stream of invective'.[84]

Many of the Australian History War campaigns were just so much wasted effort. That is to say, a willingness to acknowledge past injustice is not inconsistent with recognising Australia's British heritage. Multiculturism, furthermore, doesn't spell the doom of European civilisation. Clark personified the latter point in that he was ahead of his time in the 1950s in recognising the importance of Asia to Australia and yet his traditions

---

82   Ryan to J.P. Parsons, 16 December 1993, Ryan Papers, NLA, MS 9897, Series 6, Box 10, Folder 5.
83   Roderick to Ryan, 28 August 1993, Ryan Papers, NLA, MS 9897, Series 6, Box 10, Box 4.
84   'Debunking a national icon', *News Weekly,* 11 Sept 1993, for quotation see p. 7; Peter Corrigan, 'Brave new worlds', *Age,* 16 October 1993 (by-line column), p. 11.

were those of Europe—its music, its institutions and its literature. Clark never really fitted into the caricature developed of him by Howard and others on the conservative side of politics. In any case, adherence to either the black-armband school or the three-cheers school is often not about history at all but a function of individual circumstance. An émigré from Nazi Germany who has gone on to prosper is more likely to view Australia as a land of opportunity—a positive view that would hardly be shared by the long-term unemployed.[85]

But that does not prevent public debate becoming polarised around adversarial binaries, which minimises the space for constructive commentary. In this way, History Wars revolve around destructive dichotomies, where the original objective or point of contention tends to get lost. Or else those involved are talking past each other, as Anna Clark noted when Henry Reynolds and Keith Windschuttle attempted, in 2000, to debate historians' accounts of the frontier wars. She found it 'excruciating':

> The two speakers couldn't engage with one another on any level. Their arguments snapped and slashed with brittle vehemence as they stood on a balcony above the audience, and they became increasingly frustrated and irate.[86]

The Climate Wars are another example of a no-holds-barred situation.[87]

Confrontational opposition is not the way to come to terms with the past, nor a means of resolving valid differences. As McKenna says, 'The time for pitting white against black, shame against pride, and one people's history against another's has had its day'—a sound principle but not one that is amenable to being put into practice.[88] Rather, damaging, unproductive and pointless confrontations are forever afoot. Yet the message should be heeded that 'a country that has the courage to look its history in the eye will be the stronger for it'.[89]

---

85   Eugene Kamenka, '"Australia Made Me" … But which Australia is Mine?', *Quadrant*, vol. 37, no. 10, October 1993, pp. 24–31.
86   Anna Clark, 'The History Wars', pp. 151–52.
87   Peter Doherty, *The Knowledge Wars*, Melbourne: MUP, 2015; Mark Butler, *Climate Wars*, Melbourne: MUP, 2017.
88   Mark McKenna, 'Moment of Truth: History and Australia's Future', *Quarterly Essay*, no. 69, January 2018, pp. 1–83, specifically p. 73. Comparable thoughts are expressed by David Cannadine, *The Undivided Past: Humanity Beyond our Differences*, New York: Alfred A. Knopf, 2013, doi.org/10.1515/ngs-2013-018.
89   McKenna, 'Moment of Truth', p. 71.

These are counsels of perfection for the Australian History Wars, with their entrenched binaries, which are most likely here to stay and to be 'dominated by a public debate that's simplistic, divisive and overly partisan'.[90] They are often driven by the print media and in ways that encourage polarised thinking by setting up adversarial scenarios where neither side yields an inch. It is called 'balance'. The media are also in a position to set the terms of a given History War by what they choose to publish or not to publish, and by what they commission and the columnists they hire. More pointedly, journalist Laura Tingle has observed that 'the culture wars … are the stock-in-trade of Rupert Murdoch's media empire'.[91] Social media now chimes to the accompaniment of the mainstream, its immediate and often unrestrained rejoinders discordantly raising the temperature. The study of history itself is the casualty. The other consideration is that nation states do not want their indiscretions publicised or their past blackened and will often resort to prescriptive interventions, the Armenian genocide being a prime example. While there is nothing wrong with historical perspectives being utilised to inform policy decisions,[92] it is singularly unhelpful when politicians hijack history, or promulgate a view of the past, to bolster their own agendas.

One such occasion was John Howard's memorable intervention, in 2004, involving a $31 billion federal package for education spread over four years. There were numerous conditions, one of which was that individual schools would not receive any windfall unless they flew the Australian flag in the prescribed manner. There was no attempt to interfere with the history syllabus as such but the stipulation 'to fly the flag' was in response to Howard's (ostensible) perception that the 'value neutral' and 'politically correct' history being taught in state schools was causing an exodus of students to their private counterparts. (How 'value neutral' history can also be 'politically correct' history is indeed a teasing question.) It was all part of a broader campaign to foster patriotism and the teaching of 'proper' values in schools—in other words, his own version of what history ought to be. It raised a storm of censure with the federal president of the Australian Education Union saying that the measure was 'a preoccupation

---

90 Anna Clark, 'The History Wars', p. 152.
91 Laura Tingle, 'The High Road: What Can Australia Learn from New Zealand', *Quarterly Essay*, no. 80, December 2020, pp. 1–112, specifically p. 4.
92 For example, Julian M. Simpson, Kath Checkland, Stephanie J. Snow, Jennifer Voorhees, Katy Rothwell and Aneez Esmail, 'Adding the Past to the Policy Mix: An Historical Approach to the Issue of Access to General Practice in England', *Contemporary British History*, vol. 32, no. 2, 2018, pp. 276–99, doi.org/10.1080/13619462.2017.1401474.

with appearances rather than substance. Issues of civics education are far more subtle, and far more wide-ranging than whether or not you have a functioning flagpole'.[93] By contrast, New Zealand's Prime Minister Jacinda Ardern wisely kept the question at arms-length when asked about a petition in 2019 from the New Zealand History Teachers' Association that the 'coherent' teaching of history be mandatory for all schools. She said that this was 'common sense' and left it at that.[94] When a comprehensive new history syllabus for schools came out two-and-a-half years later, Ardern continued to deflect controversy by announcing the teachers would get the support they needed to implement such sweeping changes.[95] It was not a matter of stifling debate but of avoiding unnecessary conflict and polarisation, and that is the way it should be, with politicians smoothing the way rather than stirring up discord. Neither should politicians attempt to impose prescriptive discourses of patriotism, wartime heroism and national greatness (or guilt for that matter) on educationalists. It is well said that 'professional historians and responsible teachers cannot "devote themselves to writing a catechism for someone's version of civil religion" and call the result history'.[96]

In his attack on Clark, Ryan did allude to the History Wars in classrooms when he claimed that his criticisms of Clark were 'for the protection of the young and innocent'.[97] The *History*, he claimed, 'might be dangerous to the mental health of young persons'.[98] These were quite spurious concerns. Instead, Ryan was motivated partly by the quest for notoriety; partly to get back at Clark for being a difficult author and a poseur to boot; partly to attack the *History* and to absolve himself from responsibility

---

93   Anna Clark, *History's Children: History Wars in the Classroom,* Sydney: NewSouth, 2008, pp. 51–53; Andra Jackson and Shane Green, 'Schools told to fly flag or lose cash', *Age,* 23 June 2004, for quotation, available at: www.theage.com.au/national/schools-told-to-fly-flag-or-lose-cash-20040623-gdy3ni.html.
94   Aaron Leaman, 'Teaching New Zealand history "common sense": Prime Minister Jacinda Ardern', 13 June 2019, available at: www.stuff.co.nz/national/politics/113459160/teaching-new-zealand-history-common-sense-prime-minister-jacinda-ardern.
95   'Teachers will get support they need to teach new history curriculum, PM says', Radio New Zealand, 7 February 2021, available at: www.rnz.co.nz/news/political/435954/teachers-will-get-support-they-need-to-teach-new-history-curriculum-pm-says. New Zealand has not had a fully blown History War—yet. But see Vincent O'Malley and Joanna Kidman, 'Settler Colonial History, Commemoration and White Backlash: Remembering the New Zealand Wars', *Settler Colonial Studies,* vol. 8, no. 3, 2018, pp. 298–313, doi.org/10.1080/2201473X.2017.1279831.
96   Gary B. Nash, Charlotte Crabtree and Ross E. Dunn, *History on Trial: Culture Wars and the Teaching of the Past,* New York: Alfred A. Knopf, 1997, p. 227.
97   Ryan, 'The Charge of the Lightweight Brigade', p. 234.
98   Ryan, 'A Reply to my Critics', p. 214.

for its propagation; partly to regain work as a columnist (this time for *Quadrant*); and partly to weigh in on behalf of the three-cheers school of history and thus ramp up the Australian History Wars.

Seen in this light, Peter Ryan was flying under false colours. He was not providing a much-needed exposé of a charlatan and his works. Rather, his attacks on Manning Clark in *Quadrant* were irresponsible and came from a self-interested polemic that debased national debate. His interventions had nothing to do with such mundane yet necessary matters as honesty, good faith and sound historical practice—and least of all with civic courage.

Appendices

Appendix 1: Pre-Ryan Material in *Quadrant* that Critiques Clark (1968–93)

These entries are arranged chronologically. The book reviews refer to C.M.H. Clark, *A History of Australia*.

1968 A.G.L. Shaw, 'Manning Clark's History of Australia', review of Volume 2 (1822–38), vol. 12, no. 4, July, pp. 74–77, 79–82.

1978 Peter Schrubb, 'Culture & Stuff', vol. 22, no. 7, July, pp. 32–34.

1979 'Opinion: A Matter of Moral Courage', vol. 23, no. 11, November, p. 61.

G.P. Shaw, 'The Manufacture of Prejudice', review of *The Manufacture of Australian History*, by Rob Pascoe, vol. 23, no. 12, December, pp. 8–12.

1980 Ronald Conway, 'The Australia Watchers: Fifty Years since Hancock', vol. 24, no. 4, April, pp. 3–12.

1981 A.D. Hope, 'Rough-Riders in the Chariot', vol. 25, no. 5, May, p. 3 (satirical poem).

H.W. Arndt, 'National Identity', vol. 25, no. 8, August, pp. 27–30.

1982 Claudio Veliz, 'Bad History', review of Volume 5 (1890–1915), vol. 26, no. 5, May, pp. 21–26.

John Carroll, 'Manning Clark's Vision Splendid', vol. 26, no. 10, October, pp. 61–64.

1984 Roger Scruton, 'The Usurpation of the State: The 1984 Latham Memorial Lecture', vol. 28, no. 11, November, pp. 9–14.

Hal Colebatch, 'Professor Manning Clark and Sir John Forrest', vol. 28, no. 12, December, pp. 60–64.

1987 P.A. Howell, 'Plutocrats in Paradise: Some New Insights into the Constitutional and Political History of South Australia', vol. 31, no. 5, May, pp. 41–48.

1988 Hal G.P. Colebatch, 'Manning Clark, My Father and "Bloody Sunday": The 1919 Fremantle Wharf Riots', vol. 32, nos 1–2, January–February, pp. 24–26.

1989 H.W. Arndt, '"Besmirched by Greed": An Insatiable Longing for Wealth?' vol. 33, no. 12, December, p. 65.

1991 H.W. Arndt, 'Does this Emperor have Clothes', vol. 35, no. 6, June, p. 27.

John Barrett, 'Manning Clark: The Historian', vol. 35, nos 7–8, July–August, pp. 7–8. Republished as 'Two Clarks', in Carl Bridge (ed.), *Manning Clark: Essays on his Place in History*, Melbourne: Melbourne University Press (MUP), pp. 113–16.

1993 John Hirst, 'Australian History and European Civilisation',, vol. 37, no. 5, May, pp. 28–38. Republished as the first part of a chapter titled 'The Whole Game Escaped Him', in Carl Bridge (ed.), *Manning Clark: Essays on his Place in History*, Melbourne: MUP, pp. 117–21.

Geoffrey Blainey, 'Drawing up a Balance Sheet of Our History', vol. 37, nos 7–8, July–August, pp. 10–15. Republished as 'The Black Armband View of History', in Geoffrey Blainey, *In Our Time: The Issues and the People of Our Century*, Melbourne: Information Australia, 1999, pp. 3–14.

Appendix 2: Selected Pre-Ryan Assessments of Clark's Life and Work (apart from reviews and contributions to *Quadrant*)

1963 Brian Fitzpatrick, 'Counter Revolution in Australian Historiography', *Meanjin Quarterly,* vol. 22, no. 2, pp. 197–213.

Bede Nairn, 'Writing Australian History', *Manna,* vol. 6, pp. 107–30.

1970 Ian Turner, 'Manning Clark: History and the Voice of Prophecy', *Overland,* vol. 44, pp. 13–20, reprinted in Turner, *Room to Manoeuvre,* Melbourne: Drummond, 1982, pp. 229–45.

1973 David Duffy, Grant Harman and Keith Swan (eds), *Historians at Work: Investigating and Recreating the Past,* Sydney: Hicks Smith & Sons.

1974 James Waldersee, *Catholic Society in New South Wales, 1788 1860,* Sydney: Sydney University Press.

1975 Leith McGillivray, 'Manning Clark: A Study in the Art and Craft of History', BA (Hons) thesis, University of Adelaide.

1977 R.W. Connell, *Ruling Class, Ruling Culture: Studies of Conflict, Power and Hegemony in Australian Life,* Cambridge: Cambridge University Press, doi.org/10.1017/CBO9781139085076.

1978 Peter C. Bosmann, 'Three approaches to Manning Clark: Tradition, Vision and Technique', BA (Hons) thesis, Griffith University.

R.W. Connell, 'Manning Clark and the Science of History', *Meanjin,* vol. 37, no. 2, pp. 262–68.

Rob Pascoe, 'The Making of Manning Clark', *National Times,* 27 May–2 June, pp. 18–20, 22–23, available at: vuir.vu.edu.au/19397/1/Pascoe_Manning_Clark__National_Times_2_June_1978_%282%29.pdf.

Michael Roe, 'Challenges to Australian Identity and Esteem in Recent Historical Writing', 1977 Eldershaw Memorial Lecture, *Tasmanian Historical Research Association—Papers & Proceedings,* vol. 63, no. 2, pp. 51–65.

Tim Rowse, *Australian Liberalism and National Character,* Melbourne: Kibble Books.

1979 John Docker, 'Manning Clark's Henry Lawson', *Labour History,* vol. 37, pp. 1–14. doi.org/10.2307/27508380.

John Lechte, *Politics and the Writing of Australian History: An Introductory Study,* Melbourne: Political Science Department, University of Melbourne.

Allan Martin, 'The Changing Perspective on Australian History', in William S. Livingston and Wm Roger Louis (eds), *Australia, New Zealand and the Pacific since the First World War,* Canberra: The Australia National University Press, pp. 9–31, available at: openresearch-repository.anu.edu.au/bitstream/1885/114738/2/b12285171.pdf.

Ailsa McLeary (ed.), 'Manning Clark and Australian Historiography', special issue of *Australia 1888,* vol. 3, pp. 4–73. Contributions by Peter Munz, C.B. Schedvin, Ailsa McLeary, Lucy Frost, Stuart Macintyre, Donald F. Miller, Alastair Davidson and C.M.H. Clark.

John A. Moses (ed.), *The Historical Disciplines and Culture in Australia: An Assessment,* Brisbane: University of Queensland Press.

Rob Pascoe, *The Manufacture of Australian History,* Melbourne: Oxford University Press.

1982 John Carroll, 'National Identity', in John Carroll (ed.), *Intruders in the Bush: The Australian Quest for Identity*, Melbourne: Oxford University Press, pp. 209–25.

Stephen Holt, *Manning Clark and Australian History, 1915–1963*, Brisbane: University of Queensland Press, esp. chapter 8 ('Critics, Compilers and Commentators', pp. 172–95).

Stuart Macintyre, 'Manning Clark's Critics', *Meanjin*, vol. 41, no. 4, pp. 442–52.

1984 Humphrey McQueen, *Gallipoli to Petrov: Arguing with Australian History*, Sydney: Allen & Unwin.

1985 John Carroll, 'The Disintegration of Australia's British Links', *IPA Review*, vol. 40, no. 2, Winter 1986, pp. 27–29.

Andrew David Wells, 'A Marxist Reappraisal of Australian Capitalism: The Rise of Anglo-Colonial Finance Capital in New South Wales and Victoria, 1830–1890', PhD thesis, The Australian National University, available at: core.ac.uk/download/pdf/156720075.pdf.

1987 Paul Carter, *The Road to Botany Bay*, London: Faber.

Ross Terrill, *The Australians: In Search of an Identity*, London: Bantam Press.

1988 Mark Hutchinson, 'Manning Clark and the Limits of Prophetability', *Lucas: An Evangelical History Review*, vol. 4, pp. 28–34, available at: drive.google.com/file/d/1qC1lzT8Q-YbLFXS0cm8HgSk7DwZUXVHo/view.

G.P. Shaw (ed.), *1988 And All That*, Brisbane: University of Queensland Press.

1990 Geoffrey Blainey, 'The Manning Clark School of History', *Scripsi*, vol. 6, no. 2, pp. 61–65.

Gerard Henderson, 'To the Garden of Eden in Red Socks', in his *Australian Answers*, Sydney: Random House Australia, pp. 99–111.

Brian Hocking (ed.), *Australian towards 2000*, Basingstoke: Macmillan Palgrave.

1991 Peter Cotton, 'Manning Clark on Life, Politics and the Quest for Grace', *National Graduate,* vol. 2, no. 1, pp. 7–8.

1992 David Carter, 'Celebrating the Nation', in Tony Bennett, Pat Buckridge, David Carter and Colin Mercer (eds), *Celebrating the Nation: A Critical Study of Australia's Bicentenary,* Sydney: Allen & Unwin, pp. 87–103 (text), 206–8 (endnotes).

Appendix 3: Articles that Discuss Manning Clark in Peter Ryan's *Quadrant* Column (1994–2014)

1994 'A Farthing Candle', vol. 38, no. 3, March, pp. 87–88.

1996 'The Labor Pantheon', vol. 40, no. 6, June, pp. 87–88.

2000 'The ADB', vol. 44, no. 6, June, pp. 87–88.

2001 'Justice Kirby's Clark', vol. 45, no. 5, May, pp. 87–88.

'The Boy from the Sir Walter Scott', vol. 45, no. 6, June, pp. 87–88.

2002 'Horror Double-Feature', *Quadrant,* vol. 46, nos 7–8, July–August 2002, pp. 111–12.

2003 'A Better Place', *Quadrant,* vol. 47, nos 1–2, January–February, pp. 119–20.

2004 'Problems with the Truth', vol. 48, no. 9, September, pp. 95–96.

2005 'Hats Off', vol. 49, no. 12, December, pp. 95–96, reprinted in Peter Ryan, *It Strikes Me: Collected Essays, 1994–2010*, Sydney: Quadrant Books, 2010, pp. 172–77.

2006 'Calibans of Culture', vol. 50, no. 4, April, pp. 95–96, reprinted in Ryan, *It Strikes Me*, pp. 190–95.

'Kokoda in Perspective', vol. 50, no. 6, June, pp. 95–96.

'Is the Uncivil War Over?' vol. 50, no. 10, October, pp. 95–96.

2008 'The Arts and Craft of the Luncheon', vol. 52, nos 1–2, January–February, pp. 127–28.

'Our Defrauded Young', vol. 52, no. 4, April, pp. 127–28, reprinted in Ryan, *It Strikes Me*, pp. 249–54.

2009 'Hollow Man of Yesterday', vol. 53, nos 1–2, January–February, pp. 126–28.

2010 'The Chatterers of Australia', vol. 54, nos 1–2, January–February, pp. 127–28, reprinted in Ryan, *It Strikes Me*, pp. 291–95.

2011 'My Life as a Leper', vol. 55, nos 1–2, January–February, pp. 127–28.

2013 'The Only Justifiable End of Eloquence', vol. 57, no. 9, September, pp. 111–12.

2014 'Heroes' Corner', vol. 58, no. 10, October, pp. 111–12.

Appendix 4: Academic (and Quasi-Academic) Coverage of Manning Clark's Life and Work (1993–2021)

The names of authors who wrote about Manning Clark and were published in *Quadrant* have been rendered in bold. Peter Ryan's references to Clark in his *Quadrant* column are itemised in Appendix 3.

Apart from some of the *Quadrant* entries, this Appendix is confined to items where Clark is discussed in his own right or else receives noteworthy mention. Passing remarks on a point of substance are also included. It excludes newspaper articles and obituaries. The contents of this Appendix demonstrate the continuing ubiquity of Manning Clark as someone of importance and relevance, such was the number and variety of his friends (and enemies!), the many contexts in which he appeared and the sheer range of his activities.

1993 Geoffrey Bolton, 'Don't smash the icon', *Bulletin*, 12 October, pp. 42–43.

Geoffrey Bolton, 'Oedipus Clark for the Nineties', *Editions*, no. 17, August–September, p. 9.

Fiona Capp, *Writers Defiled: Security Surveillance of Australian Authors and Intellectuals, 1920–1960,* Melbourne: McPhee Gribble.

Rosamund Dalziell, 'The Shaming of Manning Clark', *Eureka Street,* vol. 8, no. 3, pp. 40–41, available at: www.eurekastreet.com.au/uploads/File/pdf/EurekaStreetClassic/Vol3No8.pdf. Reprinted from the *Canberra Times,* 16 October, p. C5.

John Hirst, 'Australian History and European Civilisation', *Quadrant,* vol. 37, no. 5, May, pp. 28–38. The first section of this essay was republished as 'The Whole Game Escaped Him', in Carl Bridge (ed.), *Manning Clark: Essays on his Place in History,* Melbourne: Melbourne University Press (hereafter MUP), 1994, pp. 117–21.

Eugene Kamenka, '"Australia Made Me" ... But which Australia is Mine?', *Quadrant,* vol. 37, no. 10, October, pp. 24–31.

Shaun Patrick Kenaelly, 'C.D. Kemp and the IPA's Foundations', *IPA Review,* vol. 46, no. 3, pp. 57–62.

Leonie Kramer, 'McAuley Traduced', *Quadrant,* vol. 37, no. 10, October, pp. 55–56.

Robert Manne, 'Manning Clark, Peter Ryan and Us', *Quadrant,* vol. 37, no. 10, October, pp. 2–3.

Maurilia Meehan, 'Spot the Invisible Man', *Australian Book Review,* vol. 156, November, pp. 34–37.

Ronald T. Ridley, *Jessie Webb: A Memoir,* Melbourne, History Department, University of Melbourne.

'Symposium: Defending Manning Clark', *Evatt Papers,* vol. 1, no. 2, pp. 13–24, with contributions by Sol Encel, Stuart Macintyre and Don Watson.

1994 Carl Bridge (ed.), *Manning Clark: Essays on his Place in History,* Melbourne: MUP. With contributions by Carl Bridge, Don Baker, Russel Ward, Stuart Macintyre, G.P. Shaw, John Rickard, P.A. Howell, S.J. Ryan, Susan Pfisterer-Smith, John Atchison, Jo Woolmington, Alan Atkinson, Susan Davies, John Warhurst, Peter Craven and Miriam Dixon; republished contributions by M.H. Ellis, John Barrett and John Hirst.

Joy Hooton, 'Australian Autobiography and the Question of National Identity: Patrick White, Barry Humphries and Manning Clark', *a/b: Auto/Biography Studies,* vol. 9, no. 1, pp. 43–63, doi.org/10.1080/08989575.1994.10846731.

Bob James, 'Untangling Issues in the Clark Debate', *Recorder: Official Organ of the Melbourne Branch of the Australian Society for the Study of Labour History,* no. 183, pp. 6–10.

Stuart Macintyre, *A History for a Nation: Ernest Scott and the Making of Australian History,* Melbourne: MUP.

Humphrey McQueen, 'Manning Clark Revisited', *ABC Radio 24 Hours,* March, pp. 54–56.

Robert Manne, 'The Puzzles of Manning Clark', *Quadrant,* vol. 38, no. 11, November, pp. 2–3.

'Clark, Manning (Charles Manning Hope) (1915–1991)', in William Wilde, Joy Hooton and Barry Andrews (eds), *The Oxford Companion to Australian Literature,* 2nd edn, Melbourne: Oxford University Press, pp. 167–68.

1995 Stuart Macintyre and Julian Thomas (ed.), *The Discovery of Australian History, 1890–1939,* Melbourne: MUP.

John A. Moses (ed.), 'Historical Disciplines in Australasia: Themes, Problems and Debates', *Australian Journal of Politics and History,* vol. 41 (special issue).

Ann Moyal, *Breakfast with Beaverbrook: Memoirs of an Independent Woman,* Sydney: Hale & Iremonger.

1996 Rosamund Dalziell, 'Patterns of Shame in Some Australian Autobiographies, 1960 to 1995', PhD thesis, The Australian National University, 1996, available at: openresearch-repository. anu.edu.au/bitstream/1885/10415/1/01Front_Dalziell.pdf.

Susan Davies (ed.), *Dear Kathleen, Dear Manning: The Correspondence of Manning Clark and Kathleen Fitzpatrick, 1949–1990,* Melbourne: MUP.

Gertjan Dijkink, *National Identity and Geopolitical Visions: Maps of Pride and Pain,* London/New York: Routledge, doi.org/10.4324/9780203437933.

Stephen Foster and Margaret M. Varghese, *The Making of the Australian National University, 1946–1996,* Sydney: Allen & Unwin. Republished in 2009 by ANU E Press, doi.org/10.22459/MANU.08.2009.

Paul Johnson, 'Australia's Fraudulent Historian', in his *To Hell with Picasso & Other Essays,* London: Weidenfeld & Nicolson.

David McCooey, *Artful Histories: Modern Australian Autobiography,* Melbourne: Cambridge University Press, doi.org/10.1017/CBO9781139084956.

Mark McKenna, *The Captive Republic: A History of Republicanism in Australia, 1877–1996,* Cambridge: Cambridge University Press.

Humphrey McQueen, 'Unusual Suspects', National Library Australian Voices Essay, *Australian Book Review*, no. 186, November, pp. 36–41.

Humphrey McQueen, 'Unusual Suspects', *Australian Book Review*, no. 186, November, pp. 36–41.

Patrick O'Brien, 'Manning Clark: The Ideology Man', APSA Paper, (copy in the Ryan Papers, National Library of Australia, MS 9897, Series 6, Box 10, folder 9).

Bob Reece, 'Don't Accept any Lifts from Professors to Wagga: Some Personal Reflections on Manning Clark', *Australian Historical Association Bulletin,* no. 83, pp. 86–92.

1997 Carl Bridge, 'Manning Clark and the Ratbag Tradition', *Journal of Australian Studies,* vol. 21, no. 54–55, pp. 91–95, doi.org/10.1080/14443059709387341.

Ian Britain, Once an Australian: Journeys with Barry Humphries, Clive James, Germaine Greer and Robert Hughes, Melbourne: Oxford University Press.

David John Carter, *A Career in Writing: Judah Waten and the Cultural Politics of a Political Career,* Toowoomba: Association for the Study of Australian Literature.

Robert Manne, 'Humphrey Bare', review of *Suspect History,* by Humphrey McQueen, *Quadrant,* vol. 41, nos 7–8, July–August, pp. 2–4.

Brian Matthews, *Pursuing Literature and History in Australia: The Fate of Henry Lawson and Manning Clark,* London: Sir Robert Menzies Centre for Australian Studies.

Humphrey McQueen, *Suspect History: Manning Clark and the Future of Australia's Past,* Adelaide: Wakefield Press.

Peter Ryan, *Lines of Fire: Manning Clark & Other Writings*, ed. A.K. Macdougall, Binalong, NSW: Clarion Editions.

Peter Shrubb, 'Fiery Lines', review of *Lines of Fire,* by Peter Ryan, *Quadrant,* vol. 41, no. 10, October, pp. 78–80.

1998 Carl Bridge, 'Clark, (Charles) Manning Hope (1915–1991)', in Graeme Davison, John Hirst and Stuart Macintyre (eds), *The Oxford Companion to Australian History,* Melbourne: Oxford University Press, 128–29.

David Carter (ed.), *Judah Waten: Fiction, Memoirs, Criticism,* Brisbane: University of Queensland Press.

Darryl McIntyre and Kay Saunders, 'Official Historian', in Tom Stannage, Kay Saunders and Richard Nile (eds), *Paul Hasluck in Australian History,* Brisbane: University of Queensland Press, pp. 46–59.

Mark McKenna, 'An Article of Faith for a Sceptical Democracy', *Eureka Street,* vol. 8, no. 2, pp. 29–33.

Wayne Smith, 'Manning Clark and the *Courier Mail*', *Quadrant,* vol. 42, no. 9, September, pp. 40–43.

1999 Rosamund Dalziell, *Shameful Autobiographies: Shame in Contemporary Australian Autobiographies and Culture,* Melbourne: MUP.

Stephen Holt, *A Short History of Manning Clark,* Sydney: Allen & Unwin.

Thelma Hunter, *Not A Dutiful Daughter: The Personal Story of a Migrant Academic*, Canberra: Ginninderra Press.

Stuart Macintyre, 'History Ain't History', *Australian Quarterly,* vol. 71, no. 6, pp. 8–11 and 40, doi.org/10.2307/20637860.

Andrew Moore, '"History without Facts": M.H. Ellis, Manning Clark and the Origins of the *Australia Dictionary of Biography*', *Journal of the Royal Australian Historical Society,* vol. 85, no. 2, pp. 71–84.

Allan Patience, 'The Treason of the Universities: Late-Modernity versus Intellectuals', *Australian Quarterly,* vol. 71, no. 2, pp. 14–23, doi.org/10.2307/20637806.

Cassandra Pybus, *The Devil and James McAuley,* Brisbane: University of Queensland Press.

2000 Kenneth R. Dutton, *Auchmuty: The Life of James Johnson Auchmuty (1909–1981),* Mount Nebo, Qld: Boombana Publications.

John Fisher, 'History Master', *Quadrant,* vol. 44, no. 4, April, pp. 58–60.

Deborah Gare, '"Breathing the Ashes of Empire": The Journeys of Four Australian Historians in Belonging, Identity and in the Australian Experience of Empire', PhD thesis, University of Western Australia, available at: api.research-repository.uwa.edu.au/portalfiles/portal/52369632/Gare_Deborah_2000.pdf.

Andrew Moore, 'The "Historical Expert": M.H. Ellis and the Historiography of the Cold War', *Australian Historical Studies,* vol. 31, no. 114, pp. 91–109, doi.org/10.1080/10314610008596117.

Raymond Watson, 'Immigration, the Untouchable', *Quadrant,* vol. 44, no. 3, March, pp. 58–65.

2001 James Griffin, 'A Big Lie: Manning Clark, Frank Hardy and "Fictitious History"', *Australian Book Review,* no. 231, June, pp. 25–28.

Michael Kirby, 'Manning Clark, "Bourgeoisie Democracy" and Strange Tales from Supreme Courts', Manning Clark Lecture, 26 March, available at: www.hcourt.gov.au/assets/publications/speeches/former-justices/kirbyj/kirbyj_manningclark.htm#_ftn26.

Michael Kirby, 'Strange Tales from Supreme Courts', *Quadrant,* vol. 45, no. 8, August, pp. 10–14.

D.A. Low (ed.), *Keith Hancock: The Legacies of an Historian,* Melbourne: MUP.

Neville Meaney, 'Britishness and Australian Identity: The Problem of Nationalism in Australian History and Historiography', *Australian Historical Studies,* vol. 32, no. 116, pp. 76–90, doi.org/10.1080/10314610108596148. Republished in James Curran and Stuart Ward (eds), *Australia and the Wider World: Selected Essays of Neville Meaney,* Sydney: Sydney University Press, pp. 23–36.

Dirk Moses, 'Coming to Terms with Genocidal Pasts in Comparative Perspective: Germany and Australia', *Aboriginal History,* vol. 25, no. 91–115, doi.org/10.22459/AH.25.2011.

Robert Murray, 'Forty Years of Manning Clark', *Quadrant*, vol. 45, no. 11, November, pp. 46–53, doi.org/10.2118/1101-0046-JPT.

Geoffrey Partington, 'Manning Clark and White Australia', *Quadrant*, vol. 45, nos 7–8, July–August, pp. 15–20.

2002 Jan Bassett, *The Facing Island: A Personal Journey*, Melbourne: MUP.

Frank G. Clarke, *The History of Australia*, Westport, CN: Greenwood Press.

James Griffin, 'Albert Jacka and the Choice of Achilles', *Quadrant*, vol. 46, nos 1–2, January–February, pp. 52–55.

Graeme Powell, *Guide to the Papers of Manning Clark in the National Library of Australia*, Canberra: National Library of Australia.

2003 Judith Brett, *Australian Liberals and the Moral Middle Class: From Alfred Deakin to John Howard*, Cambridge: Cambridge University Press, doi.org/10.1017/CBO9780511481642.

Deborah Gare, Geoffrey Bolton, Stuart Macintyre and Tom Stannage (eds), *The Fuss That Never Ended: The Life and Work of Geoffrey Bolton*, Melbourne: MUP.

Stuart Macintyre, 'The History Wars', *Sydney Papers*, Winter/Spring, pp. 77–83, available at: www.evatt.org.au/post/the-history-wars.

Stuart Macintyre and Anna Clark, *The History Wars*, Melbourne: MUP, 2nd edition published in 2004.

Mark McKenna, '"I wonder whether I belong": Manning Clark and the Politics of Australian History', *Australian Historical Studies*, vol. 34, no. 132, pp. 364–83, doi.org/10.1080/10314610308596260.

John McLaren, *Free Radicals of the Left in Postwar Melbourne*, Melbourne: Australian Scholarly Publishing.

2004 Hal G.P. Colebatch, 'Manning Clark and Judah Waten', *National Observer*, vol. 60, Autumn, pp. 23–31.

Robert Manne, 'On the Manning Clark Affair' (1996), in his *Left Right Left: Political Essays, 1977–2005*, Melbourne: Black Inc, 2004, pp. 81–91.

Geoffrey Partington, 'Stumped for Grace', *Quadrant*, vol. 48, no. 12, December, pp. 56–57.

Jill Waterhouse, *University House As They Experienced It: A History, 1954–2004*, Canberra: University House, The Australian National University.

2004–05 Graeme Powell, 'The Manning Clark Archives', *Australian Book Review*, no. 267, December–January, p. 10.

2005 Fay Anderson, *An Historian's Life: Max Crawford and the Politics of Academic Freedom*, Melbourne: MUP.

Jim Meagher, 'Jim McClelland', *Quadrant*, vol. 49, no. 6, June, pp. 16–18.

Ann Moyal, *Alan Moorehead: A Rediscovery*, Canberra: National Library of Australia.

Craig Murray, 'Intellectuals in the Australian Press', PhD thesis, University of Queensland, available at: eprints.qut.edu.au/16022/1/Craig_Murray_Thesis.pdf.

Jeremy D. Popkin, *History, Historians & Autobiography*, Chicago/London: University of Chicago Press.

Stuart Ward, '"Culture up to our Arseholes": Projecting Post-Imperial Australia', *Australian Journal of History and Politics*, vol. 51, no. 1, pp. 53–66, doi.org/10.1111/j.1467-8497.2005.00360.x.

2006 Fay Anderson and Stuart Macintyre (eds), *The Life of the Past: The Discipline of History at the University of Melbourne, 1855–2005*, Melbourne: Department of History, University of Melbourne.

Hal G.P. Colebatch, 'Sir Hal Colebatch and the Missing Secret Army', *Quadrant*, vol. 50, no. 4, April, pp. 31–34.

Hal G.P. Colebatch, 'Manning Clark, Courage and Meeting Soviet Man', *Adelaide Review*, October, pp. 6–7.

Frank Devine, 'A Conversation with Geoffrey Blainey', *Quadrant*, vol. 50, no. 10, October, pp. 48–52.

John Howard, 'A Tribute to *Quadrant*', *Quadrant*, vol. 50, no. 11, November, pp. 22–24.

Jonathan Hyslop, 'Colonial Intellectuals at the End of Empire: Manning Clark's Australia and Guy Butler's South Africa', *KLEIO: African Historical Review,* vol. 38, no. 1, pp. 25–39, doi.org/10.1080/00232080685310031.

Barry Jones, *A Thinking Reed*, Sydney: Allen & Unwin.

Brij V. Lal and Allison Ley (eds), *The Coombs: A House of Memories*, Canberra: Research School of Pacific Studies, The Australian National University. Republished by ANU Press, 2014, doi.org/10.22459/C.2014.

Robert Murray, 'Commonsense History', *Quadrant,* vol. 50, no. 10, October, pp. 34–36.

John Thompson, *The Patrician and the Bloke: Geoffrey Serle and the Making of Australian History,* Canberra: Pandanus Press.

2006–07 David Campbell, 'Double Lives: Three Australian Fellow-travellers in the Cold War', *National Observer,* vol. 71, Summer, pp. 42–56, available at: www.thefreelibrary.com/Double+lives%3A+three+Australian+fellow-travellers+in+the+Cold+War.-a0160220526.

2007 Judith Brett, *Robert Menzies' Forgotten People,* 2nd edn, Melbourne: MUP.

Eduardo Marks de Marques, 'Around 1988: History and/as Fiction and the Australian Bicentenary', PhD thesis, University of Queensland, 2007, available at: www.academia.edu/1561143/Around_1988_History_And_as_Fiction_And_the_Australian_Bicentenary.

Stuart Macintyre and Sheila Fitzpatrick (eds), *Against the Grain: Brian Fitzpatrick and Manning Clark in Australian History and Politics,* Melbourne: MUP. Chapters on Clark by Stuart Macintyre, Roger Douglas, Mark McKenna, Nicholas Brown, Jill Roe, Peter Fitzpatrick and Katerina Clark.

Brian Matthews, 'What Dymphna Knew: Manning Clark and *Kristallnacht*', *Australian Book Review,* no. 291, March, pp. 18–24.

Mark McKenna, 'Being There: The Strange History of Manning Clark', *The Monthly*, no. 21, March, pp. 22–37. Republished as: 'Being There', in Drusilla Modjeska (ed.), *The Best Australian Essays 2007*, Melbourne: Black Inc., 2007, pp. 199–226. See also: 'Once More with Feeling: The Personal Voice of Manning Clark', in Stuart Macintyre and Sheila Fitzpatrick (eds), *Against the Grain: Brian Fitzpatrick and Manning Clark in Australian History and Politics*, Melbourne: MUP, 2007, pp. 191–22; 'Once More with Feeling: The Strange History of Manning Clark', in Amit Sarwal and Reema Sarwal (eds), *Fact & Fiction: Readings in Australian Literature*, New Delhi: Authorspress, 2008, pp. 323–53.

Brenda Niall, *Life Class: The Education of a Biographer*, Melbourne: MUP, 2007.

Anne O'Brien, 'Rethinking Blasphemy: Religious Ideas in the Writings of W.K. Hancock, Manning Clark and Russel Ward', *Australian Historical Studies*, vol. 38, no. 130, pp. 228–42, doi.org/10.1080/10314610708601244.

Jeremy Popkin, 'Ego-Histoire Down Under: Australian Historian-Autobiographers', *Australian Historical Studies*, vol. 38, no. 129, pp. 106–23. doi.org/10.1080/10314610708601234.

Roslyn Russell, 'Finding Manning Clark in the Letters', *National Library of Australia News*, vol. 18, no. 1, pp. 15–18, webarchive.nla.gov.au/awa/20120205171953/http://pandora.nla.gov.au/pan/131760/20120120-0944/www.nla.gov.au/pub/nlanews/2007/oct07/story-4.pdf.

2007–08 Samantha Young, 'Manning Clark. Writing History to Understand the World We Live In', *Double Dialogues*, vol. 8, n.p., available at: www.doubledialogues.com/article/manning-clark-writing-history-to-understand-the-world-we-live-in/.

2008 Susan Magarey, 'Three Questions for Biographers: Public or Private? Individual or Society? Truth or Beauty?' *Journal of Historical Biography*, vol. 4, Autumn, pp. 1–26, available at: www.ufv.ca/jhb/Volume_4/Volume_4_Magarey.pdf.

Brian Matthews, *Manning Clark: A Life*, Sydney: Allen & Unwin.

Mark McKenna, *Notes from the Underground: Writing the Biography of Manning Clark*, Kathleen Fitzpatrick Lecture, Melbourne: School of Historical Studies, University of Melbourne.

Eric Richards, *Destination Australia: Migration to Australia since 1901*, Sydney: UNSW Press.

Roslyn Russell (ed.), *Ever, Manning: Selected Letters of Manning Clark, 1938–1991*, Sydney: Allen & Unwin.

2009 Bain Attwood and Tom Griffiths (eds), *Frontier, Race, Nation: Henry Reynolds and Australian History*, Melbourne: Australian Scholarly Publishing.

Ann Curthoys and Ann McGrath, *How to Write History that People Want to Read*, Sydney: UNSW Press. Another edition was published in Basingstoke by Palgrave Macmillan, 2011, doi.org/10.4467/20844069ph.20.010.12464.

Jim George and Kim Huynh (eds), *The Culture Wars: Australian and American Politics in the 21st Century*, Melbourne: Palgrave Macmillan Australia.

Jude van Konkelenberg, 'Australia's Cold War University: The Relationship between The Australian National University's Research School of Pacific Studies and the Federal Government, 1946–1975', PhD thesis, University of Adelaide, available at: digital.library.adelaide.edu.au/dspace/handle/2440/63714.

John McLaren, *Journey without Arrival: The Life and Writing of Vincent Buckley*, Melbourne: Australian Scholarly Publishing.

Peter Reeve, 'Masters of History: Three Students of Trinity College' (W.K. Hancock, Manning Clark and Chester Wilmot), *Victorian Historical Journal*, vol. 80, no. 1, pp. 76–90.

2010 **Mervyn F. Bendle**, 'Anzac in Ashes', *Quadrant*, vol. 54, no. 4, April, pp. 3–10.

Hal G.P. Colebatch, 'Australian Freedom-haters. *Quadrant*, vol. 54, no. 9, September, pp. 18–20.

James Curran and Stuart Ward, *The Unknown Nation: Australia after Empire*, Melbourne: MUP.

Jim Davidson, *A Three-Cornered Life: The Historian WK Hancock*, Sydney: UNSW Press.

Ross Fitzgerald, *My Name is Ross: An Alcoholic's Journey*, Sydney: NewSouth.

Sheila Fitzpatrick, *My Father's Daughter: Memories of an Australian Childhood*, Melbourne: MUP.

Peter Hruby, *Dangerous Dreamers: The Australian Anti-Democratic Left and Czechoslovak Agents,* Bloomington, IN: iUniverse.

Stuart Macintyre, *The Poor Relation: A History of Social Sciences in Australia,* Melbourne: Melbourne University Press.

Peter Ryan, *Final Proof: Memoirs of a Publisher,* Sydney: Quadrant Books.

2011 **David Bird**, 'Coming to Terms with the "German Question"', *Quadrant,* vol. 55, no. 8, August, pp. 52–55.

Sophie Cunningham, *Melbourne,* Sydney, NewSouth.

Mark McKenna, *An Eye for Eternity: The Life of Manning Clark,* Melbourne: Miegunyah Press.

Peter Ryan, *It Strikes Me: Collected Essays, 1994–2010,* Sydney: Quadrant.

David Walker, *Not Dark Yet: A Personal History,* Sydney: Giramondo.

2012 David Bird, *Nazi Dreamtime: Australian Enthusiasts for Hitler's Germany,* Melbourne: Australian Scholarly Publishing and London: Anthem Press.

Milton Cameron, *Experiments in Modern Living: Scientists' Houses in Canberra, 1950–1970,* Canberra: ANU E Press, doi.org/10.22459/EML.05.2012.

Carolyn Holbrook, 'Marxism for Beginner Nations: Radical Nationalist Historians and the Great War', *Labour History,* vol. 103, pp. 123–44, doi.org/10.5263/labourhistory.103.0123.

Bruce Mansfield, *Summer Is Almost Over: A Memoir,* Canberra, Barton Books.

Mark McKenna, 'History and Australia: A Foundational Past?', Annual History Lecture, History Council of New South Wales, 8 August, available at: historycouncilnsw.org.au/wp-content/uploads/2013/01/2012-AHL-McKenna.pdf.

Doug Munro, *J.C. Beaglehole: Public Intellectual, Critical Conscience,* Wellington: Steele Roberts.

Peter Ryan, *It Strikes Me: Collected Essays, 1994–2010,* Sydney: Quadrant Books.

John Tidey, *Class Act: A Life of Creighton Burns,* Melbourne: Australian Scholarly Publishing.

2013 Alison Bashford and Stuart Macintyre (eds), *The Cambridge History of Australia,* 2 vols, Melbourne: Cambridge University Press, doi.org/10.1017/CHO9781107445758.

Rollo Hesketh, 'A.A. Phillips and the "Cultural Cringe": Creating an "Australian Tradition"', *Meanjin,* vol. 72, no. 3, pp. 92–103.

Elizabeth Kleinhenz, *A Brimming Cup: The Life of Kathleen Fitzpatrick*, Melbourne: Melbourne University Press.

Ai Kobayashi, *W. Macmahon Ball: Politics for the People*, Melbourne: Australian Scholarly Publishing.

Mark McKenna, 'After Manning Clark', *Meanjin,* vol. 72, no. 1, pp. 84–94.

Mark McKenna, 'Six Pack: Volume One of *A History of Australia* is Published', in Tanya Dalziell and Paul Genoni (eds), *Telling Stories: Australian Life and Literature 1935–2012,* Melbourne: Monash University Publishing, pp. 240–46.

Claudio Véliz, 'The Infamous Omissions from Australian History: *In Memoriam* Kenneth Minogue', *Quadrant,* vol. 57, no. 10, October, pp. 7–12.

2014 Geoffrey Bolton, *Paul Hasluck: A Life*, Perth: UWA Publishing.

Hal G.P. Colebatch, 'The Truth About Menzies and the Second World War', *Quadrant,* vol. 58, nos 7–8, July–August, pp. 18–21.

Carolyn Holbrook, *Anzac: The Unauthorised Biography,* Sydney: UNSW Press.

Ann Moyal, *A Woman of Influence: Science, Men & History,* Perth: UWA Publishing.

Wilfrid Prest (ed.), *Pasts Present: History at Australia's Third University*, Adelaide: Wakefield Press.

Alison Richards, 'Your History: Manning Clark's *History of Australia* and the End of the New Wave', *Australasian Drama Studies,* vol. 64, pp. 177–98.

Biff Ward, *In My Mother's Hands: A Disturbing Memoir of Family Life*, Sydney: Allen & Unwin.

2015 **Philip Ayres**, 'The Worlds of Claudio Véliz, Part II', *Quadrant,* vol. 59, nos 1–2, January–February, pp. 58–64.

Frank Bongiorno, 'Manning Clark Now', *Australian Folklore,* vol. 30, pp. 81–92, available at: journals.kvasirpublishing.com/af/article/view/167/255.

Glenn Davies, 'The History Man: Manning Clark Centenary—1915-2015', *Independent Australia,* 11 March, n.p., available at: independentaustralia.net/australia/australia-display/the-history-man-manning-clark-centenary-1915-2015,7465.

Christine de Matos, 'Fictorians: Historians who 'Lie' about the Past, and Like It', *Text: The Journal of the Australian Association Writing Programs,* (special issue Website Series), no. 28, pp. 1–20, available at: www.textjournal.com.au/speciss/issue28/deMatos.pdf.

Alan Fewster, 'Manning Clark and the Man in Black', *Inside Story,* 25 May, available at: insidestory.org.au/manning-clark-and-the-man-in-black/.

Tom Griffiths, 'The Intriguing Dance of History and Fiction', *Text: The Journal of the Australian Association Writing Programs,* (special issue Website Series), no. 28, pp. 1–21, available at: www.textjournal.com.au/speciss/issue28/Griffiths.pdf.

Mark McKenna, 'Clark, Charles Manning (1915–1991)', *Australian Dictionary of Biography,* National Centre of Biography, The Australian National University, available at: adb.anu.edu.au/biography/clark-charles-manning-225/text29719.

Mark McKenna, 'Elective Affinities: Manning Clark, Patrick White and Sidney Nolan', in Ian Henderson and Anouk Lang (eds), *Patrick White Beyond the Grave: New Critical Perspectives,* London: Anthem Press, pp. 81–100.

Peter Monteath and Valerie Munt, *Red Professor: The Cold War Life of Fred Rose,* Adelaide: Wakefield Press.

Camilla Nelson, 'Archival Poetics: Writing History from the Fragments', special issue: Camilla Nelson and Christine de Matos (eds), *Fictional histories and historical fictions: Writing history in the twenty-first century,* Website Series, *Text: The Journal of the Australian Association Writing Programs* no. 28, pp. 1–14, available at: www.textjournal.com.au/speciss/issue28/Nelson.pdf.

Donald Wright, *Donald Creighton: A Life in History,* Toronto, University of Toronto Press.

2016 Judith Armstrong, *Dymphna,* Melbourne: Australian Scholarly Publishing.

Tom Griffiths, *The Art of Time Travel: Historians and Their Craft,* Melbourne: Black, Inc.

Thornton McCamish, *Our Man Elsewhere: In Search of Alan Moorehead,* Melbourne: Black Inc.

Mark McKenna, '"National Awakening", Autobiography, and the Invention of Manning Clark', *Life Writing,* vol. 13, no. 2, pp. 207–20, doi.org/10.1080/14484528.2016.116 2263. Republished in Astrid Rasch (ed.), *Life Writing after Empire,* Abington/New York: Routledge, pp. 207–20; also republished, with minor changes as '"A Gigantic Confession of Life": Autobiography, "National Awakening" and the Invention of Manning Clark', in Doug Munro and John G. Reid (eds), *Clio's Lives: Biographies and Autobiographies of Historians,* Canberra: ANU Press, 2017, pp. 81–102, doi.org/10.22459/CL.10.2017.05.

Mark McKenna, *Writing the Life of Manning Clark: The Challenges of Biography,* Trevor Reece Memorial Lecture 2011, London: Menzies Centre for Australian Studies.

Doug Munro, '"How illuminating it has been": Matthews and McKenna and their Biographies of Manning Clark', in Philip Payton (ed.), *Emigrants & Historians: Essays in Honour of Eric Richards,* Adelaide: Wakefield Press, pp. 98–131 (text) and 169–75 (endnotes), available at: honesthistory.net.au/wp/wp-content/uploads/Munro_MatthewsMcKenna.pdf.

Sheridan Palmer, *Hegel's Owl: The Life of Bernard Smith,* Sydney: Power Publications.

Jill Roe, *Our Fathers Cleared the Bush: Remembering Eyre Peninsula,* Adelaide: Wakefield Press.

Jane Sloane, 'Shane Howard: Spirit of Place', *Australian Quarterly,* vol. 87, no. 2, pp. 26–33 and 40.

Mark St Leon, 'Adopted Apprentices: Juvenile Recruitment in Australian Circuses, 1847–1942', *Labour History,* no. 110, 2016, pp. 97–124, doi.org/10.5263/labourhistory.110.0097.

2017 Jim Berryman, 'The Theme of Civilisation in Manning Clark's *History of Australia*', *History Australia*, vol. 14, no. 1, pp. 82–98, doi.org/10.1080/14490854.2017.1286706.

Ross Fitzgerald, 'Manning Clark and the Vanishing Archaeologist', *Quadrant*, vol. 61, nos 7–8, July–August, pp. 82–84.

Bruce Grant, *Subtle Moments: Scenes on a Life's Journey*, Melbourne: Monash University Publishing.

Robert Lehane, *Verity: A Remarkable Woman's Journey*, Melbourne: Australian Scholarly Publishing.

Donato Longo, 'The Fin-De-Siècle Academy and its Discontents: Austin Gough and the Betrayal of the Intellectuals', *Journal of Labor and Society*, vol. 20, no. 3, pp. 285–305, doi.org/10.1111/wusa.12293.

Bruce R. Pass, 'A Shy Hope in the Heart? Religious Journalism in Australia and the Kuyperian Legacy', *Stellenbosch Theological Journal*, vol. 3, no. 1, 2017, pp. 327–42, doi.org/10.17570/stj.2017.v3n1.a15.

2018 Malcolm Allbrook and Melanie Nolan, 'Australian Historians and Biography', *Australian Journal of Biography and History*, vol. 1, pp. 3–21, doi.org/10.22459/AJBH.2018.01.

Graeme Davison (ed.), *Hugh Stretton: Select Writings*, Melbourne, La Trobe University Press in conjunction with Black Inc.

Rollo Hesketh, '"In Search of a National Identity": Australian Intellectuals and the "Cultural Cringe", 1940–1972', PhD thesis, University of Sydney, available at: ses.library.usyd.edu.au/bitstream/2123/19619/1/hesketh_rbcb_thesis.pdf.

Len Richardson, 'Patrick O'Farrell and the Making of Harry Holland: Militant Socialist', *Labour History*, no. 115, pp. 27–46, doi.org/10.5263/labourhistory.115.0027.

2019 Harry Allen, 'The First University Positions in Prehistorical Archaeology in New Zealand and Australia', *Bulletin of the History of Archaeology*, vol. 29, no. 1, n.p., doi.org/10.5334/bha-606.

Geoffrey Blainey, *Before I Forget: An Early Memoir*, Melbourne: Hamish Hamilton.

Stephen A. Chavura, John Gascoigne and Ian Tregenza (eds), *Reason, Religion and the Australian Polity: A Secular State?* Abingdon/New York: Routledge, doi.org/10.4324/9780429467059.

Mark McKenna, 'In Search of Emily', in Joy Damosi and Judith Smart (eds), *Contesting Australian History: Essays in Honour of Marilyn Lake,* Melbourne: Monash University Publishing, pp. 107–20.

'Special: Remembering the *ANU Historical Journal* (1964–87)' *ANU Historical Journal II,* vol. 1, 2019, pp. 3–54. Contributions by Rosemary Auchmuty, Ian Britain, Alastair Davidson, Ron Fraser, Doug Munro, Caroline Turner and Jill Waterhouse, doi.org/10.22459/ANUHJII.2019.

2020 Richard Allsop, *Geoffrey Blainey: Writer, Historian, Controversialist,* Melbourne: Monash University Publishing.

Peter Browne and Seumas Spark (eds), *'I Wonder': The Life and Work of Ken Inglis,* Melbourne: Monash University Publishing.

Ross Fitzgerald, 'Manning Clark and the Webbs', *Quadrant,* vol. 64, nos 7–8, July–August, pp. 94–95.

Robert Murray, 'The Punch and Sparkle of Peter Ryan', review of *Ryan's Luck,* by John Tidey, *Quadrant,* vol. 64, no. 12, December, pp. 91–93.

Jonathan Persse, *David Campbell: A Life of the Poet,* Melbourne: Australian Scholarly Publishing.

John Tidey, *Ryan's Luck: A Life of Peter Ryan MM,* Melbourne: Arcadia (an imprint of Australian Scholarly Publishing).

John Young, *Going Down Another Lane*, Franklin, TAS: Ashwood Books.

2021 Don Longo, *A Historian Against the Current: The Life and Work of Austin Gough*, Adelaide: Wakefield Press.

Kate White, 'Australian Political Biography and Biographers: Revisiting Australian Political Biography', *Australian Journal of Biography and History,* vol. 5, pp. 1–20, doi.org/10.22459/AJBH.05.2021.01.

Select Bibliography

Archival Sources

Manuscript sources

The most important are:

Papers of Dymphna Clark, National Library of Australia, MS 9873.

Papers of Manning Clark, National Library of Australia, MS 7550.

Papers of Peter Ryan, National Library of Australia, MS 9897.

Records of Melbourne University Press, University of Melbourne Archives, 2003.0134.

Other manuscript material

Papers of W. Macmahon Ball, National Library of Australia, MS 7851.

Papers of Axel Clark, National Library of Australia, MS Acc11.079.

Papers of Stuart Macintyre, National Library of Australia, MS 9389.

Archive of J.M. Main, Special Collections, Flinders University Library, PGp 2.

Papers of A.W. Martin, National Library of Australia, MS 9802.

Papers of John Molony, National Library of Australia, MS 6634.

Papers of Douglas Pike, National Library of Australia, MS 6869.

Peter Allen Ryan, Service file, National Archives of Australia, Canberra, B883, X128541.

Peter Allen Ryan, ASIO file, vol 1, 1952–72, National Archives of Australia, Canberra, A6119, 2616, available at: recordsearch.naa.gov.au/SearchN Retrieve/Interface/ViewImage.aspx?B=3901342.

Papers of John Tregenza, Special Collections, Barr Smith Library, University of Adelaide, MSS 0047.

Interviews

Dymphna Clark, interviewed by Heather Rusden, 13 February 1997, National Library of Australia, ORAL TRC 3548, available at: nla.gov.au/nla.obj-217338911/listen.

Katerina and Axel Clark, interviewed by Susan Marsden, 19 June 2001, National Library of Australia, ORAL TRC 4770.

'Making History: Mark McKenna on Manning Clark' (interviewed by Michael Cathcart), Wheeler Centre, Melbourne, 6 June 2011.

Peter Ryan interviewed by John Farquarson, 10–11 October 2000, National Library of Australia, ORAL TRC-4631.

Reviews of C.M.H. Clark, *A History of Australia*

The listing below itemises the review articles and reviews cited in the footnotes of this book. It is but a small selection of the total reviews that the *History* attracted. These can be found in two places. Melbourne University Press collected reviews of the *History* placed them in scrapbooks. Records of Melbourne University Press, 2003.0134, UM992. Copies of most of the reviews are also in the Papers of Manning Clark, National Library of Australia, MS 7550, Series 18, Boxes 156–160.

Stuart Macintyre, 'Manning Clark's Critics', *Meanjin,* vol. 44, no. 4, 1982, pp. 442–52, has assessed the reception of the first five volumes of the *History*, to which readers can refer for specific details.

Volumes 1–4

Robert Kubicek, *Pacific Affairs,* vol. 53, no. 2, 1980, pp. 378–80, doi.org/10.2307/2757518.

Bruce Mansfield, 'A History the Lotus has Eaten: Manning Clark's Australia', *Teaching History,* vol. 13, no. 1, 1979, pp. 3–12.

Volumes 1–6

Robert Murray, 'Forty Years of Manning Clark', *Quadrant,* vol. 45, no. 11, November 2001, pp. 46–53.

Volume 1 (From Earliest Times to the Age of Macquarie)

Jill Conway, 'A Vision of Australian History', *Journal of the Royal Australian Historical Society,* vol. 49, no. 6, 1964, pp. 453–59.

Malcolm Ellis, 'History without Facts', *Bulletin,* 22 September 1962, pp. 36–37, reprinted in Carl Bridge (ed.), *Manning Clark: Essays on his Place in History,* Melbourne: Melbourne University Press, 1994, pp. 70–77.

D.K. Fieldhouse, *History: Journal of the Historical Association*, vol. 49, no. 165, 1964, pp. 133–34.

J.W. Forsyth, 'Clio Etwas Gebuckt: Professor Clark's "The Forerunners"', *Journal of the Royal Australian Historical Society,* vol. 49, no. 6, 1964, pp. 423–52.

John McManners, 'Creeds in the Cradle', *Nation,* 20 October 1962, pp. 19–21.

Patrick O'Farrell, *Irish Historical Studies,* vol. 15, no. 57, 1966, pp. 93–95, doi.org/10.1017/S0021121400035045.

Michael Roe, *Quadrant,* vol. 7, no. 1, Summer 1962–63, pp. 73–76.

Stuart Sayers, 'A new history of Australia: "restless human forces and passions"', *Age,* 8 September 1962, p. 17.

A.G.L. Shaw, 'Clark's History of Australia', *Meanjin Quarterly,* vol. 22, no. 1, 1963, pp. 117–19.

O.H.K. Spate, *Australian Journal of Politics and History,* vol. 9, no. 2, 1963, pp. 267–69, doi.org/10.1111/j.1467-8497.1963.tb01066.x.

Robin W. Winks, *American Historical Review,* vol. 69, no. 4, 1964, pp. 1067–68, doi.org/10.2307/1842969.

Volume 2 (1822–1838)

K.J. Cable, *Australian Economic History Review,* vol. 8, no. 2, 1968, pp. 164–66.

'Currency lads and lasses', *Times Literary Supplement,* 2 January 1969, p. 11.

Hazel King, *Journal of Religious History,* vol. 5, no. 2, 1968, pp. 180–82, doi.org/10.1111/j.1467-9809.1968.tb00502.x.

Patrick O'Farrell, *Irish Historical Studies,* vol. 17, no. 66, 1970, pp. 289–90, doi.org/10.1017/S0021121400111551.

L.L. Robson, 'Once More with Feeling: Manning Clark's History of Australia', *Meanjin Quarterly*, vol. 27, no. 4, 1968, pp. 497–502.

Volume 3 (1824–1851)

Geoffrey Serle, 'One Man's Window on Our Past: Manning Clark's Third Volume', *Meanjin Quarterly*, vol. 33, no. 1, 1974, pp. 86–88.

Volume 4 (1851–1888)

Brian Dickey, 'History with a personal touch', *Advertiser* (Adelaide), 8 April 1978, p. 21.

W.F. Mandle, 'Through a Glass Compassionately', *Australian Book Review*, no. 1, June 1978, pp. 1 and 4.

Volume 5 (1890–1915)

Geoffrey Blainey, 'Towards History', *Hemisphere*, September–October 1982, pp. 98–99.

Geoffrey Bolton, 'Through a Glass Darkly', *Australian Book Review*, no. 37, 1981, pp. 3–4.

F.G. Clarke, *American Historical Review*, vol. 87, no. 5, 1982, pp. 1450–51, doi.org/10.2307/1857052.

Patrick Coady, 'Manning's imagination transcends history', *Catholic Weekly*, 17 January 1982 (clipping provided by Clive Moore).

Tony Griffiths, 'A bitter history', *Age Monthly Review*, December 1981, pp. 21–22.

Donald Horne, 'Australia fails its test', *Sydney Morning Herald*, 10 October 1981, p. 45.

Edward Kynaston, 'Turning history's pages—cliche by cliche', *Weekend Australian Magazine*, 24–25 October 1981, p. 10.

Stuart Macintyre, 'Clark's epic history sweeps to new peak', *Age*, 10 October 1981, p. 25.

Noel McLachlan, 'Manning Clark's Australian History', *Arena*, vol. 60, 1982, pp. 172–75.

George Parsons, *Journal of Australian Studies*, vol. 7, no. 13. 1983, pp. 95–96.

John Rickard, *New Zealand Journal of History*, vol. 17, no. 1, 1983, pp. 90–92, available at: www.nzjh.auckland.ac.nz/document.php?wid=1132&action=null.

Malcolm Thomis, 'Author's ideal is too elusive', *Courier-Mail*, 9 January 1982, p. 24.

Claudio Veliz, 'Bad History', *Quadrant*, vol. 26, no. 5, May 1982, pp. 21–26.

Chris Wallace-Crabbe, 'Manning Clark['s] Troubled Landscape, with figures', *Scripsi*, Summer/Autumn 1982, pp. 86–89.

Volume 6 (1916–1935)

Geoffrey Blainey, 'Speaking volumes of history', *Herald Sun*, 24 August 1987, p. 11.

Helen Bourke, 'Above the Mainstream: Manning Clark's History of Australia', *Overland*, no. 109, 1987, pp. 21–24.

Edmund Campion, 'Manning Clark', *Scripsi*, vol. 5, no. 2, 1989, 183–87.

Peter Cochrane, *Journal of the Royal Australian Historical Society*, vol. 74, no. 2, 1988, pp. 170–74.

Bill Cope, *Labour History*, no. 55, 1988, pp. 92–94, doi.org/10.2307/27508902.

Beverley Kingston, *Australian Historical Studies*, vol. 23, no. 91, 1988, pp. 204–5, doi.org/10.1080/10314618808595805.

John Lack, 'Manning Clark's History', *Arena*, no. 82, 1988, pp. 168–73.

Humphrey McQueen, *Continuum: Journal of Media & Cultural Studies*, vol. 1, no. 2, 1988, pp. 134–40, doi.org/10.1080/10304318809359344.

Colin Roderick, 'Not quite the history of Australia', *Courier-Mail Weekend*, 26 September 1987, p. 5.

Michael Roe, *Tasmanian Historical Research Association—Papers & Proceedings*, vol. 34, no. 4, 1987, pp. 131–32.

A.G.L. Shaw, 'Clark completes his history', *Age*, 5 September 1987, p. 12.

www.ingramcontent.com/pod-product-compliance
Lightning Source LLC
Chambersburg PA
CBHW042043240426
43667CB00048B/2967